THE
NATION
IS
BURDENED

Roger D. Masters

Alfred · A · Knopf

NEW YORK

1967

THE
NATION
IS
BURDENED

AMERICAN

FOREIGN POLICY

IN A

CHANGING

WORLD

THIS IS A BORZOI BOOK

PUBLISHED BY ALFRED A. KNOPF, INC.

Chapter iv has appeared in somewhat different form in *The Yale Review*, LV: 3 (Spring 1966). Portions of Chapter v have appeared in *The New Republic* (December 4, 1965) and in *Commonweal* (July 8, 1966).

Again I saw that under the sun the race is not to the swift, nor the battle to the strong, nor bread to the wise, nor riches to the intelligent, nor favor to the men of skill; but time and chance happen to them all. . . . Wisdom is better than weapons of war, but one sinner destroys much good.

Ecclesiastes, IX: 11-18.

Preface

BEING NEITHER an academic specialist in foreign policy nor a journalist, I have wondered more than once while writing this book whether I had sufficient knowledge to analyze American foreign policy adequately. All I dare affirm is that the result is not free from fault.

I have not, however, tried to set down a fully developed and comprehensive guide to every problem facing the United States as a world power. Instead, I wanted to raise the kinds of questions that seem most relevant to an intelligent understanding and formulation of American policies in a changing world. My proposed alternatives may be inadequate, but the issues are real and often misunderstood.

Readers who find my logic or evidence controversial will therefore probably be fulfilling my intention, which is to encourage deeper and more open-minded thought about the role of the United States in international politics over the coming fifty years. If the study of political philosophy can provide guidance to the conduct of foreign policy, it is mainly that there is no substitute for a prudential consideration of the realities of power; no great society can survive if its policies toward others are dominated by passion or ideology.

I shall forbear from thanking by name those friends and colleagues who were kind enough to comment on various parts of my manuscript, often correcting errors of substance and style; since errors doubtless remain, it would be unfair to impute to them an unwanted responsibility. Permission to publish material that has previously appeared in *The New Republic, The Yale Review,* and *Commonweal* is hereby gratefully acknowledged.

Contents

PART I: THE FUTURE LIES AHEAD

Ch. 1: The Aims of Foreign Policy   3

Ch. 2: The Evolution of World Politics   15

Ch. 3: Nuclear Diffusion and World Peace   44

Ch. 4: Goals for American Power   84

PART II: A NEW LOOK AT THE PRESENT

Ch. 5: Western Europe and the
Atlantic Alliance   123

Ch. 6: The Soviet Union and the
Communist World   167

Ch. 7: Asia and the Rising Power of China   204

Ch. 8: Economic Development and
International Organizations   246

PART III: THE PAST IN THE LIGHT OF THE FUTURE

Ch. 9: American Traditions and
World Politics   279

Conclusion   310

Index   follows page 320

PART I

THE

FUTURE

LIES AHEAD

———

America is therefore the land of the future,
where, in the ages that lie before us, the burden
of the World's History shall reveal itself . . .

G. W. F. HEGEL, *The Philosophy of History*

The Aims of Foreign Policy

ONCE UPON A TIME there was a country with no entangling alliances. To Americans today, our past freedom from foreign involvement must indeed seem a fairy tale—a dangerous fairy tale in the age of nuclear weapons and world upheaval, communist wars of national liberation and American commitments abroad. As any reasonable citizen is aware, the United States is irrevocably concerned with world politics because what happens overseas directly affects our own existence.

These observations, however commonplace, require some thought, because the United States is also a democracy, based on the principle that enlightened public opinion can and should determine the actions of government. It is not enough that we know the latest developments in Vietnam, Central America, or Europe as they are reported in the morning newspaper; we must have opinions about foreign affairs that permit us to judge day-to-day events. Moreover, the question is not that we be "for" or "against" the current policies of the President—enlightened citizens need reasons that are not habitual reflexes.

Principles and opinions that have been taken for granted over the last twenty years are increasingly being challenged everywhere. A new generation of political leadership is coming to power throughout the world; those who ruled during World War II and its aftermath are passing from the scene if not already gone. Since the problems of a new era will be confronted by new men, in the United States as elsewhere, the experiences of the first half of the twentieth century may not be the best guide to the choices we must now make.

One striking aspect of recent American politics has been the sudden involvement and activism of young people, an age group that was widely criticized only a few years ago for its indifference. Those educated since 1940 view America's future from a different perspective than their elders and are often dissatisfied with the goals and methods of the past. While youthful critics are frequently disdained by older and presumably wiser citizens, this reaction may only reveal the need for fresh approaches to our problems. It is from this perspective that the present book has been written.

Never before has the course of human events seemed to move so rapidly. In the last twenty years, a totally new kind of weapon has transformed military strategy and altered the aspect of major war; scores of new nations have emerged as sovereign states; an international organization devoted to maintaining the peace has been erected and is now threatened with impotence; the cold war between communism and Western democracy, which was not even foreseen by most commentators during World War II, has continuously evolved through phases of direct confrontation in Europe, peaceful coexistence, and challenges to American power in the underdeveloped countries (whether in nearby Cuba or faraway Vietnam). Yesterday's enemies (Germany and Japan) are today American allies; who is to say that today's enemies may not shift sides in the future?

We run the risk of totally misunderstanding current events if we react to them in terms of the problems and attitudes of the past. It may be disastrous to equate the threats posed by world communism and Nazism merely because both represent totalitarian forms of government hostile to American democracy. Hitler's racist ideas could be exported to Africa and Asia only with difficulty; Marxism, especially as reformulated by Lenin and Mao Tse-tung, claims to be a scientific formula that can be used by any nation—and particularly by any backward nation—seeking to control its destiny.

Military strategy exemplifies the dangerous tendency to be trapped by past habits. It has often been noted that armies frequently prepare and fight wars on the basis of a strategy that—had it been employed—would have won the last war; frequently this strategy turns out to be irrelevant to the changed conditions in which it is actually used. The French, prior to World War II, built the Maginot Line, a device suited to the military needs of World War I. Unfortunately this defensive line was totally ineffective against the kind of warfare based on tanks and rapid movement that took place in 1939-40; the Maginot Line is today a symbol of outmoded strategy incapable of meeting real military challenges.

Lest it be thought that we are incapable of making the same mistakes again, some recent parallels will be revealing. President Truman's intervention in the Korean War was based in large part on the recollection of the disaster of Munich; to that extent we learned well the lessons of history. But the military strategy used in the Korean War failed to take advantage of the overwhelming superiority in nuclear weapons enjoyed by the United States in 1950-52; for this reason, General MacArthur's desire to destroy Communist supply lines north of the Yalu River was rejected as too dangerous.[1] The

[1] This is not to say that MacArthur's strategy would necessarily have had the effect of winning the war without a risk of Soviet intervention, but it does indicate the extent to which our decision to fight in Korea under the UN flag may have induced certain strategic decisions that are at least debatable. See Morton Halperin: *Limited War in the Nuclear Age* (New York: Wiley; 1963), esp. pp. 50-7.

result was a stalemate in Korea and the continued danger represented by the division of that country.

Frustration over this outcome is not entirely irrelevant to the war in Vietnam, and perhaps explains the acceptance of a policy of bombing Communist military targets in the North as a means of winning the war in the South. But the situation in Vietnam is radically different from that in Korea for several important reasons. The balance of nuclear power has changed since 1952; now the Russians have invulnerable nuclear weapons and the Chinese themselves have begun to develop the atomic bomb. This means that in Vietnam we face limits in expanding the war which did not exist in Korea. In addition the nature of the conflict itself is quite different. Whereas the Korean War was more or less a "classic" war with a defined battle line or front, South Vietnam is a guerrilla action in which American positions, no matter how secure they may seem, are subject to harassment or attack by subversive elements among the population we claim to be defending.

Under these conditions a strategy that might have been decisive in Korea could well have unexpected consequences. Some would say that the bombing of North Vietnam has a different objective than the proposed attacks on Communist supply lines north of the Yalu and that the extension of the Vietnam war was intended to produce negotiations, not total victory. But the long-run effects of this tactic remain to be seen, and the only way to consider them is to analyze the conflict in Vietnam as a new kind of war, typical of future problems rather than past experience.

The debate created by the war in Vietnam has reflected increasing doubts throughout the country concerning American foreign policy. Political allegiances that once were solid have been undermined; although both parties have been divided, sharpest criticism of the Democratic administration has come from its own supporters. America's new status as a world power has thus directly affected our political system, making clearly thought-out attitudes a necessity.

Since foreign policy debates are particularly vulnerable to

emotional, unthinking reflexes, failure to examine new issues with an open mind is dangerous and can lead to passionate extremism and irreconcilable controversy. Although this problem arises even on local issues, where relevant facts are accessible in daily experience, it is even more serious with respect to American commitments throughout the world. Radio, TV, and newspaper reporting has increasingly become a nationwide industry which, particularly in the area of foreign policy, may unwittingly present a partial or biased view of events.

The importance of the selection of facts and interpretations in news reporting becomes evident as soon as one travels outside the United States. For example, the Frenchman receives information concerning the war in Vietnam that gives a completely different impression from American news reporting. Whether or not one is "right" and the other "wrong," obviously the news can be—and if the complaints of some journalists are to be believed, is—manipulated by those in power. Since the American political system depends on the ability of its citizens to judge those who govern, the failure to develop independent, nonpartisan ways of thinking about foreign affairs results in an abdication of power to those in office.

At a time when American military and political strength is at its height, it is especially important that the American people control the use of this power; to do so, we cannot allow ourselves to react on the basis of ignorance. The experience of Nazi Germany proves that a people can be "intoxicated" by what it is told; many observers would say that the Gaullist government in France achieved the same effects, especially in the course of the war in Algeria. It could happen here—and lest it should, we have an obligation to consider afresh the objectives and means suited to American foreign policy in the nuclear age.

More than two thousand years ago, Aristotle began one of his most famous treatises with the remark that ". . . every action and pursuit is thought to aim at some good." Military strategy and, more broadly, politics, were two of his examples. It is perhaps useful to recall this simple truth, for we can hardly judge what is or should be done by our country and our government until we have decided the "good" toward which we aim.

It is notoriously risky to talk about the kind of world in which we hope our children will live; like Fourth of July oratory, platitudes are cheap. Freedom, democracy, and peace are lofty—but often empty—words. Dictatorships have been established by men who claimed to support the cause of freedom, communist states say they are democratic, and slaves can live in peace. The ideals of a decent life formulated by our civilization (and envied in the new or underdeveloped nations) are well enough known; what we most commonly lack is not general principles, but concrete objectives relevant to specific foreign policy choices. Should the United States use military force to prevent communist take-overs in foreign countries? What is the future of our alliance with Western Europe? Does the United Nations have a role to play, and if so, how can it be effective? In order to answer such questions, we must first decide what our aims are in an era of rapid change.

Nor is it enough to have clearly announced policies for the present or near future. We may be quite well agreed that the NATO alliance is necessary or that communist subversion in South Vietnam must be ended, but the next fifty years could well bring about the decision of our European allies to leave NATO, and are almost certain to see the rise of Chinese nuclear power in Asia. To build for the future, we must think in terms of the world at the end of the present century, not at the end of the present year.

What, then, should we want in foreign politics? It is easier to say what our long-range objectives should *not* be than to define them. A few years ago, when the question of "national goals" was temporarily fashionable, a Rockefeller Committee report summarized our objectives as "a world at peace, based on separate political entities acting as a community."[2] Few would quarrel with such a proposition, but how is it to be realized? Peace is only possible if some states do not feel—rightly or wrongly—entitled to the territory or aggrieved at the policies of their neighbors. Free nations are not immune from making war, as a glance at history reveals: fortunately they defend themselves when threatened by hostile powers; unfortunately they sometimes attack others when carried away by passion or led by demagogues. Who can assure us that none of these conditions will ever arise? And what is the best defense against the uncertainties of the future?

Peace is not in itself a goal of foreign policy precisely because it is the result of an effective foreign policy. We properly seek to avoid war because, under modern conditions, it seems incompatible with acceptable standards of human life; but no one nation can prevent the outbreak of international violence, as the United States has discovered from Korea to Suez and from Cuba to Vietnam. Nor can we annihilate all nations that we distrust or find threatening us; even if it were morally respectable to wipe 750 million Communist Chinese lives from the face of the earth with nuclear weapons, could we do so without the risk of being destroyed ourselves?

Although the present state of the world may be tolerable to the United States, the goals of American foreign policy cannot be based on a blind fear of changes in the status quo. Similarly, although our system of government is certainly worth defending without compromise, moral ideals cannot always be realized in political practice. That the principles of Western democracy are not suited to every country in the world, regardless of its stage of economic development or its history, was proven by the adoption of British parliamentary institutions in Ghana, a country which rapidly fell under the control of a single political party led by an all-powerful ruler, ousted in turn by a military coup. Blanket

[2] *The Mid-Century Challenge to U.S. Foreign Policy,* Panel I Report of the Rockefeller Brothers Fund Special Studies Project (Garden City, N. Y.: Doubleday; 1959), p. 15.

endorsement of a high-sounding principle like national self-determination may, moreover, simply mask the hard truths of power: a communist regime in Cuba would hardly be more palatable to the United States if it had been elected by popular vote.

To think ahead, practically and constructively, is never easy. It requires a major effort of freeing one's mind from the clichés and habits that spare us from thought in day-to-day existence. Even more difficult, this effort assumes that it is possible to speak with some certainty of the range of possibilities that will confront us in coming years. Is it feasible to discuss foreign politics in long-range terms?

Nothing is more common than the popular reaction of surprise at major events and changes in international affairs. Although it was apparently foreseen by certain members of the administration—and predicted by some commentators—the Japanese attack on Pearl Harbor on December 7, 1941, was a shock to American public opinion. Of course, some major events affecting world politics, such as the assassination of President Kennedy, are impossible to predict, but others are more easily foreseeable. Competent observers long ago forecast the development of nuclear weapons by China or the attempts of French President de Gaulle to establish closer relations with Russia (to cite but two recent developments).

An example will helpfully refresh our memories of the extraordinary changes in recent history. Almost every generation in this century has seen a radical shift in the American attitude to Russia. Prior to World War I, we were relatively aloof from the Czarist regime; immediately after the Communist government was established in 1917, we were opposed to it (at least in principle). Not until 1933 was the Soviet Union formally recognized by the United States, yet in World War II it became our ally. By the late 1940's we were engaged in a cold war with communist Russia, only to sign the Test Ban and Hot Line treaties in 1963, suggesting the mutual acceptance of "peaceful coexistence" at least as far as direct confrontations are concerned. And of course, Soviet-American relations continue to evolve.

None of the past stages was permanent, although at each moment most Americans found it hard to realize that change was inevitable. To give an example of the kind of thinking necessary if we are to consider the future with an open mind, let us conceive of the possibility that our relations with Peking might follow the same pattern as those with Moscow. At present, the United States does not formally recognize the existence of the effective government on mainland China; it was only after about sixteen years that we extended diplomatic recognition to the Soviet Union. Assuming that history repeats itself, we would recognize Mao's regime in the next few years. More shocking, since about ten years after the establishment of Russo-American diplomatic relations we became allies, the historical analogy would produce an alliance between Red China and the United States in the mid-1970's.

While the past can never be used to predict the future in such a simplistic way, the foregoing parallel is instructive in two respects. First, it reminds us that time brings extraordinary shifts in the alliances between political powers. In eighteenth-century Europe it was traditionally accepted that France be allied with Prussia and England with Austria; suddenly, in 1756, there occurred a "reversal of alliances" in which these four major powers changed partners. Although informed opinion was not fully prepared for this event, it was in many ways a reasonable response to altered conditions in international affairs. Perhaps the decisive aspects of world politics today will remain unchanged for several decades, but it would be very daring to assert that we live in settled times; common sense suggests that we examine the future without assuming that it will be identical to the present.

Second, the analogy between our alliance with Russia during World War II and possible American attitudes toward China reminds us that, in foreign affairs, a country may be compelled to ally with powers it dislikes in order to preserve itself. Anticommunism at any price is not a sufficient goal for American foreign policy because the price could be the destruction of our society if not of the entire civilized world. Even "His Most Christian Majesty," the King of France, allied with the "infidel" Turks—not to mention the Protestant Swedes—while defending the principles of Catholicism in the sixteenth and seventeenth centuries.

There is a further reason why anticommunism is not in itself a sufficient goal for the United States. We may have forgotten that opposition to Soviet communism was the basis of Hitler's appeal to many Germans in the early 1930's; after he came to power, his regime was tolerated if not encouraged by some as a bulwark against the "red threat." Indeed, there are commentators who argue that this logic contributed to Western passivity (particularly on the part of the Papacy) in the face of Nazi atrocities. Whether or not these charges are true, the results of Hitler's brand of anticommunism should be sobering: the principles of Karl Marx are not the only source of tyranny and war in the twentieth century.

Observers have long noted that American opinions about world affairs tend to paint a picture in black and white moral terms. We fought World War I "to make the world safe for democracy," but then refused to play a role in power politics because of our traditional distrust of the immoral motives of other nations. The result was that the world was not safe for democracy—or indeed any form of government that was opposed to the expansionist goals of the Axis powers. We fought World War II to end totalitarianism, but after bringing our enemies to an unconditional surrender we found that our ally in this battle was a communist power as totalitarian within and expansionist abroad as Nazi Germany. For the last two decades we have been responding to this threat, often equating all sources of evil with international communism.

Our error in World War II was that—unlike Churchill, for example—Americans took it for granted that the Soviet Union would be a "reasonable" ally in peace as it had been in war; since the sole enemy was fascist totalitarianism, any ally opposed to this evil was presumably trustworthy. If we are to learn from history, our postwar disillusion should teach us the fallacy of assuming that there is but one kind of enemy. If, as one leading administration spokesman put it, "we do not intend to see any people fall under the control of totalitarianism," the United States cannot limit its concerns to the danger of communism; foreign tension would not vanish even if the communist movement were to disappear tomorrow.

For these reasons American objectives cannot be defined solely in terms of the kind of government that most obviously challenges us at the moment. Twice already in this century such logic has proved disastrous. However important the moral incompatibility between given regimes and our own, we can neither preserve ourselves nor defend Western democracy if we ignore the distribution of power that restrains threats to the peace at any point on the globe. Distasteful as the fact may be, the goals of American foreign policy cannot be divorced from the likely balance of power in world affairs over the coming decades.

This, then, should be the goal of the United States in international politics: a distribution of power in the world that permits the preservation of American democracy and the protection of similar ideals wherever possible. A world-wide anticommunist crusade, like the medieval crusades, risks exhausting the United States (as France was exhausted) while leaving the infidel as strongly entrenched as were the Mohammedans after Christian attempts to liberate the Holy Land failed.

But even if it is appropriate to speak in terms of balance of power, how are we to predict likely changes in the future? In a world of flux, it seems futile to try to foresee which nations will attack their neighbors, which will be split by civil war, and which will be reliable allies. Although detailed predictions are hazardous, we can say a great deal about the most striking trends of contemporary events. On the basis of the apparent pattern of evolution in world affairs, perhaps a reasonably accurate picture of American foreign policy goals can be drawn.

The foregoing remarks should justify a re-examination of prevailing American attitudes about world politics. They also suggest that if an analysis of foreign affairs is to free us from dangerous illusions, it must reverse the approach so often taken on these matters. The customary way of discussing American policies is to begin with a description of the past, on the basis of which the present is analyzed; the future is most often left to take care of itself or mentioned by way of a conclusion. But since what has happened in the past may well be a poor guide to the future, perhaps it would be more logical to begin with what lies ahead. If we can discover the kinds of challenges the United States will face in the next fifty years as well as the most appropriate ways of responding to them, present events will take on new meaning and present policies will be easier to judge. Even the past can best be understood in the light of the future.

CHAPTER TWO

The Evolution

of World Politics

To SPEAK of the likely course of coming events may seem akin
to prophecy or astrology because most predictions seem impossible to verify. We need not be concerned, however, with
detailed forecasts of which party will control the American
national government in 1980, who will succeed General de
Gaulle as president of France, etc.; although such events will
surely affect the course of international affairs, they will not
be the sole factors influencing foreign policy. At a broader
level of generality, many characteristics of the future are not
as difficult to predict as many assume.

Modern industrial and scientific technology, wherever fully
established, will be more or less irreversible; a nation like
the United States may be wiped out in a thermonuclear war,
but as long as this does not happen our society will presumably
not return to the technological level of the Stone or Iron
ages. In descriptions of world politics, the distinction between
the rich, industrial nations of the northern hemisphere and

the poor, underdeveloped or backward societies of the southern hemisphere is increasingly used to supplement the bipolar division of East and West, communist and democratic nations, with which we have become familiar since 1945. Given the high probability that the human race will not, short of a cataclysm, abandon the knowledge and control over physical nature developed in the last two centuries, we must consider the differing effects of modern technology on industrialized and underdeveloped societies.

Within the highly advanced nations, the consequences of modern science and industry are more drastic than we are in the habit of admitting. The way of life of Americans has probably changed to a greater degree since 1900 than did the lives of human beings during the preceding twenty centuries. Consider the effects of the automobile and the airplane, communication through the mass media (radio, motion pictures, telephones, and television), the widespread development and use of consumer durable goods, such as the refrigerator, central heating, advanced sanitary conveniences (running hot water, indoor toilets, etc.): in countless ways, the individual's daily activities in an industrial society differ from those of people who lived, or still live, in pre-modern societies.

While we take our own way of life for granted—and indeed, virtually consider it natural—the uniqueness of modern society must be properly understood. We have become dependent upon a vast and highly interrelated complex of industries and services for the satisfaction of everyday needs; what would have been unheard-of luxuries for the caveman or medieval peasant become necessities in civilized societies. Without long-distance transportation on a scale undreamed of even 150 years ago, our highly urbanized populations would probably face starvation; without assured sources of power from electricity and petroleum, our industrial plants would break down and our entire economic system collapse. This total dependence on modern technology was, of course, made apparent to millions of Americans when the northeastern section of the

United States was deprived of electric power on November 9, 1965.

Such obvious facts deserve emphasis because they reflect two political factors that are likely to continue—and indeed, increase—in importance over the next half century and more. First, the remarkable vulnerability of highly industrialized societies to certain forms of military attack, particularly from nuclear weapons, radically increases the impact of world politics; the issue of war or peace, while it has always affected civilized societies, has become particularly prominent now that science has produced the means of the total and mutual destruction of combatants. Second, nuclear war threatens to be more devastating to an industrialized society than to a backward or agrarian one, in which a pre-scientific technology results in the virtual autonomy of human life at the level of the farm village.

This second point deserves particular attention because it implies a political weakness of the most powerful nations of the world in their relations with backward societies. Whereas the United States may be able to deter the Soviet Union from certain actions, similar threats will be of lesser effect on an agrarian society with few likely targets for a nuclear attack; because, in order to disrupt Chinese society totally, a nuclear strike would have to be many times larger than one having the same effects on Russia, Communist China may be able to adopt seemingly risky policies that the USSR dare not.

An example of the sense of security produced by backwardness is readily presented by North Vietnam. American bombardment of that country was selectively focused on the transportation system—roads, bridges, railroad facilities, and the like—for many months. Were the United States subjected to similar attacks, our economic system would undoubtedly have suffered grave dislocation; in contrast, the North Vietnamese, however harassed, have been able to continue to feed their population.

The increased power provided by modern technology is

thus not everywhere of the same political or military utility. Although our advanced firepower and mobility may permit us to counter guerrilla activity in South Vietnam more effectively than the French efforts in the 1950's, substantial parts of the population in backward nations may oppose us and feel relatively sure that our nuclear weapons will not be used against them. In this sense, the further development of technology and science by the advanced nations of the West does not provide a political cure to all problems, nor does it even assure us control over the weaker and less developed societies of the earth.

Self-sustaining industrial growth has come to be taken for granted in developed societies; we assume that our economy is operating satisfactorily only when it grows at a proper rate each year. Such growth is possible, of course, not merely because of technological and scientific discoveries; equally essential is a source of capital investment in the development and production of more advanced goods and services. The higher an industrial nation's standard of living, moreover, the easier further capital investment and continued industrial growth.

The internal dynamics of advanced economic systems therefore give them an advantage over backward or underdeveloped societies that is cumulative and may even be insuperable. Whereas an agricultural people can find resources for capital investment only by means of foreign investment or a more or less forced redistribution of wealth from farming to the industrial sectors of the economy, neither is absolutely necessary within an already developed nation. But foreign sources of capital may be insufficient for industrialization, and the transfer of resources from agriculture to industry encounters, in a backward society, the farmer's or peasant's reluctance to reduce his standard of living below what is often a near-subsistence level at best.

Many underdeveloped societies do contain enclaves of

wealth in the hands of landowners, merchants, a traditional upper-class or newly formed elites, but without massive foreign assistance these sources may be insufficient to finance the necessary capital investment. The experience of industrialization in the Soviet Union shows that forced mobilization of agricultural production and a redirection of its product toward industrial uses becomes, at least to some degree, a necessity. Yet there may be limits on this device which make industrialization extremely difficult if not impossible to achieve in some societies.

The possibility that the gap between industrialized and underdeveloped nations will increase over the next fifty years can be more fully indicated by considering the process of industrialization in the last two centuries. Techniques of factory production, based on the application of mechanical devices run by nonhuman sources of energy, where first introduced on a significant scale in England in the last half of the eighteenth century. The process was slow but continuous, and took place in a society with considerable amounts of unused capital and a pool of educated personnel capable of inventing and maintaining the new technology.

The spread of industrialization was in part the result of contact between the English, who were developing these new methods of production, and neighboring nations in which the prerequisites for industrial development were almost as fully present as in Great Britain. Thus, in the late eighteenth century, French industry began to develop (with the central government encouraging or itself undertaking the establishment of new industrial enterprises to a greater degree than in England). In the nineteenth century, this process continued not only in England and France but elsewhere on the continent and in the United States. And, it might be added, an important factor encouraging the spread of heavy industry was its evident connection with military and hence political power.

If one compares conditions in various European countries at the outset of industrialization, striking features emerge. By contrast with England's experience in the eighteenth century, successive countries undergoing the Industrial Revolution did so at a later stage of technology; whereas the first experience of modern industry was on the level of small factories, primarily in textile weaving, continuous advances produced a new form of larger scale industry, characterized by the industrial production of iron and steel, and ultimately by railroads.

The scale of technology required to begin industrial growth has thus steadily increased since the beginning of the nineteenth century, so that a newly industrializing country must begin at a higher level of sophistication than its predecessors. For example, when Japan began to industrialize during the second half of the nineteenth century, it was adopting techniques (e.g., in the production of iron, transportation, etc.) far more complex than those at first used in Great Britain.

As a result, the more recent the beginning of industrialization, the greater is the original capital investment needed by a country, the more complex the technology that must be employed, and the more necessary a pool of technically trained engineers capable of running the new industrial plants. Ironically, as modern technology spreads to hitherto underdeveloped societies, it becomes the less likely that these advantages will be as readily available as they were in Western Europe and the United States.

For example, education in the West prior to the Industrial Revolution produced, almost as a matter of course, a certain (although limited) number of scientists and mechanical inventors; at the same time, there was sufficient literacy and enlightenment so that many individuals were willing to embark on radically new ways of producing things. In contrast, those countries yet to be industrialized tend to have more traditional orientations; apart from the impact of colonialism, which produced a small class trained in the Western manner, most inhabitants of backward societies in Asia and Africa are accustomed to work much as their ancestors did.

As the adoption of modern technology has spread through

the world, the chances of successful industrial development have therefore been reduced for two complementary reasons: on the one hand, the skills and capital resources necessary for industrialization are less and less to be encountered prior to the beginnings of development; on the other, these skills and resources are needed all the more, for the continuous evolution of technology has meanwhile increased the admission fee for entry into the class of modern nations.

The dilemma of ever-increasing requirements for industrialization in societies that have less and less ability to meet them is seen in the way modern technology has spread during the twentieth century. Russia did not begin to develop the rudiments of modern industry until the latter part of the nineteenth century; even then it was an overwhelmingly peasant society into which the Czarist government, by central decision, introduced a few heavy industries (largely as a means of playing a role in world politics). After the communist revolution, the USSR—utilizing the industry so developed as a base—became a first-ranking industrial power by means of centrally planned investment enforced by a totalitarian regime. Even so, this industrialization presupposed some contact with the West prior to this century, and indeed the germs of an industrial plant.

The same preconditions, though to a lesser degree, have been the basis of industrial development in China (especially in Manchuria) and India, although in both cases it was Western investment—through national concessions in China or British colonialism in India—that produced the core from which further development could arise in the second half of the twentieth century. Yet a comparison between Russia, whose decisive industrial development occurred in the first half of this century, and India and China (both of which are now attempting to achieve the same status) shows how the further advance of Western technology faces ever-increasing obstacles; without totalitarian control, even a nation with rich natural resources may fail to become fully industrialized.

The continued spread of Western technology and industry,

insofar as it is to produce nations with self-sustaining and totally modern economies, is becoming increasingly difficult. We can therefore expect that the gap between the rich and the poor nations will grow wider. Although poorer nations will be able to acquire more products of modern technology, most particularly military equipment, we should have no illusions concerning the enormous difficulties involved in the development of stable industrial societies in the currently underdeveloped regions of the world.

This problem is of particular importance because it indicates a source of tension in the future of world politics that is quite independent of the cold war. Since the industrial superpowers cannot always control recalcitrant backward peoples and the latter seek rapid industrialization under particularly unpromising circumstances, international conflict can hardly be expected to disappear in the next half century, even if the balance of nuclear terror deters great powers from a major war.

The process by which advanced technology is being diffused must be seen as the latest epoch in the history of the human race, a species distinguished from other animals by its extensive use of tools. The earliest implements were sharpened pebble-tools apparently used to make wooden weapons (in part to kill animals for food); bones of animals also served this purpose. In other words, technology seems related not merely with the means of gaining food but also with the production of weapons. It was only a related step, made centuries ago, to learn that weapons could be used to attack other men as well as animals. This intimate connection between the progress of technology and the art of making weapons deserves particular attention in the nuclear age, for the crisis of modern technology—which has simultaneously produced the means for making human life more comfortable and for destroying it utterly—is but a radical form of an ancient problem.

The evolutionary origins of man's attempt to conquer nature with technology lead one to doubt that infinite prog-

indicate that national economies, even if highly industrialized, must combine—at least to the degree represented by the Common Market—in order to challenge the two continental-scale powers. Because the economic and political aspects of size in modernized society should not be confused, it is necessary to consider both the character of industrial society and the status of nationalism as a political force.

On the purely technological and industrial side, self-sustaining economic growth requires adequate research, development and capital investment, manufacture capable of realizing the economies of scale made possible by recent technology, and —as a corollary—extensive distribution and servicing networks for the resulting output. As modern technology has progressed, the ever-increasing scale of efficient production thus places pressure on political or social institutions that would prevent the industrial plant of a developed society from operating at its optimum level.

This process is most clearly evident in Western Europe, where the development of the European Coal and Steel Community, followed by the Common Market, is sufficiently well known; the development of analogous institutions in Eastern Europe—the Soviet-sponsored COMECON—perhaps reveals the same pressures to a lesser degree. It would, however, be a gross error to overstate the political implications of the need to secure larger markets for capital investment and product distribution. Although recent statistics reveal that a highly industrialized nation-state must increasingly trade with other industrialized states, because the underdeveloped countries are often irrelevant as markets for the most sophisticated modern products, it need not follow that political union is necessary to satisfy the demands of a continental-scale industrial technology.

On the contrary, it appears that nationalism is far from dead; the existence of a community of interests and feelings plays an important role in economically developed society. A common language and traditions, permitting different classes and interests to "understand each other" both literally and

giances) may oppose rapid modernization that destroys their influence.

As a result, the path of adopting Western technology in the underdeveloped parts of the world will be very difficult. Just as Japan and Russia were modernized under sharply different regimes, there is probably no single method which could be successful in all developing societies; depending on specific circumstances, military rule, autocratic control by a single party, or systems that show more deference to traditional standards may arise as alternatives or be combined in varying proportions. We must expect that many regimes will fail to master the problems posed by the contact of backward societies with the industrially advanced nations of the northern hemisphere. And we must expect that, for some underdeveloped nations, foreign war will be a means of producing the internal cohesiveness needed to gain domestic support for those in power.

The difficulties created by the spread of modern industrial technology to backward societies are aggravated by the smallness of many new nations. A self-sustaining industrial economy requires a larger market and social base than is provided by most nation-states; the two nuclear superpowers which have successfully translated their industrial potential into dominance in world politics are best described as "continent-states." Whereas international relations were controlled by the nations of Europe from the end of the fifteenth century until World War II, in the twentieth century decisive influence has passed to formerly peripheral powers; the United States and Russia, once of marginal importance in the European power balance, became pivotal because without them other European states were incapable of containing an aggressive, industrial Germany. As one observer concluded, "to say that the European age [of world politics] has closed is to imply that the nation-state is no longer the dominant political form." [2]

The dynamics of economic development in Western Europe

[2] George Lichtheim: *Europe and America* (London: Thames and Hudson; 1963), p. 6.

Asia, Africa, or South America (where certain forms of imitating Western life are apparent, at least on the surface); the more important problems face the peasant, farmer, or village merchant who has as yet perceived only the most superficial aspects of modern life. For these traditionally oriented people, time-honored modes of family planning and daily living must suddenly be altered in a radical way.

The resulting political pressures will often be inconsistent with the democratic procedures known to us in the West. We are accustomed to government by popular consent, but it cannot be expected that a relatively illiterate people will readily overthrow its traditions for a kind of social planning that is only imperfectly understood even in industrial nations. Even if democracy manages to persist in the developing nations, it will probably take different forms than in the West, exhibiting a tendency toward a more autocratic, centrally planned society.

Such considerations have led observers to believe that backward societies might adopt communist institutions and ideas —not because of communist subversion alone, but also because of an ideology that could be used to mobilize a backward populace. Even where communism is not officially adopted, rulers seem virtually certain to introduce an ideology which justifies the sacrifice of parochial interests to the needs and commands of the society as interpreted by its government (thereby permitting the regime to control traditional elite groups).

It is not, however, a foregone conclusion that highly centralized government (especially of a quasi-totalitarian or autocratic sort) will be the most effective method of satisfying the complex problems facing backward societies. While central rulers will be tempted to force their subjects to conform to radically new ways, their very haste—backed up by military power or a seemingly omnipotent political party—may produce confusion, error, and failure. In some areas, successful change may be impossible unless it is produced through the cooperation of traditional sectors of the society, even though such groups (based on tribal or religious customs and alle-

at the same time, the increasing population absorbs increases in the productivity of non-agricultural goods, consuming output which would have to be invested if self-sustaining economic growth is to be achieved. The difficulty becomes clear when we realize that even developed economies often have difficulty in expanding steadily at a rate of over 3 per cent a year, so that population increases of that scale threaten to make it perpetually impossible for a backward nation to industrialize successfully.

There are two means by which population explosion in backward countries could be—and must be—controlled. First, large-scale birth control programs (rendered possible and inexpensive by scientific and medical advances in the West) could bring the birth rate into a better balance with the suddenly reduced death rate. Second, more advanced techniques of agriculture, developed within industrialized society on the basis of better scientific knowledge of crops and fertilizers, could be used to increase the output of existing land and farm workers. Intensive use of such means has permitted Japanese agriculture to increase enormously the yield per acre; such methods could presumably be used elsewhere as well.

New methods of birth control and agricultural production do not face the same obstacles as general industrialization: a combination of foreign aid and domestic resources should be able to supply the capital and manpower needed by underdeveloped societies (for in this case the advances of scientific technology are an advantage, reducing the cost of imitating the West). The prime concern is a human one: family planning and new modes of farming strike at the most parochial, "grass roots" level of life in pre-modern societies. In order to introduce methods of birth control and modern agriculture on a sufficiently vast scale, it is necessary to alter the habits and prejudices of peoples who have hitherto had the least preparation for such changes.

The crucial impact of modern technology on backward societies may therefore not take place in the urban centers of

sideration. In the last half century, industrialized civilization has extended the average life expectancy of man. Developments in medicine have greatly decreased infant mortality, eradicated many contagious diseases, and produced totally new methods of improving public health. The use of these techniques in a hitherto backward society does not require (as does the establishment of industrial plants) a large capital investment or even large numbers of locally trained personnel; in an underdeveloped nation, foreign resources are capable, with moderate investments in men and material that are within domestic means, of radically reducing the death rate.

In highly industrialized countries, the impact of modern medicine, with its reduction of the death rate, has been counterbalanced by lower birth rates than are found in backward societies. This is completely understandable, for high birth rates in agrarian societies are necessary, given equally high death rates, if the population is to subsist; since the process of lowering the death rate has been relatively slow and steady in the West, the adjustment in the form of correspondingly lower birth rates has taken place without massive dislocations.

Although it is sometimes forgotten that the Industrial Revolution in the West was also accompanied by increased population, European cities in the eighteenth and nineteenth centuries had high death rates and often grew as the result of migrations of farmers and peasants. The problem is more serious among those peoples yet to be industrialized, for in Asia, South America, and Africa we see both migration to urban areas and a generalized increase in life expectancy. Because medicine has taken such gigantic strides—and because the people affected, being less highly developed, have often had such high birth rates—the introduction of Western medicine has produced the frequently discussed population explosion.

Populations that are expanding rapidly, sometimes at rates of 3 per cent a year, place great pressure on food supplies;

ress is virtually assured by modern science. Our technology is merely a human invention which, like genetic mutation in other species, serves to preserve man in a changing environment. But many species have ceased to exist after flourishing for eons; there is even evidence that some of man's apelike ancestors developed tools only to become extinct. The same fate may await man himself; our industrial civilization could decline or disintegrate (as did the highly developed civilizations of the Egyptians, the Assyrians, etc.), or the human race itself may be destroyed by some future cataclysm. Although nuclear war is the most easily imagined example of such a catastrophe, industrial civilization is becoming increasingly vulnerable to any massive disruption, even from natural events.[1]

It is in this sobering perspective that the gap between the highly developed industrial societies of the northern hemisphere and the more backward peoples must be considered. Since mankind faces problems of unprecedented complexity and difficulty, it is folly to assume that any one nation, however powerful, can itself determine the course of history. But the advanced nations must still consider the impact of their actions on the planet as a whole, for failure to resolve those economic, political, and social problems that are within our control may be more disastrous than ever before.

The threat to world peace and stability posed by the underdeveloped nations is so acute that it deserves further con-

[1] "If we are able in the decade ahead to avoid thermonuclear war, and if the present underdeveloped areas of the world are able to carry out successful industrialization programs, we shall approach the time when the world will be completely industrialized. . . . As man approaches this phase of his culture he may well reach a point of no return—a point in time beyond which a major disruption to the world-wide industrial network would be irreversible. . . . Our technology will permit us to continue without [easily accessible natural resources] as long as industrial civilization keeps functioning. But if for any reason disaster strikes and the industrial network is destroyed, it seems doubtful that we shall ever again be able to lift ourselves above the agrarian level of existence." Harrison Brown, James Bonner, and John Weir: *The Next Hundred Years* (New York: Viking Press; 1963), p. 151.

figuratively, make it much easier to control the complex and divisive issues created by modern technology. This is especially clear when we realize the extent to which governmental intervention, planning, and regulation is necessary in any industrialized society, if only to avoid the extremes of unemployment and depression or inflation.

Even in the United States, where the persistence of nineteenth-century ideologies creates suspicion of governmental planning, the federal government must continually intervene in the market economy to prevent disaster. This is not merely a question of Keynesian economics, which has begun to be acknowledged, at least in principle, as a necessity; in more direct and pervasive ways, any administration in Washington now feels compelled to restrain price or wage increases that threaten to release an inflationary cycle, and to discourage strikes that would disrupt the economy as a whole. The general commitment to full employment makes this task increasingly difficult because rapid economic growth in an uncontrolled market economy tends to result in cyclical unemployment; efforts to combine increased output with economic stability require restraints on the share of the Gross National Product claimed by both labor and management.

Since governmental planning in one form or another becomes absolutely essential if a highly industrialized economy is not to collapse or produce rapid inflation, the political prerequisite of a cohesive social community becomes more important in industrial societies than in less developed ones (where deep regional, ethnic, or linguistic conflicts can be tolerated because they do not disrupt an essentially agrarian economy—or be suppressed by brute force in extreme cases). This may explain why linguistic and cultural separatism has become an explosive issue in such advanced countries as Canada and Belgium, for it is exceedingly difficult to implement central economic planning without relying upon the kind of consensus most fully provided by a common national bond.

Even within the most fully industrialized societies, therefore, important political conflicts are created by the very features of economic development that seem most attractive to the backward societies. Moreover, the technical imperatives of large-scale economic organization need not inevitably produce, especially in Western Europe, a continental political community; on the contrary, European desires for supranational political institutions reflect a need for governmental control over economic processes which may not be possible in a multinational area (where commonly shared values are to some extent undercut by divergent languages and traditions).

The present limits of national communities are not, of course, naturally fixed. In a broad historical perspective, the cohesion characteristic of the nation-state was also found in the Greek city-states of the fifth century B.C. or the Italian city-states of the Renaissance; the rise of nations as the most stable, autonomous political communities is a phenomenon of the last five centuries, and has only been fully realized on the basis of a technology that transcended the agrarian mode of livelihood characteristic of both early river-valley civilizations (Egypt, Assyria, China, etc.) and primitive or medieval, essentially village-centered, social life.

Whatever the technological prerequisites for stable forms of a civilized political community, the modern age presents something of a paradox. It was within the national state that the modern industrial economy arose, yet this technology seems to outstrip the political limits of all but the most extensive and most ethnically divergent nation-states; pressures for supranational political units of continental scale reflect a need for the internal cohesion characteristic of nations. The nation is a typically European phenomenon, yet both the United States and Russia are in a sense extra-European states.

These considerations do not incline the thoughtful observer to optimism. They indicate a weakness of developed national societies of less than continental scale and suggest great obstacles in the way of Western European political union; they also indicate that underdeveloped countries face additional obstacles in their search for political stability and rapid economic growth. Since we will deal with the former problem in more detail in Chapter v, it is worth concentrating here on the contradiction between the economic and the political prerequisites of development.

Whereas the continental scale of optimum industrial development militates against national limits for governmental policies—as has been seen by those planners who propose an African or Latin American "Common Market"—the social problems created by rapid development seem to require the kind of internal cohesion found only within a nation-state. Hence economic development simultaneously presupposes something like a national consciousness and consensus, and tends to break these customary bonds in search of a stable community of continental extent.

The primacy of nationalism in the newly developing societies is particularly evident if one considers the ideologies accepted by those attempting to modernize and industrialize their countries. Within the communist bloc, it appears that Marxism is taking on an increasingly nationalist tone; in uncommitted states, rulers often combine a degree of anti-colonialist nationalism with at least verbal acceptance of socialism (by which they often merely mean centralized planning). Whether the ideology is national communism or a version of socialist nationalism, the emphasis is decidedly on the unique or sacred character of the nation-state, for only by thus enhancing the status of the political community are rulers able to promote rapid economic and social change under unpromising conditions.

At the same time, phenomena like "Arab nationalism" or pan-Africanism reveal a quest for regional or continental identity as a means of increasing the impact of backward societies in international politics, and of broadening the area within which development will take place. But although the states comprising these regions were often the result of arbitrary colonial boundaries, they find themselves in conflict with each other as soon as specific policy issues are discussed; since backward nations either compete for the same foreign resources in order to begin their development or have radically different interests (or both), the national imperative tends to outweigh the vague cultural and geographical ties on which broader political communities might be based.

Under these circumstances, effective political and economic development seems more of a mirage than a likely result of present efforts. Given the obstacles to the emergence of a new continental scale power in Western Europe, which is already highly developed, it is unlikely that many of the less developed societies will challenge the United States and Soviet Russia in the next century; only where backward societies have inherited something like continental boundaries from the colonial era does this seem even possible. This would imply that China and India are the most probable poles of power in the underdeveloped world, with the possible addition of Brazil or Argentina. But problems in these countries today indicate that the difficulties are by no means trivial, and the likelihood of a painful century of transition toward industrialization is great.

Were these obstacles the sum of the challenge facing the human race in the next century, one might be tempted to find hope in the supremacy of the two continental superpowers; with their vast industrial establishments as hostages to each other's nuclear forces, limited agreements to avoid mutually destructive thermonuclear war would seem to be a way of preserving the peace. Some intelligent observers have concluded that the present bipolar international system has not only been more stable than usually admitted, but that it is likely to persist (if only because no states will attain the degree of power now held by the United States and Soviet Russia).[3]

[3] See Kenneth Waltz: "The Stability of a Bipolar World," *Daedalus* (Summer 1964), pp. 881-909.

At this point, however, one must consider the diffusion of military technology, and more particularly the spread of those most threatening products of modern science, nuclear weapons and strategic delivery capabilities. Unlike the prerequisites of a fully developed industrial economy, which are often lacking in hitherto backward societies, certain aspects of modern military technology are quite easily exported and utilized by states incapable of self-sustaining economic growth. Since even nuclear warheads can conceivably be possessed by a country that does not have the means of producing them, the obstacles facing a backward society seeking industrial development do not necessarily guarantee its passivity.

Despite popular fascination with nuclear weapons, the most important military product of modern technology may well lie in "conventional armaments." This term is actually misleading, for it masks the technological revolution which, completely apart from nuclear explosives, has changed the political impact of military power. As recently as the nineteenth century, revolution by masses, even when armed merely with rifles or sticks, could seriously threaten a ruler backed by an organized army; cannon could be brought to bear against the rebels within cities, but they could set up barricades that could be stormed with difficulty.

A comparison of the Hungarian revolution of 1956 with the revolt of the Paris Commune in 1870 reveals the extent to which the now "conventional" weapons have increased the vulnerability of discontented urban populations. The machine gun, tank, and airplane have given a government which controls a reasonably well-equipped army a tremendous advantage over any popular movement lacking similar weapons. The consequence is an extremely important shift in the strategy of revolutionary warfare; instead of mass action centered in cities, guerrilla action by relatively small and widely dispersed units, capitalizing on mobility and popular sanctuary, has become increasingly attractive as a means of overthrowing unpopular governments.

Although this typically modern strategy was used effectively in the battles of Lexington and Concord, the development of military technology since 1776 has had several significant consequences. (1) The means of warfare available to an organized army are, aside from nuclear weapons, more powerful than ever before; (2) the use of small arms against concentrations of higher firepower, reinforced by tanks and airplanes, is only possible in dispersed conflict; as a result, a successful rebellion presupposes a wider popular organization and a less centralized military confrontation with those in power; (3) despite the apparent superiority of the ruling military, governments are particularly vulnerable to any rebellion that is joined by part of its own armed forces; (4) in any event, the triumph of modern technology has diffused a vast range of so-called "conventional" arms and made them easily available to potential rebels as well as to those in power.

In some cases since World War II, as in Greece, Malaya, and Guatemala, established governments have succeeded, with considerable foreign assistance, in defeating domestic revolutions based on guerrilla tactics; in others, where both sides have been subsidized relatively equally (as in Yemen, Laos, and Cyprus), military battles have been fought to a statemate; finally, there have been successful guerrilla wars, of which the best known are the victories of Mao Tse-tung in China and Castro in Cuba. As these examples show, the diffusion of modern conventional weapons does not permit one to predict the outcome of internal political conflict, nor are there any strategic formulas which are certain to succeed everywhere.

Although these aspects of modern industrial technology need not fundamentally alter the relationship of force between a government and its people, the scale of violence and organization required for a military take-over has been radically increased. As a consequence, the logistics of revolution have become somewhat more complex, giving a great advantage to those who seek to organize subversion on a systematic basis and increasing the tendency of rebels to rely on ideology. Whether in the form of anticolonialism, in attempts to subvert a nominally independent government, or in the process of rapid economic development, backward societies are easily influenced by ideological appeals that promise great rewards from the use of violence. The prospect of an improved life and an end to injustice is especially effective among peoples subject to the "rising cycle of expectations"—i.e., to those fully aware of their own inferiority by comparison to the highly industrialized nations of the world.

This dependence on radical ideologies is particularly dangerous both because the minimal arsenal needed for a revolt can often be acquired without difficulty and because nationalist or peasant movements of discontent are subject to infiltration from abroad. Although these factors may give an advantage to communist states that are willing to supply arms and training to revolutionary leaders, existing regimes can respond by adopting their own nationalistic ideology, repressing dissent, and seeking support from non-communist allies. As a result, major powers may often be tempted to intervene in the domestic conflicts that seem inevitable in unstable and backward societies.

Intervention in foreign civil wars is, of course, an ancient strategy; whether during the Peloponnesian War between Sparta and Athens or in the European state system of the seventeenth and eighteenth centuries, assistance to rebels in an enemy country (or its ally) was a traditional means of increasing power. American independence was won in part because the French used this device. But modern technology, when combined with the instability of underdeveloped political systems, makes this strategy more attractive in the last half of the twentieth century.

The diffusion of conventional weapons will therefore increase the likelihood of domestic violence in the developing countries.[4] The United States, or any other industrialized nation, cannot be assured that it will keep a friendly government in power by means of military assistance, if only because the armed forces in a backward society are themselves open

[4] For evidence of this probability, see Bruce M. Russett: *Trends in World Politics* (New York: Macmillan; 1965), pp. 120-1, 135-7.

to subversion or internal division. In addition, open intervention may create the unwanted risk of a direct confrontation
between major powers.

Even if the United States so desired, it could not bring
its vast fire-power to bear on every revolutionary movement
that was potentially anti-American; as the war in Vietnam
has shown, such an effort can be both costly and domestically
controversial. As a consequence, we will be forced to select
those instances in which American intervention seems justified.
Such a choice cannot be merely ideological, for the use of a
radical rhetoric (be it openly communist or of the "extreme
left") will be widespread. It follows that the most relevant
standard for our policy is a judgment of the effects of revolutionary violence on the global balance of power. The meaning
of this objective will be spelled out further in Chapter iv
(and applied in Part II) of this book.

While the diffusion of military technology has important
internal consequences in underdeveloped nations (especially
because it limits the control available to the superpowers), it
also affects the relations between such governments. Since
conventional military forces, including tanks, bombers, and
machine guns, can be acquired by a nation lacking an autonomous industrial base, modern warfare can be waged by relatively weak powers. Moreover, as the Indo-Pakistani war over
Kashmir showed, such combat can threaten to undermine the
international balance of power.

The first consideration deserving mention is the relative
ease with which minor powers can be exhausted in conventional wars with their neighbors. There is evidence, for example, that New Delhi and Karachi were willing to accede,
at least formally, to the UN cease-fire in Kashmir because they
realized their mutual inability to score a decisive victory
and found continued major fighting too costly. The awareness
of relative weakness, even when a minor power has considerable armed forces, has doubtless contributed to the reluctance
of Egypt and other Arab states to unleash a large-scale attack

on Israel (and to the similar restraint of Sukarno in Indonesia's confrontation with Malaysia before the military reversed his policies).

Second, the threat of great-power intervention serves as an additional check on minor powers. This restraint operates in a curiously dual fashion: each minor power threatens its rival with the prospect of gaining assistance from a major power in case of hostilities, but the minor powers themselves are reluctant to take this step for fear of becoming satellites of the power they call upon for support. Superpowers seek to deter their rivals from intervention by the threat of doing likewise, and are caught in the contradictory pressures of supporting friendly regimes while avoiding open commitment in a minor war that could escalate.

Such restraints operate more heavily on the major powers than on their weaker allies. As long as one superpower intervenes indirectly and has a likelihood of victory, the other is tempted to limit its involvement to declaratory support (and perhaps the shipment of arms); Russian reluctance to oppose the United States directly in the Congo is a case in point. These restraints may even lead one superpower to disown an ally or sharply reduce its commitment in order to avoid a direct confrontation with its major enemy (as in the Suez and Cuban missile crises).

Under these complex circumstances, aggressive minor powers will increasingly be tempted to develop military forces that would give them the upper hand without having to rely on extensive foreign support. This strategy is profitable for a minor power because it can hope to fight its rivals without outside intervention thanks to mutual deterrence between the superpowers. But such military buildups also have advantages for an aggressive superpower that seeks to undermine its rival without being committed to direct intervention.

The strategic impact of modern weapons on rivalry among the minor powers is revealed by several examples. First, the attempts of Egypt to gain dominance in the Middle East, especially by embarking on the production of short-range missiles which would permit an attack on Israel (whose conventional military strength has twice been more than a match for the Egyptian army). Nasser can hope that, bolstered by foreign aid, he can develop a military potential that ultimately promises victory; he can also hope that in case of a war against Israel, Egypt can again count on Soviet threats to prevent or neutralize American intervention.

A second example is provided by India and Pakistan. Each has sought to use cold-war tensions as a means of receiving modern armaments from the superpowers; both were compelled to use such weapons when war broke out (although it appears that the Pakistanis were the first to do so). The quest for more powerful allies willing to support an aggressive move led the Pakistanis to rely on China (at least tacitly), just as the Israelis were combined, though more openly, with Great Britain and France in their attack on the Suez Canal.

In both instances, the United States and Soviet Russia apparently shared an interest in limiting the extent of violence between minor powers. But this parallel concern for avoiding a direct confrontation is strictly limited; in both cases, intermediate powers did support an aggressive move by a relatively small country. Moreover, in each case the two superpowers had different long-range interests in the area concerned and so acted differently.

The Soviet Union, while insisting on the end of hostilities in the Suez and Kashmir crises, maintained an apparently benevolent attitude toward the Egyptians and Indians; on both occasions Moscow saw an advantage in encouraging a nonaligned minor power that could serve its purpose in the global balance of power. Since the United States has tended to make the restoration of peace an end in itself, the American position has been less clear to the parties involved and our dependence on the UN has been correspondingly greater than that of the Russians. This strategy, justified as an impartial concern that favors neither local enemy, may be a way of getting other states to support our policies. But reliance on the UN may also weaken our ability to manipulate events (especially since anticolonialist, underdeveloped countries are increasingly able to control the General Assembly).

To avoid being outmaneuvered by the Soviet Union, American responses to violence in the underdeveloped parts of the world must take more explicit account of the effects of our actions on the global power balance. This requisite of a sober foreign policy is particularly important because the diffusion of conventional military capabilities, in a period of unrest and instability in the so-called "gray areas," makes minor wars more likely as time goes on. We must learn to live in a world of violence.

The most widely recognized problem created by the spread of modern technology—the proliferation of nuclear weapons—should be considered in this context, for it is really an extreme case of a more general process. Minor or secondary powers may be unable to bring sufficient conventional arms to bear on their rivals; since such weapons are easily obtained even by nonindustrial states, local enemies can often develop roughly equal conventional military capacities by purchase or foreign aid.

Under these circumstances, the temptation to develop nuclear weapons cannot be ignored. Fear of nuclear proliferation has of course been an important restraint, especially since invulnerable missile systems are still extremely expensive. Since minor powers do not want their rivals to acquire nuclear weapons and fear that acquisition of such forces would induce others to do likewise, most backward societies have publicly attacked the principle of nuclear dissemination.

Many statesmen have taken hope in this fact and have urged the need of an international agreement forbidding the spread of nuclear weapons. Before considering the advantages of such an agreement, let us see whether restraints on diffusion are truly possible. While most nonnuclear powers have refrained from developing national striking forces, a few have not done so. France and Great Britain, both industrialized powers of far from superpower status (and both relatively secure under the American nuclear umbrella), embarked on the production of nuclear capabilities; the Chinese have done the same. More significantly, some leaders in India and Japan have begun to consider seriously the advantages of joining the nuclear club.

The example of even one large but not fully developed Asian state—China—seeking to become a nuclear power shows how hard it is to check nuclear diffusion. If an industrialized state is determined, for whatever reasons, to join the nuclear club, not much can be done over the long run to stop it (other than to subject its test sites and nuclear plants to military attack). Moreover, as developing countries industrialize, more candidates for the nuclear club can be expected to arise. The history of disarmament and arms control shows that no state will enter or abide by agreements that contradict its view of national self-interest.

As nuclear energy is increasingly used to generate electricity in some of the more advantageously situated but not fully developed countries, the technology of the atom is diffused throughout the world. "Proliferation has reached a stage where India could achieve a first fission test within 18 months from the decision being taken; Canada within two years; West Germany within three years; Israel, Sweden, Italy and Japan within five years; and Czechoslovakia, East Germany, Rumania, Yugoslavia, Spain, Australia, South Africa, Pakistan, and possibly Indonesia and the United Arab Republic within 10."[5] Whether any or all of these states actually develops nuclear weapons will be determined by a political decision based on considerations of power and self-interest, not by scientific or industrial ability alone.

To date, nuclear proliferation has been restrained within the industrialized societies of the Western alliance by the American commitment to defend Europe and the relatively high cost of independent production. These factors did not deter the British and French, however, and it would be dangerous to assume that either is certain to persist indefinitely. Even if a nation is unlikely to acquire a nuclear capability that is as extensive and invulnerable as the strategic forces of the

[5] Andrew Martin and Wayland Young: "Proliferation," *Disarmament and Arms Control*, III (August 1965), 108. Some observers would place Japan in the category of two to two and one-half years.

superpowers, the possession of a minimal deterrent may seem attractive to statesmen who feel that otherwise their country will be insecure.

Outside of Western Europe, the probability of nuclear proliferation varies widely. Industrialized, technically competent nations seem more likely to embark on the production of atomic weapons whenever the reduction of their cost and the perceived needs of self-defense favor entry into the nuclear club. Although large or aggressive developing countries like India and China are somewhat less favored with respect to the industrial capabilities required, their self-interest in acquiring nuclear weapons (especially when rivals have done so) may be greater than in a Western Europe now defended by three nuclear powers. In contrast, most underdeveloped societies of Africa and Latin America will probably find the acquisition of nuclear weapons economically difficult and strategically unnecessary so long as costs are high and aggressive neighbors don't start the race.

The unequal temptations to utilize the evolving knowledge of nuclear technology apply equally to the means of producing other new military weapons as well (notably missiles). Japan is pushing forward in a program to launch a satellite, and will surely have effective long-range missiles in a few years. Egypt has been able to construct some missiles, although the assistance of foreign technicians, notably from West Germany, has been necessary. Since it is hard to envision a means of checking the diffusion of technological information (much of which is already available in scientific journals), the possibility of some proliferation of nonconventional armaments seems high. Even if an anti-proliferation treaty is signed, extraordinarily vigorous controls and enforcement powers would be required to prevent a determined state from becoming a nuclear power.

Although nuclear diffusion must be considered as but one aspect in the evolution of world politics, the spread of nuclear weapons seems both unavoidable and terribly dangerous. For this reason, questions of military, and especially nuclear, strategy have unprecedented importance; these problems will therefore be considered in detail in the next chapter. But before so doing, it may be useful to summarize the trends sketched thus far.

It is unlikely that many underdeveloped economies will attain the military capability now shared by the superpowers; excepting a united Western Europe, which would have the industrial base and technical skill to become something of a superpower should it gain political unity, few challengers to the United States and Soviet Russia are discernible. Although China has a good chance of attaining superpower status in the next half century, few other underdeveloped societies seem headed in this direction.

One reason for this is the continental scale needed for continuously self-sustaining economic growth; since something like national cohesion seems both necessary for modernization and a check on the fullest industrial development, not many backward societies are likely to develop an economy capable of supporting a first-rate military establishment. The probability of continued evolution of military technology by the superpowers reinforces this conclusion.

Even if the superpowers maintain an absolute superiority over all other states, however, it does not follow that the bipolar pattern established since 1945 will persist unchanged throughout the next half century. On the contrary, we will probably see the emergence of a number of second-level powers capable of minimal nuclear deterrents and industrialization that will distinguish them from the most backward states. Projections of current rates of economic growth bear out such a forecast.[6]

Because the gap between the most and least developed societies seems likely to grow wider, however, conditions within the relatively backward regions will continue to be unstable. The superpowers will be less able to control events in world politics, for they will be challenged by intermediate powers,

[6] See Russett: *Trends in World Politics*, pp. 120, 144.

at least with respect to local conflicts, and the poorest states will be encountering political, economic, and military threats that superpowers cannot resolve by themselves.

There are many indications that the bipolar confrontation of the United States and Russia, which forced vulnerable states to ally with a superpower while neutrals played one against the other, has recently been weakened; the attempts of France and China to establish independent policies, without totally abandoning the protection of a nominally allied superpower, show how far rigid bipolarity has declined. A continuation of current trends will doubtless reinforce this diffusion of power to second-rank states.

As to the future, let us concentrate on the strategic implications of a general dispersion of power in the next half century. Ideologies are not a clear guide to these changes, for the principles of Western democracy or Marxism-Leninism are not necessarily suited to the particular conditions of every developing society; as bipolarity declines, it becomes more difficult to describe political conflict as uniquely an issue of communism versus freedom. The persisting elements of ideological hostility between East and West are therefore best understood by placing them in a broader context of the evolution of the global balance of power in a period of technological, economic, and political change.

CHAPTER THREE

Nuclear Diffusion
and World Peace

IT HAS OFTEN been suggested that the era of nation-states is coming to an end; continental-scale political units seem to be necessitated by the modern industrial technology that alone confers major-power status. But few such continent states are likely to emerge during the remainder of this century because the potentialities for economic and political development are not everywhere present and nationalism seems to be increasingly important in underdeveloped parts of the world.

As a result, the erosion of bipolarity need not produce the kind of multipower balance that characterized international relations in the eighteenth and nineteenth centuries. Among other things, such a balance of power, which was also approximated among the Italian city-states of the fifteenth century, implies the relative equality of at least four or five major powers; only if Western Europe, China (and perhaps India) were to attain superpower status would this condition for the traditional balance-of-power relationship exist. Hence, at least for the immediate future, we must expect a situation between strict bipolarity and a multipower balance of roughly equal political communities.

Historical examples in which a dominant form of political community, such as the Greek or Italian city-states, disintegrated in the face of larger-scale powers show that it is not easy to foresee the consequences. After the great bipolar confrontation between Athens and Sparta in the Peloponnesian War (fifth century B.C.), the Greek city-states rapidly fell under the sway of Macedonian power; ultimately Rome conquered the Mediterranean basin and established a world empire. The fifteenth-century balance of power in Italy gave way to a conflict between the national monarchies of France and Spain, ultimately producing a century of religious wars in which the national state fully emerged and permitted a return to a multipower balance.

A continuously evolving technology may conceivably lead to a break-through permitting one power to establish world-wide dominance (and perhaps empire); also possible is a time of troubles in which international politics remains suspended between bipolarity and a multipower rivalry of roughly equal states. Since the latter seems somewhat more likely, let us consider the results of the emergence of intermediate powers that are neither as strong as the continental superpowers nor as weak as the most backward societies.

The aftermath of World War II was marked by an enormous qualitative difference between the strength of the two leading states and the relative helplessness of virtually every other country in the world. In a sense, the nations of Western Europe had but little advantage over the most underdeveloped societies; it was this weakness, largely caused by the exhaustion of two major wars in a half century, that led to the collapse of European empires.

Now that the process of decolonization has been largely completed, Western European states have recovered to the point of establishing an independent basis of strength; industrialized countries like Japan and large but developing states like China show signs of increasing their power over that of the most underdeveloped societies. It is therefore necessary to specify in detail the characteristic differences in political and military strength that seem most likely to develop over the next half century.

It is not enough to describe all states as either superpowers (or nuclear powers) and weak or secondary powers. A more realistic approach would be to distinguish four levels of power, each of which depends on a given state's relative strength vis-à-vis its neighbors as well as its absolute degree of economic and military development. For most purposes, these categories can be defined in terms of a country's offensive and defensive potential.

First-ranking or super powers—thus far the United States and the USSR—are those that can totally devastate any attacking country after having borne the brunt of an all-out military strike. In practical terms, this capacity implies the possession of invulnerable, so-called "second-strike" nuclear forces (land-based and well-protected intercontinental missiles or mobile submarines with Polaris-type weapons). The mere possession of relatively limited stockpiles of nuclear missiles is not sufficient to give a country superpower status, which at present seems only accessible to highly industrialized states of continental scale.

Second-ranking powers can be described as those incapable of destroying a superpower after receiving an all-out attack (although they may inflict marginal damage), but can devastate a third-ranking power without receiving more than marginal harm from the victim. Although the acquisition of nuclear capabilities seems the most characteristic means of attaining secondary-power status, large conventional armies may serve the same purpose. France and China are both secondary powers even though the latter acquired this status before developing an operational delivery system for nuclear weapons.

In this view, third-level powers are those that could be destroyed by either first- or second-rank powers without being able to make an effective military response by themselves. Such third-ranking states would be distinguished from a fourth level, however, because the latter would be too weak to attack any foreign enemy, no matter how impotent, whereas third-level powers could conduct military aggression against equivalent or weaker states. Just now, India and Pakistan are third-level powers, whereas Burma is of the fourth rank.

These categories of power are not based solely on measures of military forces or economic development; although such factors as the gross national product are vital components of political power, a state's opportunities and goals in foreign politics are also highly relevant. For example, countries devoted to the preservation of the status quo and having little possibility to increase their power by violent means, like the United States or Great Britain, require somewhat larger military forces and gross national product to balance an aggressive state, like China, which has tempting opportunities for increasing its control over weaker countries.

Although the distinction between the levels of power of various states is not entirely relative, the will and desire to use force against rivals is extremely important in assessing military strategy. Too often this factor has been completely overlooked in American writings that concentrate on the technological details of a state's armed forces. History has shown that a highly developed, rich society can be in effect weaker than a less wealthy but more aggressive state simply because the latter is willing to take far greater risks in the use of force.

The above categories of power are useful because they indicate that while few states are likely to become superpowers, some third-rank states will probably increase their power by one degree. The dual factors of nuclear proliferation and the rise of second-rank powers must be considered together if the weakening of bipolarity is to be properly assessed. American strategic analysts have spoken of nuclear diffusion as the

"Nth Country Problem" (without reference to the specific powers most likely to acquire nuclear capability). However, analysis of military technology and strategy as parts of a process of historical and political evolution leads one to question this view.

When analyzed in purely strategic terms, the argument can easily be made that the spread of nuclear weapons to "Nth countries" creates an overwhelming danger to mankind. Assuming that all or most states have at least some atomic bombs, the likelihood of nuclear war becomes exceedingly great; since it could conceivably become difficult if not impossible to identify with certainty which nation attacked first, every state would be radically insecure. Alliances would be relatively useless, for no country could increase its ability to protect itself against sneak attack by gaining an ally, nor could it add to its offensive power without at the same time risking involvement in its allies' quarrels.[1]

The situation imagined as the result of proliferation has therefore been compared to the "war of all against all" described by the English philosopher Hobbes, for every state could inflict devastation on any other state (and would risk being destroyed in turn). Hobbes described life under such conditions of "continual fear and danger of violent death" as "solitary, poor, nasty, brutish, mean, and short"; no wonder this view of nuclear proliferation appears to be the greatest evil imaginable. Compared to such an unstable world, the current bipolar confrontation of the United States and Russia seems tame indeed.

The crucial assumption of this "Nth Country" approach is dubious, however, because nuclear technology does not equalize the war-making potential of every state, nor can all states acquire the same kind of strategic capabilities. Even assuming extensive diffusion of nuclear weapons, there may be a great difference between the kind of invulnerable missile forces now held by the superpowers and the less effective delivery systems of weaker states.

[1] See, for example, Morton Kaplan: *System and Process in International Politics* (New York: Wiley; 1957), pp. 50-2.

Whereas the United States can now destroy Soviet society even after being subjected to a massive Russian nuclear attack, a relatively backward society that possesses a few missiles with atomic warheads will presumably not have this ability. Continued research and development, and especially the installation of antimissile defenses may even widen this gap. As a result, the threat of reciprocal annihilation that deters the superpowers from attacking each other need not operate in the same way on weaker powers.

Other restraints would exist, however, after general nuclear proliferation. A state with minimal nuclear forces is not likely to attack one of the superpowers directly except under massive provocation—and even then only on the assumption that this attack will trigger war between the superpowers themselves. Because a superpower need not, and probably would not, defend a weaker nuclear state whose aggressive actions threatened to produce a global holocaust, the less powerful nations would run a double risk in using atomic weapons. They might be devastated by a superpower while other major powers refrained from intervention; alternatively, a third minor power might retaliate, assuming that the original aggressor did not have a sufficient arsenal to respond effectively and that the superpowers would remain aloof.

Although prediction of these matters is extremely difficult in the abstract, both the United States and the Soviet Union appear increasingly reluctant to engage in a nuclear exchange for the sake of any ally. As the Cuban missile crisis showed, the fear of mutual destruction does not prevent one superpower from attempting to modify the existing power balance, but it does introduce great restraints in how far such a superpower will risk all-out nuclear war with its equal.

Restraints do not flow from any formal treaty but from the calculated self-interest of a reasonable statesman faced with a possible enemy attack that would destroy his own society. The balance of terror is of course uncomfortable: who knows whether an irrational ruler or his uncontrolled lieutenants will misjudge the consequences of an action and unleash total war? But recent experience shows that the more powerful a nation with nuclear weapons, the less it is inclined to risk using its nuclear forces even in a selective way.

The actual behavior of the nuclear superpowers is thus at variance with some of the strategic conceptions often advanced in the United States. Whereas in practice statesmen are reluctant to use atomic weapons (however much they may have threatened to do so), American strategic theory has come to accept the idea of a "flexible response"—that is, the conduct of less than all-out nuclear warfare. In other words, our strategic doctrines consider varied degrees of nuclear retaliation despite the fact that public opinion—and rulers themselves—tend to treat nuclear war as an all-or-nothing matter. The attitude of the average citizen is hardly absurd, moreover, because the risks of escalation are all too evident.

It is the extreme character of major thermonuclear war, therefore, that creates the most decisive limit on the unstabilizing effects of nuclear diffusion. Whereas fundamentally agrarian, backward societies may find the prospect of nuclear attack less appalling (because they have few targets for strategic attack), industrialized states could be demoted to the status of minor powers even if they survive. Hence the superpowers have an interest in limiting their intervention in conflicts between lesser powers, whether nuclear weapons are used or not, since to do otherwise would be self-defeating.

In this context, we should consider the prospects of nuclear diffusion from a rather unconventional angle. The kind of strategic calculation usual in analyzing the Nth country problem seems most relevant to the policy making of a single power; when applied to more complex issues, this approach may be misleading because a number of states are simultaneously calculating their strategies (often on differing assumptions). To appreciate this situation fully, let us compare the rivalry between nuclear superpowers to the economic competition between two, three, or four giant industrial firms, each fearing a major price war that could cause mutual bankruptcy.

Economists have studied in detail the kind of rivalry among a small number of extremely powerful companies that dominate the production of a particular product (such as automobiles or petroleum); they call this situation "oligopoly" if there are several such firms, "duopoly" if only two. In this kind of market, each company tries to increase its share of sales, but each is also aware that major competitors will react to large price changes. So giant firms tend to make tacit or under-the-table agreements to limit their rivalry in prices—and to try to make their products seem different to consumers (through advertising, service, etc.).[1]

The similarities between economic competition and international politics may seem tenuous, but they are revealing. In both, the risk of unrestrained hostility ("price war" in the one case, nuclear war in the other) is mutually unsatisfactory; in both, there is a temptation to compete according to more or less unwritten rules of the game to minimize these dangers. The parallel for advertising in oligopolistic industries is the emphasis on political ideology in the international arena. Moreover, in many oligopolies there are smaller firms, operating under the "umbrella" of industrial giants, who exist on the sufferance of the larger competitors (because rivals will retaliate if one major firm tries to absorb too many of these smaller companies).

If one looks at the stability of different oligopolistic industries with an eye to the analogy of world politics, surprising consequences follow. Duopoly—the bipolar competition between two all-encompassing firms—is one of the most unstable forms of competition under certain theoretical assumptions; when increases of the output or power of each firm are against the interest of its rival, it is difficult to predict the balance of power between the two rivals. While agreements between the duopolists are always possible as a means of limiting serious conflict, such cooperation is fragile unless the two companies

[1] For a statement of the economic theories here briefly summarized, see William Fellner: *Competition Among the Few* (New York: Knopf; 1949); and Martin Shubik: *Strategy and Market Structure* (New York: Wiley; 1959).

virtually combine their forces and act as one. Short of such an agreement, it is relatively easy for each firm to observe and calculate the gains of the other, creating the risk of violent price war.

In contrast, tacit agreements to limit competition, without which rivalry leads to mutual disaster, may be more stable in an oligopoly with four or five major companies. This follows because probing actions by one firm do not necessarily undermine the desire to keep price competition from getting out of hand; even where a number of small firms operate under the "umbrella" of the largest ones, relative price stability seems to be consistent with continued increases in output and technological advances.

Beyond a certain point, however, an increase in the number of major firms has radically different results. When there are many producers of roughly equal size, no individual can control the prices on the market as a whole; without governmental controls, each individual's attempt to make and sell more of his product frequently causes a decline in price which can be disastrous to all. This situation, which is approximated in modern agriculture without governmental intervention, is called "pure competition" by economists, and is often highly unstable (as unregulated farm prices or the recurring booms and depressions in nineteenth century America graphically reveal).

In recent decades, the growth and vitality of American industry have greatly depended on the large size of our leading industrial firms and the failure of the American economy to conform to the image of free competition among a large number of small producers. Popular prejudices to the contrary, the possibility of tacit price fixing by such giant companies as General Motors, Ford, and Chrysler (who are careful not to start price wars among themselves) has led to both increased stability and greater innovation than would have been possible if our leading industrial firms had less individual power.[2]

[2] See John Kenneth Galbraith: *American Capitalism: The Concept of Countervailing Power* (Boston: Houghton Mifflin; 1952).

The significance of this digression into economic theory is clear when one considers the similarities between international politics and economic competition.[3] The common assumption that nuclear proliferation will produce a kind of "war of all against all" corresponds roughly to the theory of "pure competition" in economics; in this situation, the relative equality of a large number of powers would stimulate uncontrolled rivalries dangerous to all and would produce demands for "governmental controls" (perhaps through the UN).

At the other extreme, the competition between the two giant firms suggests the precarious but real possibilities for stability in a bipolar international confrontation. As the economic analogy reveals, a two-power confrontation can best be stabilized by tacit or explicit agreements to limit competition; nuclear deterrence and such Russo-American agreements as the test ban and hot line indicate the kinds of mechanisms that prevent all-out war today.

From this perspective, the emergence of new nuclear powers could either heighten or lessen the instability of world politics, depending on the particular nations involved. Relatively weak and vulnerable nations that have a great interest in aggressive policies (in the hope that the two superpowers would continue to deter each other) pose a greater threat than larger and more developed communities that could become secondary but truly major powers or even superpowers. For example, an Egypt armed with nuclear weapons, even of a primitive kind, would probably be more of a danger to world peace because of its weakness than a Western European community that could sooner or later become a superpower.

Should new continental states approximate the strength of the two superpowers, international relations might become like the state of affairs in the American automobile industry. Rivalry persists between General Motors, Ford, Chrysler, American Motors, and smaller domestic and foreign producers; although General Motors is the largest, and General Motors

[3] For a somewhat different application of economic theories to international politics, see Kenneth Boulding: *Conflict and Defense* (New York: Harper; 1961), esp. pp. 274-5.

and Ford are each substantially more powerful than Chrysler, the lesser firms are able to stay in business and even make marginal increases in their sales. At the same time, it is extremely difficult for a new company to enter the market due to the economic advantages of size, as is shown by ill-fated attempts to introduce Kaiser and Tucker automobiles.

This analogy may seem fanciful, but it suggests a great deal about the calculations of relative power and the likelihood of total war in an international system composed of four or five nuclear superpowers. Just as advertising attempts to show that each product is unique, ideology and propaganda would have the function of distinguishing each power from its rivals; in this sense, propaganda is a substitute for forms of violence that are unpromising due to the risks of nuclear war.[4] Just as America's industrial giants are constantly investing in research and development and constantly changing the quality of their product, the superpowers seem destined to continue their economic progress; in both cases, modern technology increases their prestige and power, which appear to be relatively secure from challenges by weaker competitors.

From this view, the gravest weakness in the future would probably be the tendency to make increased production (presumably a means to human betterment) something of an end in itself. Just as the continued production of more and more automobiles creates increasing problems in American life, especially because our cities are strangled by traffic, the perpetual quest for greater and greater industrial output and technological progress may have adverse effects on the moral and political foundations of human existence.

Apart from such possibilities, which are outside the scope of this book, the comparison between economic competition and international politics indicates that rivalry among three or four superpowers, conducted within tacitly or explicitly

[4] Although some scholars have spoken of the "end of ideology" in the industrial age, it appears that such a development is not highly likely and may even be undesirable. See Joseph La Palombara: "Decline of Ideology: A Dissent and an Interpretation," *American Political Science Review*, LX (March 1966), 5-16.

accepted limits, could be relatively peaceful and stable. Such a world order could, of course, break down at any time, just as the American economy could again lapse into depression; the certainty of peace would be no more assured than is continued economic growth in the United States. But even this possibility shows that the threats to stability may be subject to rational control; since businessmen and labor leaders alike have come to admit the need for governmental planning, if only to prevent economic crises, we may assume that statesmen would also be able to cooperate, especially under the aegis of the UN.

Despite the likelihood of violence in and between the underdeveloped nations, general war need not break out as long as the major powers restrain their intervention in such conflicts; world politics need not be tranquil in order to be stable.[5] Major powers could therefore be expected to continue their efforts to influence favorably the various underdeveloped societies and even to attempt to subvert or control their governments. Newly industrializing countries could be expected to bid for increased power, just as foreign producers attempt—often successfully—to gain a share of the American market. But as long as the first-ranking powers continue to develop on a strong economic basis and to compete with each other, the mutual recognition of a common interest would restrain this rivalry and preclude all-out nuclear war.

It will be argued that the proliferation of nuclear weapons would undermine this prediction; after all, General Motors does not threaten to destroy the plants of the Chrysler Corporation. Paradoxically enough, however, the spread of atomic weapons increases the relevance of a comparison between world politics and an oligopoly like the American automobile industry. In the prenuclear age, statesmen could believe, al-

---

[5] "War on the grand scale and peace in its true sense may be buried side by side." General André Beaufre: *An Introduction to Strategy* (New York: Praeger; 1965), p. 104.

though often mistakenly, that increases in the power of any other state were necessarily decreases in their own power; the size of the world "pie" often seemed relatively fixed, the only question being the size of the slices for each nation. Under these circumstances, there are few common interests shared by all rivals regardless of their power; the strongest state has little interest in restraining its aggressiveness, since it can always hope to seize the entire pie by becoming a world empire.

This kind of cutthroat competition, in which Louis XIV, Napoleon, and Hitler tried to establish hegemony over Europe, becomes harder when even the most powerful state is subject to devastation should its power exceed the limits tolerable to other major powers. When one power's gains caused another power's losses, the only way to check a major aggressor was for its potential victims to ally in order to prevent world conquest. Such combinations are, however, limited by the purely negative character of their common interest; as the strains within the alliances against Louis XIV, Napoleon, and Hitler revealed, as soon as the aggressor is defeated (if not before), the allies fall out among themselves because they disagree on individual goals.[6]

In contrast, an awareness that all rivals can gain by a particular outcome changes the strategic calculation in a fundamental way. When there are common interests recog-

[6] Strategists, when they discuss this kind of competition, often speak in terms of "game theory." According to this mathematical approach to rivalry, when the stakes of conflict are relatively fixed, world politics can be described as a "constant-sum game." In one variety of such games—called a "zero-sum game"—the gains of the winners are necessarily losses of the other states, so that the total of gains and losses is zero. Under these conditions, it is often possible to calculate in theory what each statesman (or player in game theory) should do to maximize his winnings or minimize his losses in face of a rival seeking to do the same thing. This kind of game therefore tends to describe conflict between more or less declared enemies, each of which expects the other to try to win as much as he can, on the assumption that cooperation is unlikely or impossible. For an introduction to game theory, see J. D. Williams: *The Compleat Strategyst* (New York: McGraw-Hill; 1954); Kaplan: *System and Process in International Politics,* Ch. ix; or Hayward Alker, Jr.: *Mathematics and Politics* (New York: Macmillan; 1965), Ch. vii.

nized by all major powers, such as the avoidance of mutual nuclear destruction, one can no longer think of the stakes of world politics as fixed; some losses for one state imply losses for the others. Virtually all states have a shared interest in avoiding all-out nuclear war in the same way that virtually all automobile producers have an interest in preventing a general depression. For example, the destruction of both the United States and Russia in a thermonuclear exchange would not only represent a disaster for the superpowers involved; it might also have grave consequences for other powers, who would be adversely affected by the level of fall-out and might prefer the status quo to a confrontation between the surviving major powers (namely, China and the countries of Western Europe).

Just as the losses of all-out war might be general, the gains of relative stability may also be shared by virtually every country in the world. As long as the superpowers do not destroy each other they are available as sources of technological and capital assistance to developing countries. Like the prospect of an increase in the total sales of automobiles, which can increase the profits of every car producer even if each company has a fixed share of the market, economic growth without violent conflict can benefit the superpowers themselves. Minimal cooperation is therefore mutually advantageous because failure to agree on rules of the game hurts everyone.[7]

The psychological difference in how these various situations are approached is particularly important. If any gain by one state is a loss to all others, a rational statesman must assume that his rival or rivals are malevolent and that he must win as much as possible at each opportunity; in contrast, this

---

[7] Strategists who utilize game theory speak of situations in which all competitors can gain (or lose) from a given action as "nonconstant sum" or "nonzero sum" games. In such games it often becomes possible and reasonable for rivals to cooperate since the size of the pie can be increased by agreements that are in the self-interest of everyone; if every state can acquire a bigger slice than it had previously, all may tolerate differences in the absolute size of the slices of various powers.

strategy is irrational if each state will lose by attempting to grab the most and gain by accepting solutions that are beneficial to all. If the second type of situation is confused with the first, mutual disaster—or unnecessary losses—will result because outcomes that are in the interest of all rivals will not tend to be chosen.[8] Sometimes there is a substitute for victory.

While open cooperation or bargaining is a useful means of avoiding cutthroat competition where it is self-defeating, a negotiated division of the spoils can sometimes be approximated by developing, from the experience of restrained rivalry, a mutual recognition of shared interests. Although General Motors could drive most of its competitors out of business by reducing prices about $400 a model, it does not do so because such extreme success would be disastrous (given adverse popular reaction to unfair competition and probable antitrust prosecution). Instead of trying to get the highest profits in the short run, auto manufacturers exhibit what has been called "limited joint profit maximization" over the long run—that is, they accept as legitimate the continued existence of their major rivals and establish mutually understood limits to their competition.

Again, the analogy to international politics is revealing. The kind of informal as well as formal agreements that stabilize the balance of terror are familiar to all since the United States and Russia have explicitly recognized their common interest in avoiding nuclear war. But just as two giant firms may have difficulty keeping agreements because the chances of gaining an unequivocal advantage on one's rival are so obvious, bipolarity is riskier than many observers admit; although South Vietnam could be dismissed as marginal to the strategic position of both superpowers, neither wants its local favorite to be totally defeated. Hence what was an essentially secondary conflict between the French and Vietnamese

[8] The classic example of this danger is the so-called "Prisoner's Dilemma" in game theory. See Kaplan: *System and Process in International Politics*, pp. 199-200; Alker: *Mathematics and Politics*, pp. 137-41, and the references there cited.

in the 1950's has become a central world preoccupation in the 1960's, throwing a chill on hoped-for signs of *détente* between Washington and Moscow.

For these reasons, a small increase in the number of nuclear powers may actually strengthen the cooperative restraints on total war. As secondary powers develop their own nuclear capabilities, still weaker powers may find security in the deterrence provided by more than one ally; for example, Italy may feel more secure against a possible Soviet invasion if both France and the United States are committed to defend it. It is true that the rise of a second Communist nuclear power seems to have increased the freedom of maneuver of countries like Rumania, whose autonomy could be put to aggressive use. But the risks in so doing are impressive insofar as no major power is willing to subject itself to nuclear destruction for the sake of a weaker ally that seeks greater power. In this sense, the weakening of traditional alliances may strengthen world peace.[9]

Since this analysis will seem overly abstract, it is necessary to apply it directly to the central problem of the future of world politics, namely the diffusion of nuclear weapons. Although states that possess nuclear weapons have up to now shown considerable caution in avoiding all-out war, the risks of irrational use of atomic armaments should not be underestimated. Because it seems highly dangerous to rely solely on

[9] George Liska, perhaps the most perceptive theorist of international politics today, has summarized the argument as follows: "The no-alliance rule . . . may prevail as a matter of expediency when all or most great powers have nuclear capability. They need not have, for the purpose, anything like nuclear parity prior to the first use of nuclear weapons in a contingency. The consequence might be a new form of deterrence; not only mutual between two nuclear powers, but also multilateral for the system as a whole. Multilateral deterrence can obtain among a few nuclear powers with comparable capabilities; or it can constrain a greater number of states with highly unequal nuclear capabilities." *Nations in Alliance* (Baltimore: Johns Hopkins; 1962), p. 269. The details of Liska's highly complex argument are of the greatest importance for specialists, and have unfortunately not received the attention they deserve.

the reasonableness of statesmen, international agreements that could increase the stability of world politics must be explored.

The most widely discussed means of controlling nuclear proliferation is an international treaty prohibiting the emergence of new members of the nuclear club. An extension of the nuclear test-ban is, of course, merely one version of such an agreement. It has already been suggested that this kind of treaty would have limited effect, since it would not bind any power that refused to sign it, nor would it prevent a signatory from breaking its commitment. Experience has shown the impossibility of binding a sovereign state when it finds a national interest in developing or increasing its military forces; unless there is some means of punishing a state that denounces or refuses to sign the treaty, that agreement becomes a worthless scrap of paper as soon as a crisis arises.[1]

It is sometimes thought that the opprobrium attached to violating an international obligation would restrain states from breaking the prohibition on acquiring nuclear weapons. Such optimism is hardly justified either by domestic law or by international experience. An aggressive ruler like Hitler is bound to ignore the vague outcries of "international public opinion" if by so doing his power can be increased; we do not count on mere opprobrium to prevent murder but insist that society provide policemen, courts, and jails to punish violations of the law.

True, a general antiproliferation treaty would increase the obstacles to acquisition of nuclear weapons by third- or fourth-ranking powers, who would be less likely to ignore the desires of the superpowers and the pressure of world opinion. Since universal nuclear diffusion could well produce a "war of all against all," this minimal result is advantageous. But the real problem lies in the attitude of secondary powers (like Japan, South Africa, or India), whose self-interest may one day dictate entry into the nuclear club. Such nations will feel that it is

[1] On the limited effectiveness of the Treaty of Washington (1922) and its successor, the Treaty of London (1930), which supposedly limited the size of naval forces, see John G. Stoessinger: *The Might of Nations*, rev. edn. (New York: Random House; 1965), pp. 337-50.

unfair to prohibit them from developing nuclear weapons while allowing the existing nuclear powers to maintain or increase their stockpiles. Thus, without a general disarmament treaty that seems at present utopian, antiproliferation agreements would not prevent the most probable cases of nuclear diffusion over the next few years.

This problem is not solved by monitoring and inspecting nuclear reactors to determine whether fissionable material is diverted from peaceful uses to weapons production. Those who want to cheat may be able to circumvent even a relatively reliable inspection system. Unless force is to be used in cases of infraction, moreover, a state that has decided to break an antiproliferation treaty may actually want other countries to know that it seeks to acquire nuclear weapons; after all, such weapons can only act as deterrents if their existence is known.

International agreements can be effective, therefore, only if all states have a great self-interest in standing by them or if violations are likely to be punished. The latter method could be used to restrain nuclear proliferation if the UN were to become a world government capable of using force against those who violate treaties or initiate aggression. Unfortunately, the history of the UN, like the League of Nations before it, shows that nation-states are unwilling to surrender sovereignty to an international organization they are incapable of controlling; the greater the power of a state, the more unwilling its leaders will be to submit to majority decisions against their own interests.

It follows that the most promising restraints on the undesirable effects of nuclear proliferation will have to depend on the interests of sovereign powers. We must therefore consider whether there are any explicit agreements or unwritten understandings that every state, or at least the nuclear powers, would have a self-interest in observing and even enforcing against other nations. Approaching the problem in this light, we find three possible areas in which a common interest might produce effective action: 1) the prohibition of gifts or sales of nuclear weapons by any member of the nuclear club to any nonnuclear power; 2) a tacit or explicit agreement not to initiate the use of nuclear weapons in warfare, at least under certain specified conditions; and 3) a guarantee from each major nuclear power to some (if not all) secondary and minor states that aggression against them would be met by force, including nuclear force if need be.

Each of these three agreements deserves analysis. The first, a prohibition on the gift or sale of nuclear weapons by states that already possess them, is clearly in the self-interest of the nuclear powers themselves. The United States, Russia, Great Britain, and France have all been reluctant to encourage nuclear proliferation by giving such weapons to other states; even the French, who have argued that diffusion is probably inevitable and is not necessarily pernicious, are opposed to the acquisition of atomic weapons by West Germany or any further powers. Although China at one point may have offered nuclear assistance to Indonesia, the only clear examples of Peking's assistance to the Indonesian government were funds for a still-unfinished meeting hall (in which the Conference of the New Emerging Forces was to take place) and a doctor to treat President Sukarno.

Since even new nuclear powers seek an exception to the general prejudice against dissemination only for themselves, not for others, it appears that there is a well-perceived interest shared by all possessors of atomic weapons. This means that a treaty prohibiting the gift or sale of nuclear weapons to nonnuclear powers is conceivable and has a chance of being observed out of self-interest. To be sure, violations of such an agreement might be difficult to detect and to punish; from this point of view, a formal treaty would add little to the already evident interests of the nuclear powers.

Indeed, if it is useful to know which nations have atomic weapons, a treaty against the sale or gift of warheads could be undesirable should it encourage clandestine actions by an aggressive power or by private individuals. It might be better if each major nuclear power reasserted its opposition to sales or gifts, pledging itself not to initiate such proliferation even

though not bound to a formal treaty. On the other hand, insofar as international opinion may demand some steps in the
direction of formal agreements, a treaty might be desirable
(especially if the Chinese could be induced to sign it).

Even if the existing nuclear powers do not initiate diffusion,
however, the nuclear club seems destined to expand in the
next generation; for this reason, attention must be directed
to the use (or rather, the nonuse) of atomic weapons. One
frequently suggested device would be an agreement by all
nuclear powers to refrain from using nuclear weapons before
a rival has done so. Such an accord, in a written treaty or on
the basis of tacit understandings, is in the self-interest of the
superpowers, who recognize the danger of reciprocal suicide.
But here one must consider the complexities of military
strategy in the nuclear age. The main function of nuclear
weapons to date has been their ability to deter or scare rival
powers; unlike most conventional weapons, which can be
used without necessarily resulting in disaster for the user,
atomic arms are more dangerous now that at least two states
have invulnerable strategic forces. This deterrent effect of
nuclear weapons depends, however, on the possibility that
one country might conceivably use them in retaliation for
nonnuclear aggression, such as a Russian attack on Western
Europe with conventional forces.

In the immediate post-World War II period, the communist
bloc had large numbers of conventional troops which the
Western powers apparently could not match; it was the threat
of American nuclear attack that restrained the Soviet Union.
NATO strategy was therefore based on the assumption that
the United States would be willing to initiate nuclear war,
an assumption that was highly credible as long as the Russians
did not themselves have a large supply of nuclear weapons
and the means of delivering them on American targets.

When this strategic balance was changed by the Soviet
acquisition of long-range missiles, nuclear deterrence came to

have a quite different meaning. As soon as Russia was capable of nuclear retaliation after an American nuclear strike, our threat to respond to a conventional attack on Western Europe by "massive retaliation" became more difficult to believe; both Moscow and our European allies have begun to wonder whether the American leaders would be willing to sacrifice their own cities for the defense of Berlin, Bonn, or Paris. Our insistence that we would do so serves, of course, to complicate matters for the Russians, but it has become less and less likely that either superpower would initiate a nuclear war that could destroy both.

In this context, the military power of NATO troops in Europe had to be strengthened. This was proposed and to a certain degree achieved on the assumption that the United States would not want to use its strategic nuclear weapons in retaliation to a conventional Soviet attack on our European allies; if so, there had to be some means, short of all-out nuclear war, to stop an aggressive move in Berlin or elsewhere along the iron curtain. Although a large increase in the number of soldiers in Europe was proposed, NATO's conventionally armed forces did not reach the levels that most strategists thought necessary to deter the USSR; indeed, the target of thirty NATO divisions has still not been fully attained.

In order to avoid the choice between a nuclear war in which the United States would be devastated and a conventional war in which Western Europe would be defeated, it was therefore proposed that American tactical nuclear weapons be used to increase the firepower of NATO's units. By so doing, it was argued, the United States would be able to pose a threat to the Soviet Union short of a mutually destructive thermonuclear exchange; battlefield atomic warheads would be able to defeat a communist land attack in Europe without forcing the Russians to bomb American cities.[2]

[2] For the classic presentation of this thesis, see Henry A. Kissinger: *Nuclear Weapons and Foreign Policy* (New York: Harper; 1957). But compare Kissinger: "Limited War: Conventional or Nuclear? A Reappraisal," in *Arms Control, Disarmament, and National Security*, ed. Donald G. Brennan (New York: Braziller; 1961), Ch. vii.

This strategy, which has been incorporated into what Secretary of Defense McNamara calls the "flexible response," implies that there are still conditions in which the United States would initiate the use of nuclear weapons. For our European allies, however, the shift from a strategy of "massive retaliation" to one of "flexible response" has been extremely uncomfortable; Frenchmen or Germans are understandably skeptical of the idea that Washington plans to fight a war in which atomic weapons would be used in Western Europe while the United States and Russia were immune from nuclear attack.

Moreover, as some of our allies have pointed out, the distinction between "strategic" and "tactical" nuclear weapons is largely irrelevant in Western Europe. The normal definition of tactical arms is that they are used on the battlefield and directed only at enemy military targets. But in Europe, population density is so great that almost any use of tactical nuclear weapons would have an enormous destructive effect on civilian population (both from the blast of the warheads and from the fall-out). Thus our allies would prefer a strategy that threatened the Soviet Union with the destruction of its cities in case of any war in Europe; it is this desire that led the French, before General de Gaulle came to power, to begin building independent nuclear forces.

One response to this dilemma has been the elaboration of what is called the strategy of "limited strategic retaliation." In this view, the United States could respond to a Soviet move on Berlin or Western Europe by launching a strictly limited nuclear attack on selected Soviet targets; we would demonstrate our resolve by delivering an atomic warhead on a single city, a military installation, or an uninhabited portion of Russian territory. Presumably the Russians would respond in kind, destroying roughly equivalent targets in the United States. Such carefully restrained and paced attacks would continue until both sides agreed to negotiate a settlement as a means of avoiding total destruction.[3]

[3] For the strategy involved, see *Limited Strategic War*, ed. Klaus Knorr and Thornton Read (New York: Praeger; 1962), and the references there cited.

Apart from more technical problems posed by limited tactical or strategic nuclear war, it is evident that such concepts reflect a difficulty in current military planning. At present it can be argued that nuclear strategy is in a transitional phase; the two superpowers continue to have overwhelmingly superior nuclear arsenals, but each has at least one nominal ally that is developing an independent nuclear striking force. Thus the proliferation of nuclear weapons seems to be connected with the fear that, under certain conditions, a superpower might be unwilling to initiate a nuclear attack on its rival. Since the very essence of nuclear deterrence lies in the threat to use such weapons first, it is the weakened credibility of these threats by either superpower that has induced France and China to join the nuclear club.

This suggests that an agreement to refrain from initiating the use of nuclear weapons could be extremely dangerous. Such a self-denying ordinance might weaken the nuclear deterrence between the superpowers; more precisely, agreement not to use nuclear weapons would remove their deterrent value in the case of conventional aggression (especially with reference to allies of the superpowers). If the United States indicated that in no circumstances would we use any form of atomic weapons before the Russians did so, given the present distribution of troops on either side of the iron curtain, we might merely invite a conventional attack on Western Europe. Only if we planned a conventional attack on China and sought to insure ourselves against Soviet nuclear retaliation would these risks be counterbalanced by a positive gain.

The danger of an agreement not to initate nuclear war is radically increased, moreover, by the fact that NATO strategy has long assumed that even in case of a "limited war" in Europe our troops would utilize tactical nuclear weapons. An agreement not to use these weapons, with which NATO's forces are now equipped, would therefore greatly cripple NATO's defensive abilities (since the Russians would have every reason to conduct warfare with all the most modern means except atomic weapons, and would have a good chance of winning).

If it were decided that an agreement not to initiate nuclear warfare is desirable, therefore, NATO strategy would have to be altered completely. The West would be forced to increase its conventional armament to enable our European allies to have a reasonable chance of defeating a Soviet offensive—an effort that would be costly and unpopular. As the fear of Soviet aggression in Europe declines, the likelihood of our allies adopting such a policy is further reduced. Moreover, the Europeans remember that major conventional wars, like the two World Wars, are hardly "limited" in the areas of battle; they would therefore probably prefer to develop their own nuclear weapons rather than plan for a conventional war.

This is the calculation made by the French, who believe that their small *force de frappe* at least makes Russia consider the risks of having some of its cities destroyed as a consequence of a conventional attack on Western Europe. Yet the French would be loath to make a blanket agreement to refrain from initiating nuclear retaliation for the same reasons that have been discussed with reference to the United States. It would seem, therefore, that a formal treaty prohibiting the first use of nuclear weapons would be against the self-interest of at least some nuclear powers (namely, those that are at a relative disadvantage with regard to their non-nuclear military forces).

Conversely, a universal agreement not to initiate nuclear war would be of the greatest advantage to those members of the nuclear club most likely to gain their objectives by conventional or guerrilla war. This explains why China, alone of the five nuclear powers, has publicly stated that it will not use atomic weapons unless attacked by them. Since a self-denying ordinance by nuclear powers would favor aggressors with large conventional armies and human resources, what originally seems to be an "equal" bargain is effectively biased in favor of our rivals and hardly in the American interest.

This conclusion need not be as dismal as it appears at first, however, because the calculus of nuclear deterrence radically discourages any nuclear power from carrying out threats to initiate nuclear war. In conflicts between major powers, the danger that one's own society will be destroyed is so great that large scale use of nuclear weapons is a measure of last resort; while a formal agreement against such actions would not be desirable for the West, it also may not be necessary. Even the selective tactical or strategic use of nuclear weapons would raise very great risks of rapid escalation, for the side that stood to lose might prefer the mutual destruction of both super-powers to its own defeat.

Such extreme reactions to a supposedly limited nuclear war would not be inevitable, because the use of small atomic war-heads on the battlefield might be sufficiently circumscribed that neither superpower would feel its homeland in danger. Nonetheless, statesmen have become accustomed to make a radical distinction between nuclear and conventional weapons; once the line between the two is crossed, it would be more difficult to prevent a nuclear power from resorting to retalia-tion on the homeland of another nuclear power.[4] This con-sideration is particularly important now that two of our Euro-pean allies possess nuclear forces. Even if NATO headquarters and Washington agreed not to attack the Soviet Union with nuclear weapons, London or Paris might prefer the risks of nuclear retaliation to a total defeat.

The same argument can be made against "limited strategic retaliation." It is extremely difficult to believe that rival super-powers would be willing to play the game of destroying each other's cities in a purely rational effort to force a negotiated settlement; once the tacitly accepted restraints on using nu-clear weapons are broken down, escalation might be exceed-ingly difficult to control. This does not mean, however, that the threat to employ limited strategic retaliation is foolish. On the contrary, it may be a useful means of making nuclear deterrence more credible, at least in some circumstances (for there are events that might justify American intervention at the cost of one of our cities that would not justify an all-out nuclear war). The difficulty, of course, is that action on the

[4] See Thomas Schelling: *The Strategy of Conflict* (Cambridge, Mass.: Harvard Univ. Press; 1960), Appendix A.

basis of such a strategy may be folly even if it is advantageous as a deterrent.

As a result, the first use of any nuclear weapons, however limited, could invite an all-out war engulfing the superpowers against their will. The only exception to this might be an attack by a nuclear power on a far weaker rival. Such uses of atomic weapons will be considered in a moment, but in direct confrontations between major nuclear powers, a formal agreement to prohibit the initiation of nuclear war is not as necessary as some observers have suggested: either such restraint will be observed as a result of calculations of self-interest (which militate against tactical or limited strategic nuclear warfare for fear of escalation), or a formal treaty would be worthless (since it would be violated whenever a state had the interest to do so, and in the meantime would weaken the Western deterrent).

Similar problems arise with reference to a Soviet proposal that would prohibit the use of nuclear weapons on the territory of any nonnuclear state. Such a provision would seem to reinforce the inhibitions on proliferation, since it points up the danger of becoming a target of nuclear attack as part of the cost of membership in the nuclear club; this obvious advantage explains the Western interest shown toward this scheme when it was first presented to the Geneva conference on nuclear disarmament.[5]

Like most disarmament proposals, however, Russia's suggestion satisfied its own national interests under the appearance of a fair and equally binding rule. Two major consequences would flow from the prohibition of nuclear strikes on nonnuclear powers: first, such a treaty would legitimate an attack on China that the Soviet Union decided to tolerate; second, it would make obsolete NATO's strategy of using tactical nuclear weapons in response to a Soviet attack on Western Germany. While the first of these implications is a reflection of the joint Russo-American interest in restraining irrational Chinese aggressiveness, the second would increase doubts

[5] See *The New York Times,* Feb. 3, 1966, p. 1.

among our allies that the United States is willing and able to defend them.

The disadvantage of the Soviet plan from the Western point of view is its tendency to divide NATO further, especially by heightening German insecurity. It would therefore be necessary to reach some satisfactory accommodation within the Western alliance *before* adhering to the Soviet proposal. But Russia's interest in an antiproliferation treaty largely stems from a desire to block increased German participation and control over NATO's nuclear forces; hence an agreement to give Germany a greater nuclear role in NATO, while it might compensate for abandonment of NATO's tactical nuclear strategy, could lead the Soviets to abandon negotiation on an antiproliferation treaty.

We seem to be trapped in a vicious circle. International control over the proliferation and use of nuclear weapons is difficult to achieve because agreements must satisfy both the interests of our various allies (in part determined by residual fears of the Soviet Union) and the desires of the Russians. Whereas Moscow would prefer agreements that increase her relative security and power, the Western alliance has been built on the principle of containing and balancing the USSR; arms-control measures are intended to make the use of nuclear weapons less likely, but NATO is designed to convince the communist bloc that our military forces will be used to counter any attack. Formal treaties seem unpromising unless the need for them has ceased to exist, at least in Europe.

To this point, therefore, the logic of self-interest tends to deter the superpowers—and other members of the nuclear club—from encouraging the spread of nuclear weapons or from using them first in warfare. International treaties could only be based upon shared attitudes, but we have seen that the cooperative element in the use of nuclear weapons is a cooperative selfishness (and not an altruistic desire to resolve problems by compromise). Under these circumstances, it is primarily unwritten or tacitly accepted rules of the game of international politics—and not unenforceable or undesirable formal agreements—that will minimize the risks of all-out nuclear war.

Restraints based on self-interest are, however, insufficient to prevent all nuclear diffusion, and among the nuclear powers some, like China, will be aggressively minded. Moreover, the logic of mutual deterrence applies most directly to industrialized societies, so that an aggressive but relatively backward country that acquires atomic weapons may take greater risks than an industrialized superpower. Thus a strategy of escalation, in which the determination to resist an aggressor is indicated by increasing conventional commitments, may not truly deter an agrarian nuclear power like China; since the threat of nuclear attack is not fully credible against a country whose main power base is not concentrated in cities, the hope of real gains in a guerrilla or conventional war may lead some of the third-generation nuclear powers to attack their weaker neighbors.

The limitations of strategic calculations suited to a confrontation of industrial superpowers are quite clear even today in Southeast Asia, and will be discussed more fully in Chapter vii. For the present, the crucial point is that nuclear diffusion offers grave threats to world peace in two ways: (1) some nuclear powers, although having only small atomic capabilities, may thereby gain a great advantage over local rivals; such countries, while totally unable to challenge a superpower, may feel tempted to use their atomic weapons to deter or limit great-power intervention in the course of guerrilla or conventional aggression; (2) the more powers possessing atomic warheads, the more likely it becomes that at some point nuclear deterrence will fail, whether by accident or by a faulty calculation; if a second-rank power uses nuclear weapons to attack a nonnuclear enemy, the resulting intervention of a superpower could lead to a general, all-out war.

Although the second of these possible conditions has given rise to the greatest fears, the first is the more probable. Assuming that a relatively minor power acquires atomic warheads as a means of altering a local balance of power, it need not follow that the new nuclear capability would at once be used in an aggressive war. The weapons stocks of a minor nuclear power will presumably be smaller and more vulnerable than those of a superpower, so that a superpower could intervene directly or indirectly (by giving some nuclear weapons to a local ally for use in retaliation against the cities of the aggressor). The widely feared anonymous use of nuclear missiles would probably work against the small aggressor, since any industrial power with long-range missiles could retaliate selectively with only marginal risk to itself.

For example, if Egypt used most of its small stock of atomic warheads to obliterate Israel, the United States, France, or Great Britain might each be the conceivable origin of two or three IRBM's that could destroy the aggressor's major cities. Other major nuclear powers, regardless of their sympathies for the Egyptians, would be understandably wary of intervening given the risks of an all-out nuclear war (especially if the country that had retaliated on Egypt was in doubt). If a small power used nuclear weapons and received devastation from a superpower that itself was not attacked, the lesson for other minor powers would be clear.

In contrast, a secondary power that acquires nuclear weapons might well use them to deter great-power involvement in a conventional or indirect local aggression. Such a strategy would be promising because, with a relatively small stockpile of warheads and delivery capabilities, a weaker nuclear power would have every reason not to use its sole means of deterring a superpower. Unused, these weapons pose the risk of triggering a nuclear war between major powers. Whereas a nuclear attack on another minor power could induce an opposed nuclear giant to retaliate (and might lead allied superpowers to disown the aggressor), nonatomic attacks would seem profitable to new members of the nuclear club, both because it would be harder for their local rivals to enlist allied support and because the risk of total defeat would be largely removed.

To continue the previous example, should Egypt acquire nuclear weapons before Israel, a conventional attack against the latter would seem highly attractive as soon as the Egyptians had any reasonable chance of winning. Western nations seeking to aid Israel could hardly do so anonymously, and might be deterred by Russian threats of a countervailing intervention; the Suez crisis shows what could happen in such a course of events. Nor would Egypt have to rely on foreign aid to prevent total defeat (as in Suez), for her willingness to use a minimal nuclear arsenal would be highly credible and might deter Israel from attempting to occupy Egypt even if this were possible.

If two rival countries of secondary rank have roughly equal nuclear forces, one or the other might launch a nuclear attack in the course of a local war; though the balance of terror might prevent hostilities from breaking out, once begun it would be tempting for the loser to risk all rather than capitulate. Should this result in the mutual destruction of the two enemies, this type of war would be a most abhorrent lesson in the risks of using nuclear weapons. It may sound cynical, but such an outcome might be the only way, short of a general cataclysm, of teaching statesmen that nuclear warfare is untenable.

It follows that the most dangerous consequence of the spread of nuclear weapons lies not so much in the risks of a total, worldwide nuclear war as in the greater probability of conventional or guerrilla attacks by a new member of the nuclear club. This conclusion is hardly cause for rejoicing, however, because one nuclear power—China—has already given us a foretaste of the threats to world peace that could result. Moreover, the relative weakness of the potential victims of such aggressors is in itself a powerful incentive for acquiring nuclear weapons (as is evident in the demands of many Indians that they develop nuclear forces in order to deter the Chinese).

Superpower guarantees have recently been proposed as a means of discouraging both nuclear proliferation and attacks upon nonnuclear countries by their nuclear rivals. For example, the United States could promise to attack China with nuclear weapons if Peking commits aggression on India. It is argued that the Russians would tolerate such retaliation and that this kind of unilateral guarantee, without binding New Delhi to a political alliance, would remove India's incentive to produce her own nuclear weapons.[6]

However, this device has several compelling shortcomings. First of all, such guarantees have not effectively prevented diffusion up to now; the last three powers to acquire nuclear weapons (Great Britain, China, and France) all benefited from a nominal guarantee of this sort, yet all three found their allies' promise of aid less than fully credible. Second, if China chooses to attack India by indirect means (e.g., by supporting a "war of national liberation" among some disaffected ethnic or linguistic group), would the United States resort to nuclear retaliation? Finally, the risks of intervention would be great for the United States, if only because the Russians might respond by a move on West Berlin supported with conventional weapons. Without prior agreement between the superpowers (be it explicit or tacit), therefore, a unilateral guarantee would not sufficiently reassure nonnuclear countries faced with nuclear enemies.[7]

This suggests the advisability of agreements between the superpowers to punish any less powerful nuclear power that commits aggression, be it nuclear or conventional. Such an agreement might be in the mutual interest of the United States and Russia, for it could—together with their continued economic and technological superiority—assure them of dominance while removing the threat of direct confrontation. Assuming a Russo-American agreement to police a world threatened by nuclear proliferation, one could even dream of a peaceful condominium of the two superpowers.

Unfortunately, the chances of a general agreement of this

[6] See Peter Barnes: "Nuclear Treaty Without Alliance," *New Leader*, Nov. 8, 1965, pp. 8-9.

[7] See Andrew Martin and Wayland Young: "Proliferation," *Arms Control and Disarmament*, III (Autumn 1965), 127-33.

kind seem slim. Bipolarity may produce a certain stability (as it has since World War II), but it is hard for two rivals whose ideologies and interests clash throughout the world to make such a global agreement; just as cartels between duopolists are risky because the advantages of cheating are often great, in a time of crisis one of the superpowers could insist on its own definition of aggression and threaten a direct confrontation if the other does not go along.

Apart from ideological differences between East and West, an agreement between Washington and Moscow to police the world jointly would reinforce the trend toward independence on the part of China, France, and others who fear that their interests would be sacrificed. It is often not realized that the test-ban and hot-line agreements had, in a lesser way, this effect. Because the rise of new powers of secondary rank is likely over the next generation, a Russo-American guarantee to defend all states against nuclear attack would probably destroy the alliances centered on each superpower; hence attempts to maintain bipolarity could well be self-defeating.

Should a united Western Europe and a more highly developed China approach the ranks of superpowers, joint guarantees by three or more continental-scale units, each armed with invulnerable nuclear weapons, might be more feasible as a means of protecting small powers against nuclear or conventional attack by their local rivals. Then disagreement among the superpowers would not assure an aggressive secondary power of its impunity to act; the superpowers would not be forced to act jointly, for one of them could be delegated to punish a small power that stepped out of line. Even without signs of agreement, one superpower would hesitate to oppose another for fear of mutual destruction to the profit of the remaining superpowers.

This kind of unilateral guarantee could approximate some of the peace-keeping features of the so-called "Concert of Europe," which came into existence after the Napoleonic wars. At that time, the major European powers (Great Britain, France, Austria, Prussia, and Russia) agreed in principle to regulate among themselves conflicts that threatened to result in general war; for example, one of the five was on occasion delegated or allowed to suppress civil wars (notably in Spain and Greece).[8] To be sure, this system broke down—in part because Great Britain withdrew from it and in part because the great powers found their common interests were outweighed by the possibilities of power gains by each country. But the risk of major nuclear war between superpowers, because it would be self-defeating for all, might prevent this outcome.[9]

The tacit delegation of peace-keeping responsibilities to a superpower has already been demonstrated in the Hungarian revolution of 1956 and the Dominican Republic crisis of 1965. Soviet mediation in the Kashmiri war between India and Pakistan is an example of a related device. Even though Moscow gained prestige by its successful diplomatic intervention, Washington tolerated and even encouraged Russia's efforts at Tashkent; mediation by a rival superpower was clearly preferable to continued violence which could have undermined India, especially had China renewed its attacks on the Himalayan frontier (as Peking threatened at one moment).

Such tacit agreements to allow one major power a preponderant role in keeping the peace have occurred elsewhere, but they are difficult to institutionalize as long as the world is viewed as essentially a bipolar confrontation of East and West. Mediation or armed intervention can prevent major changes in the global balance of power, but they are most effective when there are more than two great powers.

For example, France has long indicated (along with India) that it would welcome the opportunity to mediate between the United States and North Vietnam in Southeast Asia; in contrast, some State Department officials have hoped that

[8] See Inis L. Claude: *Swords into Plowshares,* 2nd edn. (New York: Random House; 1959), pp. 23-8.

[9] For a more detailed analysis of the conceivable stability of a world composed of four or five superpowers, see Roger D. Masters: "A Multi-Bloc Model of the International System," *American Political Science Review,* LV (December 1961), 780-98; Liska: *Nations in Alliance,* Ch. vi.

Moscow could intervene. Unhappily, the Soviet Union is ill equipped to act as a mediator between a communist state and the United States, for it fears being branded as "revisionist" by Peking. French mediation, on the other hand, would presuppose an increase in the power of France in addition to the kind of independence from Washington that de Gaulle has tried to achieve.

Since superpower mediation or intervention is most likely to succeed in conflicts to which another superpower is not a party, such devices for managing the peace would be greatly reinforced by the emergence of new major powers. In the immediate future, Soviet or American attempts to repeat the Tashkent precedent are possible, though at a cost to the prestige of the superpower that delegates peace-keeping functions to its rival. Over the longer range, a diffusion of power may make these methods more acceptable, for a larger number of possible mediators would be available and the risks of a tacitly delegated guarantee would be somewhat reduced.

There is, moreover, a slightly different form of guarantee that has promise in an era of nuclear diffusion. In previous periods, major states sometimes promised to defend a country in the event that it was attacked by any coalition of two or more rivals. This kind of guarantee is relatively unambiguous, for a joint attack by two states is more easily defined than aggression (especially indirect aggression); it would also be consistent with the interests of nuclear powers, for it discourages other states with nuclear weapons from attempting to increase their offensive capabilities by means of alliance. Since nuclear weapons tend to reduce an aggressor's need for allies, the guarantee against coalition could conceivably deter nuclear powers from involvement in wars between minor states.[1]

For example, an American guarantee to defend Israel against

[1] For more details on the conception of a guarantee against a coalition and its applicability in a nuclear age, see Liska: *Nations in Alliance*, pp. 32-3; 135-8; 269-72.

any coalition of two or more enemies would dissuade Russia from openly supporting Egypt in an attack on the Israelis. Since a guarantee against a coalition does not name the potential enemies, it does not require political ties that bind the protected state; indeed, it can extend identical guarantees to opposed powers. Hence the United States could guarantee Egypt in the same way as Israel, thus indicating its willingness to stabilize the entire Middle East. Given a possible repetition of the alignment in the Suez crisis, during which France, Great Britain, and Israel attacked Egypt, this guarantee could be as welcome to the Egyptians as to the Israelis.

The main weakness of guarantees against a coalition of aggressors is that they presuppose a relative equality between rival states. To continue our example, as long as Egypt and Israel have roughly equivalent military capabilities (be they conventional or nuclear), such guarantees by great powers may discourage violence in the Middle East. But with gross inequalities of power, successful deterrence is less likely. Hence an American (or Russian) guarantee to defend both Syria and Israel against any coalition of two or more states might only encourage the Israelis to attack the Syrians in the hope that Egypt would not dare to intervene. Yet such a calculation would be highly risky, for the Egyptians might risk great-power intervention, especially if the Russians could be expected to counterbalance an American or Western European effort in support of Israel.

It follows that guarantees against coalition are most effective when offered to states that can defend themselves against any single local rival. New members of the nuclear club with local rivals of nearly equal power would be the most likely beneficiaries of superpower guarantees; if India can balance China's conventional and nuclear capacity on her own, American or Russian guarantees against coalition attacks on India could prevent Peking from seeking an offensive alliance with Pakistan. Hence this means of reinforcing the peace may only operate after a certain degree of nuclear proliferation has taken place, and cannot substitute for a rough parity of military strength between potential aggressors and their victims.

The long-range possibilities of superpower guarantees against attack should not be overestimated. Although such devices would be most appropriate in a world composed of at least four industrialized continent-states, as yet this configuration of power does not exist (and might never emerge). Before the time when the United States and Russia cease to be the only superpowers, unilateral or joint guarantees against aggression can be of only marginal utility, especially because they are relatively ineffective against guerrilla warfare. And since indirect aggression seems to be the most promising means for an expansionist power to undermine its rivals, we must expect both continued violence between minor powers and new attempts to join the nuclear club.

Some readers will object that there has been a most appalling omission in this discussion of nuclear weapons. Many Americans sincerely believe that the solution to the terrifying instabilities of a nuclear era lies in disarmament. It has been argued here that we must expect more nuclear proliferation, not disarmament; is this not unrealistic, given the danger that a nuclear war will lead to the suicide of the human race?

Anyone who has studied the history of warfare or of disarmament negotiations must admit that efforts to disarm hostile powers or prevent them from developing new weapons are usually futile. One author has recently argued that this occurs because men have a natural instinct to make weapons and use them to kill.[2] Be that as it may, disarmament has never fully succeeded in the past for good reasons derived from the nature of politics itself.

Men seek to further their own desires or goals by cooperation within political societies; except for interludes when most of the civilized world was conquered and controlled by a single empire, political communities have engaged in persistent and often violent rivalries. Outsiders often seem to threaten the

[2] Robert Ardrey: *African Genesis* (New York: Atheneum; 1961).

way of life of a society, especially if rival states are more powerful. Conversely, dissatisfied rulers seek to resolve their own needs by defeating other societies and seizing their resources.

Weapons are a means to this end, not the fundamental cause of hostilities between states. Both the United States and Great Britain are nuclear powers, but neither views the other as a threat; when close ties exist between states, based on common interests, no degree of military preparedness seeems threatening. But as a French statesman once said, "the agreement between any two interests presupposes opposition to a third"; in many cases, friendship between states is reinforced by (if not based upon) hostility to a common enemy. Since offensive weapons provide the means of attaining or preserving the interests of a political community, they cannot be abolished unless persisting common interests between societies have emerged.[3] It follows that general disarmament would be possible only if all fundamental political disputes between states gave way to a genuine community of interests.

Short of a world state, nations cannot be expected to disarm because it is never in the universal self-interest of all rulers or societies to do so. Any disarmament proposal must affect each state equally if governments are to accept and abide by it. But as experience amply shows, any formula for disarmament has an unequal effect on the various powers in the world at any one time.[4] Lest this seem an arbitrary statement, let us consider the effects of an enforced agreement to destroy all nuclear weapons.

The day such a treaty went into effect, it would leave the United States and Western Europe at the mercy of the Soviet Union and China with their superior numbers of conventionally armed troops. Even an agreement to disband formal mili-

---

[3] See Karl W. Deutsch, et al.: *Political Community and the North Atlantic Area* (Princeton, N. J.: Princeton Univ. Press; 1957).

[4] Cf. Thucydides: *History of the Peloponnesian War*, I, 89-93 (the most widely available tr. is the Modern Library ed. [New York: Random House; 1951], pp. 51-4); Hans Morgenthau: *Politics Among Nations* (New York: Knopf; 1953), Ch. xxi.

tary units would not reverse this consequence; totalitarian societies could mask continued military readiness in the form of a citizens' militia or police force. Short of a world government, therefore, "general and complete disarmament" would ensure the permament supremacy of the major communist powers (which is of course why Khrushchev proposed it at a time when Russia was the dominant power in the communist bloc).

Just as nuclear disarmament—or general disarmament—would effectively favor some powers and harm others, virtually any other disarmament agreement would have different effects on the interests of various states. The Baruch Plan, proposed by the United States when we had a nuclear monopoly, would have meant that this country was the only one with nuclear-weapons technology; hence we would have had a permanent advantage in case international controls broke down. In any event, our proposal to give all nuclear weapons to the UN assumed that the international organization would never adopt views to which we were opposed. Since Moscow shared this assumption in the late 1940's, the Russians quite understandably blocked the implementation of our proposal.

Given the necessary inequality of any disarmament treaty, states that signed such an agreement against their own interests would be tempted to cheat. Since only the most thoroughgoing inspection system, tantamount to world government, could ferret out nuclear weapons that were retained in violation of a disarmament treaty, cheating could pay off handsomely; law-abiding nations would surrender their stockpiles, leaving only the most aggressive and dangerous states in possession of nuclear arms. Clearly nothing would be more likely to produce a war in which these weapons would be used.

To be sure, all nuclear powers might cheat more or less to the same degree. Or, what amounts to the same thing, an agreement could be made to lower nuclear stockpiles to a fixed but small number of warheads. Even if the superpowers reduced their nuclear forces to roughly equal levels, however, the results could well be disastrous, because the current balance of terror rests on the certainty that the two major nuclear powers can destroy each other even after suffering a nuclear attack. If there were but few weapons on each side, the chance that a surprise attack would wipe out all the rival's weapons would increase greatly; under these circumstances, minor inequalities between the nuclear forces of the superpowers might be sufficient to trigger a major war.[5]

The sobering reality is that the most frequently proposed agreements designed to check or mitigate the effects of nuclear proliferation are not likely to be of great value. Disarmament is largely a vain hope as long as something like world government does not exist, and with a world government disarmament is hardly necessary as a distinct goal. Without hitherto unheard-of enforcement powers, a general treaty banning the acquisition or testing of nuclear weapons could not bind any state that wished to violate it. An agreement by all nuclear powers not to initiate the use of nuclear weapons would have undesirable and perhaps disastrous effects on the credibility of the American deterrent. A guarantee by nuclear powers to defend weaker states seems unpromising unless it is made jointly, and such an agreement apparently requires the emergence of new superpowers that are willing to share the responsibility for policing the world. While some agreements to control the use of arms or to create nonnuclear zones in Africa and Latin America are possible, one of the most promising devices for stabilizing international politics—a guarantee against attack on a second-level state by any coalition—probably presupposes further diffusion of nuclear or conventional weapons if it is to operate effectively.

If we are willing to tolerate a greatly increased amount of nonnuclear warfare and violence, these conclusions need not mean that a third world war waged with nuclear missiles is inevitable. They do indicate, however, that the United States must reconsider its foreign commitments. The future seems

---

[5] As Thomas Schelling argues, "a limitation on the number of missiles would appear to be more stabilizing, *the larger the number permitted.*" *The Strategy of Conflict*, p. 236.

highly risky if we continue to assume that all forms of aggression must be met with force, for no single superpower is likely to control the destiny of the globe by itself. Nuclear diffusion thus places a primacy on a clear understanding of the foreign-policy goals appropriate to a rapidly evolving age. Despite this fact, far too little attention has been given to the long-term objectives that the United States should set for itself as a major power.

CHAPTER FOUR

Goals for

American Power

In a world of rapid change, American power is not meaningful unless it is directed to long-range goals. To plan ahead solely in terms of the next few years may be folly if the results are doomed to become obsolete as soon as they are attained. It is therefore necessary to consider the various objectives that the United States could set for itself as a major world power. By analyzing the possibility of achieving such aims, we can gain a clearer idea of the limits of American policy in different areas at present as well as in the future.

Early in the cold war, American policy-makers established the objective of containing communism. As this goal was formulated by George Kennan in his famous "X" article in *Foreign Affairs* (1947),[1] the prime task of American policy was to prevent Soviet advances into Western Europe. At that

---

[1] The article, entitled "The Sources of Soviet Conduct," is repr. in Kennan's *American Diplomacy: 1900-1950* (New York: Mentor Books; 1952), pp. 89-106.

time, Kennan assumed that if Stalin were prevented from extending his power farther to the West, the communist desire for territorial expansion would die down as the Soviet Union became more industrialized and more conservative internally. To some extent, this objective has been achieved; the communists have not advanced into Western Europe, and since the Khrushchev era the Soviet Union has shown a noticeable tendency toward moderation under the slogan of "peaceful coexistence."

Despite its success—or perhaps because of it—Kennan's containment policy is now totally obsolete. Although the test-ban treaty and the hot line prove the possibility of agreements between the United States and Russia, it would be wrong to assume that communism has ceased to be a threat to the West. But almost immediately after Kennan formulated the idea of containment, two events took place which indicated the changing character of the communist danger and the impossibility of this policy as a permanent goal.

The first was Marshal Tito's successful assertion of the independence of a national communist movement in Yugoslavia. This event, foreshadowing the subsequent loosening of ties between the Soviet Union and her East European satellites, showed the possibility of influencing or moderating Soviet policies by distinguishing between various members of the communist bloc. Insofar as Moscow can no longer dictate its will to all other communist states and parties, the orientation of American policy toward the isolation or containment of the Soviet Union is clearly insufficient; as Kennan himself has since insisted, if we equate all communism with Russian communism, we reinforce the ties within the communist bloc and lose valuable freedom of maneuver.[2]

The limits on Russia's ability to control her allies have become particularly important as a result of another event shortly after Kennan first stated the American containment

---

[2] See *On Dealing with the Communist World* (New York: Harper and Row; 1964), in which Kennan does not even speak of "containment" as the American goal.

policy. By coming to power in China, Mao Tse-tung set in motion what has since become a profound split in the communist bloc. This largely unforeseen development has rendered the original concept of containment difficult if not impossible to achieve, for advances of the worldwide communist movement can no longer be checked simply by reaching agreements with the USSR.

In addition to indications that the United States and Russia could agree to a settlement in Vietnam were if not for the intransigeance of the Chinese, the decisive proof of the obsolescence of the original containment policy is available ninety miles from American shores. Whatever criticism may be raised against our failure to block Castro's rise to power in Cuba, it remains true that the prevention of communist advances into Western Europe has not precluded communist gains elsewhere. The reason for this, of course, is that the nature of the challenge is radically different. China is a peasant society which, contrary to the predictions of Marx, has become communist in an era marked by the economic growth and political stability of capitalist states. It is in other underdeveloped or backward societies, and not in the highly industrialized nations of the West, that communism appears to have its greatest chances of success in the near future.

Communism, or left-wing radicalism supported by communists, can therefore become a potent force in any backward society whose political institutions are unstable. This is equally true whether the society is nominally independent, as in South America, or still a colonial possession, like the Portuguese colonies in Africa. The objective of containment must therefore be analyzed in terms of perpetually blocking further communist gains in backward countries, modeled on the revolutions in China and Cuba.

In the short run, given the present American superiority in nuclear weapons and air power, it is entirely possible for the United States to prevent by force a communist take-over in a country where American military intervention can be decisive. The case of the Dominican Republic is apparently persuasive in this respect, for the presence of thirty thousand American troops on that island apparently prevented what many thought would be an immediate left-wing coup.

In the longer run, however, the United States cannot permanently be expected to prevent communist expansion throughout the world by military means for at least three reasons. First, threats may occur in so many countries simultaneously that it would be almost impossible for the United States to intervene in every society where a serious risk of communist subversion existed. To be convinced of this, imagine a communist or left-wing coup in a large South American country like Argentina, requiring a sizable intervention by American troops at a time when we were still heavily committed in Vietnam.

Second, it is not clear that military intervention is in all cases an appropriate response to communist subversion, particularly in countries where the peasantry and urban lower classes have deep-seated grievances against a conservative oligarchy. Such circumstances seem particularly suited to the type of guerrilla warfare that brought the communists to power in China and Cuba, and that first France and now the United States have struggled to defeat in Vietnam. Even where such a rebellion is suppressed (as in Greece, Malaya, or Guatemala), stability presumes the emergence of a government with a reasonably general degree of popular support. As long as this condition and the reforms necessary to maintain it cannot be achieved by American military intervention, our capacity to assure the survival of regimes favorable to the West is limited.

The third reason why we cannot prevent all further communist take-overs in backward societies lies within the United States itself. How long will the American public underwrite military interventions that involve a considerable loss of life as well as economic sacrifice? Faced with a series of such crises, the temptation to hold Moscow or Peking responsible for subversion would become virtually overwhelming. In South Vietnam, inability to gain rapid victory in a guerrilla war led to escalation in order to force North Vietnam and China to negotiate—and in the process created demands that the United States attack China directly; similar threats elsewhere in the world, where American impotence to achieve immediate military control would be even more apparent, would probably produce the same result.

The goal of global containment in the last half of the twentieth century is therefore virtually impossible to attain unless the United States establishes a worldwide "hegemony." Although such a goal has been imputed to us by President de Gaulle, Americans tend to deny that it is our objective. Yet to establish a unilateral American responsibility for the prevention of all communist take-overs presumes that the United States can effectively stop such regimes from coming to power anywhere in the world. This was not the case when Kennan first formulated the goal of containment, for he was primarily concerned with Western Europe at a time when the United States had a monopoly of operational nuclear weapons, and the countries threatened from without had a firm will to remain independently anticommunist. Under those conditions, communism could only advance by a Soviet military intervention which we could deter by the threat of nuclear retaliation.

At present, not only has the nature of the political challenge changed, but the rise of a nuclear stalemate has altered the character of deterrence, forcing us to rely on a combination of political and military means in order to check communist advances. Yet even if we still had a monopoly of nuclear weapons, we could not prevent left-wing revolutions throughout the world without employing military force on a hitherto unprecedented scale. Nuclear weapons cannot resolve political crises in underdeveloped nations because, unless the country involved is wiped from the map, at the conclusion of hostilities some political settlement must be found. In short, we have no permanent way of preventing the rise of hostile governments in Africa, Asia, and South America.

A recent variation on the concept of "containment" deserves

a final comment. It is increasingly said that while we no longer need to contain world communism as a whole, our policy should be oriented to the containment of Red China; even some who favor recognizing Peking speak of "containment without isolation." Just as the United States successfully checked Soviet advances into Western Europe immediately following World War II, so now we should block further encroachment by the Chinese in Southeast Asia.

The difficulty with the idea of containment, even if applied only to an aggressive China, is reflected in the enormous difference between the nations of Western Europe that joined NATO in 1949 and the Southeast Asian states that seem vulnerable to Chinese dominance. In terms of industrial potential, domestic political stability, and willingness to be formally aligned with the United States, it seems hard to equate Burma, Laos, and Cambodia with Great Britain, France, and Italy; although both Germany and Vietnam have become divided nations, the Bonn regime has never faced an internal movement comparable to the Vietcong.

More fundamentally, it can be argued that the image of world politics implied by the word "containment" is faulty and dangerous. If this concept, as applied to China, means that any and all advances by Peking must necessarily be met by force, containment in Southeast Asia faces the same obstacles as have been indicated on a more global basis. If, on the other hand, it merely means that increases in Chinese power should be neutralized or restrained so that world peace and America's vital interests are not directly threatened, we would be well advised to speak of balancing China, not containing her.

While this may appear to be a verbal quibble, the notion of containing China is dangerous because it implies that we do not consider Peking to be a legitimate power—and hence that we expect a major confrontation unless the Chinese adopt our views of international politics. Such a preconception unnecessarily limits our freedom of maneuver, and in the process exaggerates the threat of China (whose policies met with a series of essentially self-inflicted reverses in 1965 and 1966).

Moreover, the notion of containing China in Southeast Asia, even without "isolating" her, makes the defense of a single geographical region our primary goal in foreign policy; as the Vietnamese crisis has revealed, we may thereby concentrate our energies on the most unprofitable battlefields at considerable cost to Russo-American relations and our position within NATO. Paris and Moscow agree with Washington that it is in their mutual interest to balance Peking, but they have not shared our view that China must be contained at all costs—and are unlikely to do so in the future.

In an era of international violence and instability, further development of the United Nations toward a world government seems a necessary alternative for many Americans. There is much that is tempting in such an objective, and indeed the ideal of a federation of states outlawing war has a long pedigree dating back to Henry IV of France and including the writings of the Abbé Saint-Pierre, Rousseau, and Kant in the eighteenth century. Could not recent experiences with international peace forces provide the core of an international order in which security is assured?

All attempts to achieve one or another form of world government have faced the same obstacle; sovereign states are reluctant to surrender their own independent authority to a supranational government whose policies they cannot be assured of controlling. In no decisive case has the UN been able to impose the will of the international community, however defined, on a reluctant great power. The United States is of course no exception to this generalization; indeed, both the United States and the Soviet Union were originally in favor of a veto in the Security Council so that the United Nations would not violate their national self-interest.

It is, of course, possible that the United Nations could develop into a world government in the next fifty years. The suitability of such an evolution as an American policy goal must be questioned, however, for several reasons. First, if the UN responds to the needs of world politics today, and especially to the desire of minor powers to influence major ones, it is as an international forum for discussion or negotiation, and not as a world government. Since experience makes a truly effective, mutual surrender of sovereignty improbable, the wisdom of placing highest priority on such an unlikely prospect can be questioned.

Second, the development of world-wide political institutions cannot be expected to end the struggle for political power in human affairs, and most particularly the conflict between communist and capitalist ideologies. As long as some of the most populous nations continue to believe firmly in the principles of Marx, Lenin, or Mao, the present struggle to determine how men live will persist, and the emergence of a more powerful UN might only exacerbate the issue by raising the stakes of victory or defeat.

Third, anthropological and historical evidence of the rise of political institutions uniting many previously independent peoples is hardly encouraging, for such developments, whether on the level of primitive African tribes or the early civilizations of the Nile, were most often based on force rather than on agreement, and usually resulted in the dominance of one small group over many subject peoples; an international community similar to the Roman Empire would not be an unmitigated blessing should it be ruled by men like Caligula, Nero, or Hitler. If a world government were to be a global tyranny, who would prefer such slavery to the risks of current freedom?

Hence we are forced to the unhappy conclusion that if world government be our objective, the form of government that Americans find desirable is unlikely, and the most probable origin of such an institution would be despicable from the standpoint of our domestic traditions. Granted that the UN serves a useful function in international affairs and that it may be able to overcome the frequent crises that have threatened to paralyze it, its development into a world government does not represent a panacea.

Perhaps, however, it is unfair to pose the question of the

future role of the UN in terms of its possible evolution into a world government; many supporters of international organization would claim far less as their goal. Between the image of international government empowered to prevent violence anywhere in the world and the uncontrolled rivalry of sovereign states, might there not be the objective of increasing the ability of the UN to mediate conflicts that create the risk of major war?

Consider the different kinds of political institutions discovered in the primitive tribes studied by anthropologists. In some cases, autonomous villages, clans, or family groups coexist without any governments at all; such tribes are called "stateless societies" because, like international politics, there is no central authority, and each group feels free to resort to violence in disputes about land, women, or previous killings. Among other primitive peoples, there are highly developed governments, with kings or chiefs who can enforce central decisions on individuals or groups within the tribe; as in a civilized society, there are political institutions and courts which normally serve as the final arbiter in internal conflicts.

Between these two types of primitive society is a third category, which can most conveniently be described by referring to medieval Europe. In the Middle Ages—and in many primitive tribes that persisted into the recent past—political authority was strangely divided: the king or central ruler had certain very real powers over his subjects, but these powers were exercised only sporadically and local authorities were for most purposes autonomous. In many instances, only when conflict between local groups threatened to get out of hand or when individuals committed extremely serious crimes did the king and the king's justice intervene.[3]

These three kinds of primitive societies have obvious parallels to world politics. International relations between sovereign states are very similar to primitive "stateless societies" because in neither is there a recognized government that could

[3] For an analysis of this type of political system, see Aiden W. Southall: *Alur Society* (London: Heffer; n.d.)

enforce a settlement on hostile groups; in many ways, world politics is indeed a kind of primitive politics.[4] The conception of the UN as a world government is based on the contrary image of centralized political rule, similar to that within a modern nation-state or some primitive kingdoms. But since the emergence of a world state seems either unlikely or undesirable from an American perspective, perhaps the intermediary condition of a medieval type could be a goal for the future development of the UN.

It is necessary to spell out a little further just what such a situation would imply. The medieval king (or the chief of any of the primitive tribes in the kind of political order being considered) was not the king of France—he was the king of the *French*. This subtle difference meant that the central ruler was not the sole, nor even the primary, political authority within a given territory; one might say, using an old terminology, that the king was suzerain but not sovereign. Most political and social decisions were not made by the king or his ministers, nor did individuals feel a direct subjection to central authority on all matters; rather, each individual was primarily a member of a less inclusive social grouping, subject to a lord who was in turn subject to a higher lord (duke, count, or baron), who was in turn subject to the king.

For example, a medieval monarch did not issue a draft call in order to raise armed forces, for there were no local draft boards established under national legislation and empowered to use national courts and police to enforce their decisions. Instead, the king relied for his troops on the lords immediately subject to him, and a duke or baron would raise the requested contingent from his own vassals. Similarly, the individual could not, at least in the early Middle Ages, appeal directly to the king's courts when he felt an injustice had been done; instead it was necessary to appeal to the courts of one's lord, though higher appeal was in some cases possible.

[4] On this comparison, which is a development of the conception of the "state of nature" in the political philosophies of Hobbes, Locke, and Rousseau (among others), see Roger D. Masters: "World Politics as a Primitive Political System," *World Politics*, XVI (1964), 595-619.

It may seem absurd to propose that the UN, if it has a long-range future, should come to approximate the status of a medieval monarch. Yet such an evolution may be a desirable and practical goal, for it would avoid the most imposing obstacles that face the development of a world government. At present, statesmen understandably reject any notion that the UN can intervene in "domestic" matters, fearing that their own power would be permanently destroyed if disgruntled citizens could appeal, directly as individuals, to a higher authority. But if international organizations are viewed as residual authorities whose decisions influence individuals only indirectly and with the tacit consent of the immediate rulers, not merely the UN but other regional groupings (like the Organization of American States) could increasingly become courts of appeal for states in conflict.

In this view, world politics may come to be structured into several levels of political institutions, each with its characteristic sphere of competence. Like the individual of an African tribe who was simultaneously a member of a family household, a lineage of his closest relatives, a clan of his most distant relatives, and the tribe as a whole, the individual would be a subject of his state, a participant (along with his fellow citizens) in a regional organization of nation-states, and ultimately a member of a world community over which the UN exercised residual powers. Whenever subordinate groups became locked in conflicts that posed too great a threat, the next largest authorities would have some claim to intervene to settle the dispute. Neighboring states that refused to settle a dispute would come before a regional grouping of which both were members, just as rival lineages within a single primitive clan could be led to compose their differences by the elders or chief of the clan as a whole; states in different regions or conflicting regional organizations would be to some extent subject to the UN, just as some tribal chiefs could intervene in conflicts between different clans.

For example, in one African tribe the chief was not empowered to settle disputes within villages, nor did he normally intervene in feuds or conflicts between villages. But when two villages engaged in a dispute and enlisted the support of rival clans, so that large-scale violence threatened to persist without a satisfactory solution, the chief would enlist the support of all other members of the tribe; failing a settlement of the dispute, the chief would then descend on both offending villages and destroy them, thereby creating a considerable incentive to listen to reason in future disputes.

Perhaps it is conceivable that the UN could develop into something like that African chief, having residual but very real peace-keeping powers. Certainly the development of international forces, supplied and financed by member states, indicates a certain trend in this direction. But the reluctance of France and the Soviet Union to pay for UN peace-keeping forces (like those used in the Congo and Cyprus) shows that the UN is still far short of the powers needed to intervene against the will of any major power or its close allies; significant increases in the authority of international organization would therefore be necessary for the UN to approximate the role of a medieval or primitive suzerain.

If such is to be our goal for the UN, we must be clear about the likely conditions for its success and the consequences. American support for international organization has hitherto rested on the assumption that our foreign-policy goals would not be flagrantly contradicted by UN decisions; with the rising importance of the Afro-Asian bloc and the likelihood that Peking will be admitted, we must anticipate defeats within the UN and consider their importance to us.

The medieval or suzerain political pattern is characteristic of situations in which human security is a dominant problem because centralized government is impossible to establish yet "stateless" anarchy overly risky. Whether due to the weakness of less inclusive political units or as a result of military technology, this basic insecurity is rendered more tolerable by the confusing and shifting system in which central political officials usually intervene only as a last resort. These conditions may develop over the next fifty years, especially as a consequence of nuclear proliferation, but it will be doubted whether such insecurity is desirable.

If the nation-state (or continent-state) can protect its subjects without risking the extermination of the human race, it could therefore be argued that conscious efforts to work toward increased authority for the UN are either unnecessary or undesirable. Such a role would be unnecessary if the states themselves could come to accept solutions based on their mutual self-interest (and particularly their desire to avoid nuclear destruction); it would be undesirable insofar as further movements in this direction might actually increase the kind of instability which seems both the condition and the natural characteristic of a medieval type of political order.

This last argument depends to a great extent on one's assessment of the probable consequences of UN suzerainty in world politics. The essential mechanisms by which medieval or primitive rulers of this kind maintained power are quite different from those within a civilized nation-state or empire, for the central ruler is usually dependent on subordinate authorities for the forces needed to make and keep the peace. In such societies, the result was a process of rivalry between subordinate authorities, each of which sought either to have a dominant role in advising the central ruler or—if defeated in this attempt—to overthrow the suzerain king or chief.

It is no accident, therefore, that the prevailing impression of medieval life is one of a time of troubles and violence. During the so-called "dark ages," the use of force to settle domestic disputes acquired a legitimacy that was later suppressed within the nation-states established by centralizing, absolute monarchs. Under a ruler who is suzerain but not sovereign, it is impossible to speak of treason: civil war becomes an accepted means of replacing a chief or king who is hostile to one of his nominally subordinate but actually very powerful subjects.

Moreover, the game of politics under such institutions places a premium on the relations between groups that are all supposedly subject to the central ruler. A medieval duke who could count on few men to assist him, and who was engaged in bitter dispute with a more powerful duke allied with other potent lords, could usually not count on the assistance of the king; often the monarch would not intervene unless the opposed forces were nearly enough equal to make his action decisive.

Even should the UN acquire powers similar to those of the medieval monarch, therefore, power relationships between states would remain a prime characteristic of world politics. A UN with increased peace-keeping forces may be able to reduce the dangers of war if rivals are roughly balanced and major powers see a common interest in compromise; such was the case in Cyprus and the Congo. Similar marginal conflicts may be moderated with the assistance of the UN in the future, but as the cease-fire between India and Pakistan revealed, mediation by a superpower like the Soviet Union can sometimes be more effective than attempts to work out detailed solutions within the General Assembly or Security Council.

It follows that the most likely means of increasing the power of the UN is not a sufficient long-range goal for American foreign policy. On the contrary, such an evolution of international organization, however useful it may be, suggests that relationships of power between various states and alliances may become even more important than in the last two centuries of world politics. This is so because a suzerain UN would act, as did the medieval monarch, on the basis of the likely sources of power that could support central action; in this sense, further increases in the UN's authority would heighten the importance of the relative strength of each state and its allies in determining the outcome of international rivalries.

The foregoing comments indicate again, as was suggested in chapter i, that the long-range goals of American foreign policy must be defined in terms of a balance of political power, which is to say patterns of political alliance and influence that preserve American ideals and interests insofar as possible. It is therefore necessary to consider the fundamental options of the United States in terms of the kinds of international alignments that could conceivably emerge between now and the end of the present century.

The first and most often considered possibility is an Atlantic community. The success of NATO in deterring Soviet aggression has suggested to many Americans that a permanent alignment between Western Europe and the United States —the cores of Western civilization—is desirable because its industrial superiority and military strength could survive any possible changes in world politics. Some have thought of this relationship as a bar-bell alliance (to use a phrase that became popular under President Kennedy), joining a united Europe and the United States as equal partners; others conceive of a single, more diffuse coalition of democratic nations.

Although we shall return in detail to the problems of the Atlantic alliance and the incompatibility of these two views, neither satisfies the long-range needs of American policy. Even assuming that an Atlantic community existed and were organized on a supranational or federal basis, so that all of the major Western states had a common policy, it is not certain that such a union could maintain the world peace. Because communist expansion could still take place in underdeveloped nations, the scope of our political goals cannot be limited to a single portion of the globe, especially that portion in closest agreement with American objectives and ideals.

An Atlantic community would only be part of a tolerable long-range political goal, and as such would have to give promise of establishing a reasonable balance of power between the states excluded from a union of the industrialized nations ringing the Atlantic. Yet a successful Atlantic community might itself contribute to international instability by grouping together so many of the most prosperous nations of the world; to those outside it, an Atlantic union would look like an effort to establish a world-wide hegemony of the industrially developed West. It is for this reason that several of our allies have attempted to maintain or create political alignments with underdeveloped countries, whether it is the British Commonwealth, the French effort to maintain influence in Africa and win it in South America, or the West German attempt to establish lasting influence in the Middle East.

These efforts reflect an additional weakness of the Atlantic community as a goal of American foreign policy—namely, the internal cleavages within that community itself. Many Europeans are acutely aware that alliance with the United States is not sufficient to preserve peace throughout a rapidly changing world. Fears of a world war arising out of American commitments in Vietnam have only driven home this point, for Americans have often implicitly (if not explicitly) viewed an Atlantic community merely as one means of containing communism at all costs. In contrast, many NATO members have admitted the inevitability of certain communist advances —and, for example, have recognized Peking.

It would therefore be impossible to establish a lasting Atlantic community without a specific agreement on the goals to be pursued by a more tightly organized Western bloc. The history of the last few years should prove that this kind of agreement is not readily available even on immediate questions like the attitude to communist take-overs in Vietnam or the Dominican Republic, not to mention larger issues concerning the orientation of South America toward Europe rather than the United States. As a result, an Atlantic community presupposes political integration, making possible a single policy based on a shared conception of a global balance of power. To the extent that American policy-makers and citizens are not willing to surrender American sovereignty to supranational institutions representing the industrialized West —and so run the risks of being outvoted in the resulting Atlantic community—this goal seems impossible to attain.

We must therefore consider other alignments of power and interest which, either independently of or in addition to an alliance with Western Europe, could serve as a stable basis of world politics in the next fifty years. The first that comes to mind is essentially a Russo-American great-power condominium, based on the assumption that the Soviet Union is the most reliable partner available for restraining other members of the communist bloc. By sharing zones of influence and reaching tacit agreements that neither superpower would challenge positions deemed crucial by the other, it is hoped that the United States and the Soviet Union could manage the danger of nuclear confrontation, restrain their own allies, and maintain world peace.

This conception, implicit in President Kennedy's "Strategy of Peace," was to a certain extent realized during the Suez and Cuban missile crises. The tacit recognition by the United States and the Russians of their common interest in preventing a nuclear holocaust has, however, very clear limits. In particular, both the United States and the USSR have an important formal ally that is reluctant to accept a permanent Russo-American condominium.

In this respect, the reactions of France and China to such events as the Moscow treaty outlawing nuclear tests are strictly parallel, for both China and France fear Russo-American agreements to the detriment of their own interests. The French insistence on an independent policy and the Chinese criticism of Khrushchev and post-Khrushchev leadership—not to mention the efforts of both to develop independent nuclear forces—have thus one common theme: both France and China have tried to show that a Russo-American condominium cannot last since neither the United States nor the Soviet Union can with assurance restrain or speak for its nominal ally. This means that a Russo-American alignment may very well be profitable on specific issues, but it cannot be a sufficient long-range goal of our foreign policy.

This conclusion is reinforced by a second factor. In a sense, the Sino-Soviet split has strengthened the world communist movement, even though it may have weakened the control of any single nation over that movement. Since individual communist parties can follow either the Russian or the

Chinese line, or play these two parties off against each other, it becomes possible for communists to take aggressive positions even if one or another communist power seeks an accommodation with the West in a given area.

This means that American alignment with Russia could conceivably encourage—rather than discourage—a radical pro-Chinese party to follow a revolutionary course of action. As a result, the strategy oriented to a *détente* with the USSR could actually increase communist gains, which the Soviet Union might ultimately be able to exploit to our disadvantage while seeming to do the opposite. Some commentators have even argued—though it seems contrary to the most likely explanation—that the Sino-Soviet split is merely a façade to lull the West. Be that as it may, it is hard to conclude that in itself a Russo-American condominium could either be established or maintained as a long-range objective conducive to a stable balance of power.

The inadequacies of either an Atlantic alliance or a Soviet-American alignment lead one to question whether any single pattern of power relationships can be established as a long-range goal. Given the increasing independence of Western Europe with regard to American commitments throughout the world, and the split within the communist camp (which renders less likely accommodations with that bloc as a whole), some might suggest that the United States seek alignments elsewhere in the world. For example, one alternative might be a development of the Alliance for Progress and the Organization of American States toward a Western Hemispheric power base for the United States. Unfortunately, the tradition of American policy in Latin America, the frustrations caused by our dominance in the hemisphere, and the bitterness felt in many quarters at such events as our originally unilateral intervention in the Dominican Republic, raise real questions concerning this possibility.

At its best, a hemispheric alignment, particularly if combined with a reduction of American commitments elsewhere in the world and reforms that could satisfy the demands of those South American workers, intellectuals, and peasants who are attracted to radicalism, might prevent further communist advances in Latin America. But absolute achievement of this goal, itself unlikely, would still not indicate how similar threats on other continents could be prevented from causing either major wars or unfavorable consequences for American power; as a result, a long-range orientation of the United States to the Western Hemisphere is hardly a sufficient means of balancing world-wide forces in international politics.

Although it is less frequently considered, perhaps an American orientation toward the Pacific might be desirable. Since both Western Europe and the Soviet Union have become highly industrialized or "have" powers, nuclear deterrence and a common interest in self-preservation can probably suffice to prevent war in Europe; the greatest threats to the present balance of power seem to arise in Asia, for the conflicts of interest between major powers could, it is hoped, be managed by astute diplomacy on all other continents. But if we are to be, as President Johnson has claimed, a "Pacific power," it is necessary to be aligned with some specific Asian states.

To create a stable global balance of power based on an alignment with Asia, it is insufficient for the United States to ally with weak nations like Thailand or the Philippines; such a Pacific orientation amounts to the establishment of a ring of client states ultimately dependent on the United States. To be stable, therefore, a long-range alignment toward the Pacific would probably require an accommodation with Communist China, the most powerful state on the Asian continent. Only in this way could we balance the diffusion of power in other areas and the possibility of entente between Russia and Western Europe aimed at reducing American power.

While so highly unlikely at the moment that it seems visionary, tactical alliance with Peking might have clear advantages for American self-interest in the future. Our attempts to isolate or contain the most revolutionary major power in the world may well be self-defeating, for the U.S. has little or no ability to deter the Chinese without defeating them militarily; the Russians are similarly unable to restrain their nominal ally. While both superpowers fear Peking, an American attack on China would probably force Moscow to support its unruly communist rival and create grave risks of a Russo-American confrontation.

Our ideological opposition to Peking has dangerously blinded us from seeing that our conflicts of interest with China are much less profound than those dividing the Russians and the Chinese. Since both major communist powers are states with territory and persisting ambitions on the Asian continent, China serves to balance the Soviet Union; even more important, any policy which removed Peking as an autonomous power would invite an unwelcome expansion of Russian influence (either by reestablishing a Sino-Soviet entente or by creating a power vacuum into which Moscow would not hesitate to move).[5]

Paradoxically, the Chinese have less to fear from a tactical alliance with a capitalist power than with a communist one, since we could never pose a threat to Chinese pretensions to lead the world communist movement. Moreover certain convergent although not identical interests may be shared by China and the United States. The Chinese wish to industrialize and modernize their society so as to become a major world

[5] Hugo Portisch, an Austrian journalist, has acutely formulated the basic power configuration: "It might take a long time for Chinese leaders to understand the world outside China, as it obviously takes a long time for the world to understand some of the motives behind China's ambitions. But eventually China's conflict with the West might be solved. . . . It will be much more difficult for the Soviets and the Chinese to find a similar basis of understanding. For both of them have their homes in Asia. The only thing that again would bring the Chinese and the Soviets together—and in a hurry—would be any major attack on Communist China. The Soviet Union, as the leading Communist power, simply could not afford to stand idly by if it did not want to see its prestige in the Communist world completely ruined overnight. . . ." "The Chinese-Soviet Gap Widens," *Saturday Review* (July 2, 1966), p. 12.

power; we find Chinese expansionism as a means to this end intolerable. But it could be argued that industrialization and full-fledged possession of nuclear forces induce a major power to a more conservative strategy; if so, the United States might have much to gain from the very developments that the Chinese desire.

Strikingly enough, the rise of the Soviet Union to the status of a world power with an awesome nuclear arsenal has reduced its willingness to resort to all-out war to achieve its aims. The recklessness with which the Chinese seem to approach nuclear weapons today directly parallels attitudes shown by the Russians at the same stage of their nuclear development; nuclear powers have shown the greatest restraints on their desire to use nuclear weapons only after they have developed weapons systems that require a sophisticated nuclear strategy.

Finally, an alliance with Red China has a certain purely abstract advantage. The United States is essentially a status quo power. Such a power is always placed at a disadvantage when faced with revolutionary challenges in spheres beyond its direct control. The natural tendency of a status quo power is to seek conservative allies, but under modern conditions this tactic seems doomed to be nothing more than a holding action. Perhaps the only means of restraining the most revolutionary forces in the world over the long run is to form an alliance with them; as the saying goes: "If you can't beat 'em, join 'em."

Astounding as this policy might appear, the United States at present faces the choice between preventive war against the Chinese or a long-range policy that recognizes China as a great nuclear power. But even if the former alternative is rejected and Americans accept China as a legitimate power, the possibilities of American alignment with Peking seem at present nil, not merely because of conflicting commitments in Vietnam, but broadly because of ideological and political positions which have become habitual. The Chinese seem to need us as their enemy, if only to maintain their Maoist revolutionary fervor, and hence would probably reject our overtures (at least in the immediate future). Similarly, American opinion is quite unprepared for a Peking-Washington alliance, regardless of the advantages it might offer.

Moreover such an alignment, even if attainable, would not exhaust American foreign-policy objectives, for it would probably imply an alteration of our attitudes toward Europe and the Soviet Union. If a Sino-American entente were to result in a unified Europe from the Atlantic to the Urals, such a reversal of alliances would hardly seem desirable to most Americans. It appears, therefore, that there is no single alignment which could hope to be a successful means of maintaining a stable global balance of power over the long run.

With the frustrations of maintaining the peace in a nuclear age, could the United States return to a policy of isolation? This suggestion, like alliance with Peking, seems so sharply opposed to prevailing American beliefs that it is usually dismissed out of hand. Nevertheless there is much to be said for a reduction of American commitments throughout the world during a period of revolutionary upheaval.

Nuclear weapons and the superiority of the American arsenal—not to mention the possibility that American weapons development will continue to outpace advances in military technology by other major powers—reduce the absolute necessity of alliances; in a sense the geographical isolation provided by the Atlantic and Pacific oceans before the twentieth century may have been regained in terms of a new kind of strategic invulnerability. Moreover, American commitments throughout the world may fail to prevent communist advances under conditions in which we will constantly be tempted to escalate our means of intervention to the point of all-out nuclear war.

Because of the highly urban concentration of the American population, such a war would be more devastating for the United States than for any other major power, with the possible exception of Western Europe. Realization of these risks has led many Europeans to be critical of America's anti-communist involvement in Southeast Asia and Latin America. If our international commitments may lead to our own destruction in the worst case, and isolation from our European allies insofar as this outcome is feared, would it not be preferable to avoid foreign entanglements? Could the United States not be content with the defense of its own territory?

This question is especially important because support for a kind of neo-isolationism appears to be emerging in the United States. At the same time that unprecedented governmental programs to reconstruct cities, aid the poor, or finance local public services have become politically acceptable, technological advances have radically increased the costs of weapons development and procurement. It seems increasingly necessary to choose between military and civilian needs (or, to use the now common phrase, "guns and butter") in establishing the federal budget. Those who most insistently demand extensive governmental action to end domestic social injustice also tend to de-emphasize the need for military and political commitments abroad; hence we may see, in future years, a left-wing neo-isolationism similar to the domestic progressivism and international isolationism of Senators Norris and Borah in the late 1930's (except that the party labels will probably differ).

Isolationism could be a goal in an era when the United States was not only militarily invulnerable but largely independent economically as well. But whereas in the nineteenth century the United States depended on Europe for imports of capital and men, both of which were not hindered by America's lack of commitment in European politics (and may have been aided by it), the American economy today is not so easily isolated. Because international commerce has become a necessity for American industry—and, it might be added, American agriculture—political isolationism could have disastrous consequences if other industrial powers were to gain markets which our producers seek to supply.

These economic factors indicate that a return to isolationism could give rise to bitter and fundamental dispute in American politics. Those who view communism as a major threat—and they are by no means confined to the right wing—will doubtless condemn a general abandonment of our commitments to defend other free peoples; the rise of a "new left" that combines neo-isolationism and extensive domestic reform will probably be strongly opposed by many Americans who feel that the latter threatens their social position and that the former is tantamount to treasonable or communist conspiracy.

Although it may be necessary and wise to reduce our formal commitments to other governments under some circumstances, isolationism does not seem to be a foreign-policy goal that would be either salutary or popularly acceptable. On the contrary, American withdrawal from collective-security pacts like SEATO can best be defended on the ground that these international obligations are ineffective; whereas isolationism implies that foreign affairs are not of major importance, the arguments used to support it ultimately refer to the most effective means by which the United States can act as a world power.

In other words, international politics would not disappear if this country turned its attention entirely inward. The needs of America's increasingly international business community, along with the necessity to defend our way of life against military threats (such as the presence of Soviet missiles in Cuba), cannot be wished out of existence. However realistic it may be to recognize that the United States must on occasion act alone in world politics, defending our interests even though our allies dissociate themselves from us, a return to the objectives of the last century is as unsatisfactory a goal for American foreign policy as the other power relationships sketched above.

All these considerations show that no particular alignment of power is satisfactory as a long-range objective for the United States. This difficulty may result from an attempt to define policy goals in too specific terms. Granted that the ultimate American objective is a stable world in which the United States and her interests can be defended without too great a risk of nuclear war, there is no reason to assume that alignment with any specific nations would necessarily and permanently be superior to any other alignment.

On the contrary, there is much to be said for the proposition that the United States should adopt as its goal a general world-wide equilibrium, adopting alliances or accommodations with any power or powers that further this objective. This may seem unpardonably vague, but such a goal was more or less the guiding theme of British foreign policy in the nineteenth century, if not before.

Two crucial questions must be answered if this proposed orientation is to be practicable. First, can the United States free itself from the largely ideological anticommunism that has rendered agreements with the Soviet Union suspect and accommodation with China virtually impossible even if in our own interest? Second, if we do adopt a radically flexible attitude toward alignments with other nations, based primarily on balance of power considerations, which trends in world politics are most relevant to our choice of policies at any given time? The first of these questions cannot be readily answered, for it depends on the will and intelligence of American political leaders and statesmen, but the reply to the second can be made with greater assurance.

Three characteristic features of the twentieth century seem destined to play a dominant role in coming years: the continuing technological revolution connected with industrialization, the resulting expansion of stable major powers to the size of continent-states, and the problems posed by the diffusion of nuclear weapons. Given these three factors, international stability could well be most fully assured by the emergence of a number of continental centers of power, each with industrial, population, and military resources like those of the United States and the Soviet Union.

From this perspective, the rise of a federated Europe with

independent nuclear capabilities and a distinct foreign policy, and the emergence of China as an industrialized nuclear power, could have stabilizing effects on world politics. As long as the United States and Russia remain the only superpowers, each must commit itself extensively for fear the other may gain predominant power; the so-called "theory of falling dominoes," applied to Vietnam, is but one manifestation of the risk of all-out war in a bipolar world where the superpowers equate losses of position with irreversible defeat.

When there are four or five major independent powers, violence on a limited scale may be more likely than in a bipolar world, but the possibilities of limiting war once it occurs are equally increased. In a bipolar situation, the maintenance of stability ultimately depends on the prudence of the United States and Russia, whereas smaller powers may find an interest in exacerbating tensions under the nuclear umbrella of an allied or benevolent superpower. When there are four or more major powers, in contrast, the consequences of major war become more uncertain even for the victor, and the possible gains from a superpower's all-out nuclear attack on any one rival very much minimized. On the contrary, victory may be self-defeating wherever the victim is a nation of considerable importance.

For example, should the United States completely destroy mainland China, the political consequence might be an alignment of all other major powers against the United States, based on fear of American hegemony. Thus we could defeat the Chinese only to find a new alliance between Russia and Europe dedicated to limiting American influence. Such an alignment might restrict American power far more severely than if we had not attacked the Chinese in the first place; in a pre-nuclear age, much the same fate was the reward of Napoleon.

Radical changes in technology and strategy in the last half of the twentieth century may tend toward the development of a number of great-power centers, all of which would have major nuclear capabilities and a base continental in scale.

Western Europe and China are the most likely candidates to join the existing superpowers (although the long-range potential of other nations, notably India, must also be considered). All of these powers need not be of equal stature, but each would be radically superior to nation-states whose military and economic potential does not permit effective action and political influence beyond their own continent.

In this kind of international system, Africa, the Middle East, and South America would be the most likely theaters of rivalry and violence because in these regions the scale of political community is not yet large enough to attain great-power standing based on self-sustaining industrial development. Over the long run, new great powers may emerge in these areas as well, but the prime problems of maintaining world peace in the next fifty years will probably be connected with great-power competition for influence among secondary or tertiary powers.

If the United States establishes as its general objective a stable balance between continental-scale major powers—essentially Western Europe, Russia, China, perhaps India, and herself—all of the specific power relationships discussed above might have a role to play in American foreign policies. Clearly, a preferential alliance with Western Europe insofar as our interests coincide is crucial for the United States, not merely as a means of defending our own political ideals, but also to assure our economic survival. Similarly, accommodation with the Soviet Union is particularly necessary because of the present nuclear superiority of the United States and Russia, and therewith our common interest in avoiding a direct nuclear confrontation; for the foreseeable future, these two powers seem assured of at least a quantitative advantage in nuclear weapons, even vis-à-vis other continental units which may achieve superpower status.

At the same time, efforts to maintain the cohesion or at least the peace within the Western Hemisphere could be justified as a particularly American responsibility under a tacit division of zones of influence between major powers. In this sense, the Soviet predominance in Eastern Europe, the special relationships between Western European powers and Africa, and the long-range influence and supremacy of the Chinese in Southeast Asia would seem to be corollaries of a relatively stable international system based on continental nuclear superpowers.

The notion of zones of influence may be repugnant to American minds, but it is consistent with the realities of world politics. This notion does not mean that all states within the zone of a nearby nuclear superpower are simply absorbed by it. On the contrary, one characteristic of the modern world is an attempt of such subordinate or satellite nations to establish countervailing ties with other major powers: Russian satellites in Eastern Europe seek trade and cultural relations with Western Europe, the United States, and China, just as South American states seek to balance their dependence on the United States by ties with Western—if not Eastern—Europe.

The decisive factor is a universal recognition that each superpower has a preferential negative role in the region of its dominance. If power gains in the area of dominance of another major power have less legitimacy than each super-power's defense of its own sphere, agreement to withdraw in case of conflict is appropriate where one superpower meets another in the latter's zone of influence.

This type of unwritten understanding of the rules of power is not pure speculation. Russian moderation in the Cuban missile crisis, for example, was the counterpart of American moderation at the time of the uprisings in Eastern Europe. In each case a nuclear giant realized the limits of its ability to intervene massively close to the frontiers of its major rival. More recently, foreign powers that condemned the American intervention in the Dominican Republic refrained from mili-tary opposition, recognizing that this conflict lay within our sphere of influence.

But, it will be asked, what are the guarantees that an ag-gressive major power—in particular, China—would retreat in case of a conflict with another superpower, especially since the aggressor could disguise its intervention in the form of subversion (appropriately called a movement of national liberation)? The converse of a division of the world into spheres of influence is that each superpower not be considered to have absolute hegemony over its zone of dominance; on the contrary, each superpower must realize that all others have an interest in making the most of their influence throughout the world. Experience shows that certain states within one major power's zone of influence cannot be prevented from aligning with a more distant one, as the Albanians have aligned with the Chinese, the Cubans with the Russians, and the Malaysians with the British. What would be necessary is a flexible policy aimed at convincing each major power that its zone of influence will be respected only if it grants a mutual respect for the zones of other major powers and a tolerance for counterbalancing interventions in marginal cases between one zone of influence and another.

Reverses in individual states may be tolerable only if it is manifestly impossible for any one superpower to gain world-wide hegemony by conquest or subversion. Hence it would be in the interest of the United States to encourage the development of new continental-scale powers, even if they were independent of us (and were not members of a Western "bloc"); the logic of power is the surest restraint against aggression. For example, the best means of limiting Chinese expansionism in the near future could be the emergence of India as an independent nuclear power, capable of deterring China's power in Asia.

The international system just described would not be one of assured peace and tranquillity, luxuries which cannot be expected in a world shaken by the technological and political changes which seem inevitable in the next fifty to one hundred years. But a realistic appreciation of power relations, freed from fixed ideological commitments or narrow definitions of our allies and enemies, would permit a more flexible response to challenges to the peace; in this way, ad hoc coalitions of the major powers could restrain violence in any particular area, or at least confine it.

Such a structure of world politics would be particularly advantageous because further nuclear proliferation is so likely, even with a formal international treaty prohibiting it. The process of diffusion can be stabilized most effectively by emphasizing tacit agreements and a sense of mutual self-interest among a small number of independent major powers (much as the giants dominating the American automobile industry refrain from price wars because they recognize their mutual interdependence).

As thoughtful observers on both sides of the Atlantic have begun to realize, deterrence may be strengthened when an aggressor must calculate not only the probable reactions of its major nuclear opponent, but also the responses of other nuclear powers that might trigger an all-out war.[6] Whereas bipolar nuclear deterrence can be undermined by hopes or fears of a surprise attack, reciprocal deterrence among four or five nuclear powers may be more stable over the long run.

This tacit awareness of the mutual interest in avoiding all-out war among major powers would not necessarily prevent a nuclear war, especially if a minor power obtained a small stockpile of atomic weapons. But if the major nuclear powers maintain a rough balance in their own capabilities and refrain from nuclear exchanges, minor powers might be deterred from nuclear adventures by two means.

First, a small power that used nuclear weapons, whether acting either on its own or as a proxy for a superpower, would risk retaliation from one or more of the other superpowers. For example, should the Egyptians want to attack the Israelis with nuclear weapons, a tacit agreement between the other major nuclear powers to punish such aggression by joint retaliation would be an impressive deterrent as long as at least one of three or four nuclear powers was likely to

[6] See Liska: *Nations in Alliance*, Ch. vi; and General André Beaufre: *Deterrence and Strategy* (New York: Praeger; 1966), Ch. iii. Cf. Albert Wohlstetter: "The Delicate Balance of Terror," *Foreign Affairs*, XXXVII (1959), 211-34.

honor its commitment. The Security Council's demand for a cease-fire between India and Pakistan indicates that such great-power agreements are conceivable.

The second means of limiting violence by minor powers hardly seems an advantage, but it must be looked at as the lesser of necessary evils. A tacit or explicit agreement among superpowers to prohibit and dissuade the initial use of nuclear weapons by other states would probably convince expansionist powers that they have a greater advantage in conventional or guerrilla aggression than in nuclear attacks. On a lesser scale of military intervention, it would be far more useful—especially for reckless nations of secondary rank—to play one nuclear giant against another as part of the fluid process of rivalry between a limited number of great-power centers. In South Vietnam, the Vietcong and North Vietnamese have already done this kind of thing.

Although the encouragement of limited war and subversion is not a welcome prospect, it is preferable to a total war fought with thermonuclear weapons. Moreover, the reduction of the stakes of conflict in a world composed of a number of superpowers must be emphasized. As we move away from a bipolar system, it becomes less certain that the subversion or conquest of any single nation could give the victor a decisive advantage. On the contrary, as allies of the superpowers continue to assert their own independence—a phenomenon already quite marked in both Eastern and Western Europe, not to mention insistence upon "nonalignment" in many underdeveloped countries—major powers will find it increasingly difficult to impose their will on secondary states, whose freedom of maneuver is in a sense assured by weakness.

While accepting the fundamental notion that American goals should be oriented to a global balance of power, some may object that the objective of a world-wide equilibrium among a small number of continental superpowers is unsatisfactory. It could be claimed that American power and wealth will continue to increase at a faster rate than any single potential rival; since the United States can use its numerical superiority in nuclear weapons to deter direct threats to our society (and outspend any other country in a technological arms race), our vast and growing industrial strength, if properly used, could permit us to defeat aggression against any ally. Hence, some have argued, the United States will dominate the coming century in world politics, and all calculations of a balance of power should be based on this essential fact.[7]

One could even speak of an American hegemony or empire as a feasible foreign-policy goal. Our global control would not be that of directly amalgamating other peoples into our own political system, as did the Romans when their republic encompassed virtually the entire civilized world; the American goal would be an indirect domination through commercial power, approximating the Athenian empire of the fifth century B.C.

Such an objective is not as ridiculous as may first appear to many Americans. Our economic power has grown faster than that of the Soviet Union or any other nation; even at identical rates of growth, our immense industrial base outstrips all others. The growing gap between rich and poor nations, moreover, makes the emergence of new challengers to our supremacy all the more difficult. Just as Athenian hegemony was the consequence of technological ingenuity and wealth, which came into play only after the Persian attempt to conquer the world has been defeated, so the rise of American power rests on our industrial strength, first clearly manifested on the international scene after World War II.

Like the Athenians, American dominance is based on the attempt to develop an alliance of states with similar political institutions, capable of defeating any hostile power; like the Athenians whose empire was built in opposition to Sparta, we have been impelled to seek increased international control by the threat of Soviet Russia (representing alien political

[7] As Lester Markel put it: "We do not yet realize that, as the great power of the West, our role is inevitable and unmistakable. We have undertaken, as the British once did, to police the world; to insure, if we can, a global peace." *The New York Times Magazine* (July 17, 1966), p. 52.

principles organized in an alliance of potentially hostile states). And like the Athenians, our position within the alliances built since 1945 depends in good part on superior military technology rather than direct conquest. Athens dominated the Delian League because only a couple of her allies had an independent naval force—and no other city-state could by itself match the Athenian navy; Great Britain and France are our only allies with independent nuclear forces, and no nation-state has a nuclear arsenal comparable to our own.

A final analogy is particularly telling. The Athenians rose to hegemony because their free and democratic society placed a priority on individual initiative, which permitted Athens to respond effectively and decisively to external challenges as they arose. Athens consequently became an imperial power as the unplanned consequence of her pragmatic and successful policies, in much the same way as the United States emerged in 1945 as the leader of the free world without having actively sought such status as a long-range goal.[8]

While historical analogies must be approached with caution, one must consider the possibility that the United States, like Athens, could acquire (and indeed has already acquired) a hegemonic empire without conquest or direct administration over our allies. Throughout Western Europe, American busi-nesses have increasingly great investments and control. Given

---

[8] The similarities between Athens in the period following the Persian wars and the United States in the last twenty years will be striking to anyone who reads Thucydides' *History of the Peloponnesian War* with care. For example, Thucydides speaks of "the enterprising and revolution-ary character of the Athenians," who are described by a speaker from Corinth as "addicted to innovation" (Modern Library edn., pp. 40, 58). As an Athenian supposedly put it in justifying his city's hegemony in Greece: "that empire we acquired by no violent means, but . . . because the allies attached themselves to us and spontaneously asked us to assume the command" (p. 43). Much the same could be said of the United States. The Peloponnesian War, like the cold war, was based on a balance of terror strategy; as Pericles said: "If they march against our country we will sail against theirs," causing simultaneous mutual destruction that would be advantageous to Athens because of its greater naval power as compared with Sparta's larger land power (p. 82). Adding nuclear weapons and air power to naval forces, the strategic situation in recent years has been surprisingly similar. Pericles' famous funeral oration (pp. 102-6) could almost be a description of the United States.

the ultimate character of nuclear deterrence, therefore, is it not conceivable that moderate but firm opposition to limited aggression could restrain communist powers while our expanding economy established an indirect global superiority that could last for generations?

Such a goal may be more feasible than American statesmen dare proclaim. Whether it is desirable, however, requires careful second thoughts. Pericles predicted that the Athenians would win the Peloponnesian War with Sparta if they could "consent not to combine schemes of fresh conquest with the conduct of the war"; he was more afraid of Athens' "own blunders than of the enemy's devices."[9] As Thucydides makes clear in the course of his *History,* it was such a scheme of "fresh conquest"—the expedition to distant Sicily—which opened the way to Athens' downfall; after the death of Pericles, Athenian democracy was undermined by the lack of a moderate and prudent leader, aware of the dangers of overcommitment abroad and passionate extremism at home.

The first question, therefore, is whether the kind of empire open to the United States is not dependent upon wise and moderate leadership for its preservation. In the nuclear age, this would seem too obvious for further comment. Although democratic government does not insure that rulers will always be wise statesmen (as is revealed, for example, by a comparison between Polk and Lincoln), the complexity of supervising an American hegemony would require that the President have ever greater power in the conduct of foreign policy. Yet the Founding Fathers, because they did not expect that those elected to the presidency would always be virtuous and wise, feared such centralization of power and attempted to guard against it.[1]

This leads to a second and even more serious objection.

[9] Ibid., p. 82.

[1] For example, see *The Federalist Papers,* No. 75: "The history of human conduct does not warrant that exalted opinion of human virtue which would make it wise in a nation to commit interests of so delicate and momentous a kind, as those which concern its intercourse with the rest of the world, to the sole disposal of a magistrate created and circumstanced as would be a President of the United States."

Our institutions were never designed for the role of an imperial power, even if empire is defined as an indirect hegemony like that of Athens; rather, our traditions of government were based on the assumption that the United States, isolated from Europe by the Atlantic Ocean, would not need to enter the "entangling alliances" required of a major world power.

Even if feasible, a foreign-policy goal of world supremacy has huge costs because such a departure from past experience could change our entire political life. This objective would imply our willingness to take enormous responsibilities in maintaining world peace; continuous tension, largely due to the quest for economic development in the nonindustrialized countries, would become commonplace. The federal government would increasingly be the only focus of all American political life as governmental planning and control were expanded and resources mobilized for putting down wars of national liberation wherever they arose.

The domestic controversies arising out of the Korean and Vietnamese wars indicate not only that the pressures of such a global policy would be great, but that opponents to our foreign commitments would run the risk of being branded as traitors. The national passion for unity in the face of threat, especially characteristic of the American response to World Wars I and II, might become a continuous phenomenon as the United States was repeatedly engaged in police actions throughout the world. Especially if foreign aggression could be attributed to communism, domestic dissent would become increasingly difficult to tolerate as it became more widespread.

Both Athenian democracy and the Roman republic were ultimately corrupted by the internal consequences of foreign empire.[2] Lest the same fate occur in our society, unaccustomed

[2] "Some critics of American policy argue that the attempt to play a role simultaneously in every part of the globe is beyond our *physical* resources. It seems to me clearly beyond our *psychological* resources. If we insist on assuming the principal responsibility for every square mile of territory at every moment of time, we will tear ourselves to pieces inwardly . . . hegemony is demoralizing in the long run." Henry Kissinger: "For a New Atlantic Alliance," *The Reporter* (July 14, 1966), p. 23.

to the role of a major power in world politics, it would seem highly undesirable to seek actively a more extensive hegemony over foreign lands. Because such an indirect empire is possible, particularly should the Soviet Union fail to defend another communist regime that we find it profitable to destroy or conquer, we must seek a global balance of power that would reduce the impact of foreign politics on our domestic institutions.

To do otherwise is to run the risk of subordinating justice within our borders to the benefits of power secured in the international arena. While it has been proposed that foreign policy be oriented to a balance of power, this does not mean that international power is the sole end of political life. As Rousseau put it, the calculations of foreign affairs which require the expansion of a society, "being only external and relative, should be subordinated" to the concerns of a legitimate and just domestic order, "which are internal and absolute" (*Social Contract*, Book II, Chapter ix). Balance between a small number of continental superpowers, unlike the further extension of American hegemony, is a foreign-policy goal that has the greatest likelihood of permitting the United States to retain its almost unparalleled domestic freedom and democracy.

There is, of course, no certainty that the type of balance-of-power system here described will come into existence before the end of the present century. Miscalculation by the United States or the USSR could produce an all-out nuclear exchange despite attempts to avoid such a mutually suicidal confrontation. Changes in weapons technology could create so great an advantage for one superpower that it would profit from its superiority by launching a preventive war of extermination. Though the Chinese have till now been extremely cautious in every confrontation with Western power, they may risk an adventure causing a major world war.

But in any of these circumstances—as well as in other possible patterns of evolution in world politics—the struggle for power and influence can be expected to persist as the decisive factor in international relations (unless the human race succeeds in exterminating itself). For this reason, the United States must adopt a long-range policy goal directed toward the development of an international system consistent with the observed trends of political, military, and economic change, and in which the limitation of war to tolerable levels is conceivable.

PART II

A NEW
LOOK AT
THE PRESENT

It is always the concern of the offensive to discover new methods by which it may seize an advantage; but it is equally the concern of the defensive, which has already made some inventions, to search and think out others.

ARISTOTLE, *Politics,* BOOK VII

It is DIFFICULT to analyze situations that are continuously evolving, for changes in policy or unforeseen events can render one's discussion obsolete at any moment. Nevertheless it should be possible to describe the various options open to the United States in such a way that, although the following anlysis may become irrelevant, we can discover general lessons arising from American commitments throughout the world. For example, whether the United States continues to fight on an increasing scale or negotiates a peace settlement in Vietnam, there will remain proponents of the alternative policy who will decry the actions chosen. Hence the following discussion should be useful *ex post facto* even if the analysis of our alternatives at the time of writing (July 1966) is bypassed by events.

CHAPTER FIVE

Western Europe and the Atlantic Alliance

It is both fitting and natural that a discussion of the specific choices facing American foreign policy begin with the question of our ties with Western Europe. Of all the alliances established since World War II, surely NATO has been the central instrument by which we have restrained Russian communism; of all the nations in the world, surely our European allies are closest to us in form of government and outlook. Together we share common traditions and beliefs, for together we form a civilization that descends from the Judeo-Christian and Graeco-Roman worlds—a civilization that has invented modern science and achieved unsurpassed political freedom for man.

During the past twenty years, in which we have borne the military and political responsibility for the preservation of the West as we know it, Americans have developed habits and attitudes that are largely unthinking reflexes. Holding an effective monopoly of nuclear weapons, and acknowledged as the dominant member of NATO (with the veto over its policies that was implied by our military superiority), the United States has come to view itself as the "leader of the Free World." Whether we like it or not, it is now absolutely necessary to reconsider this image of ourselves and our relation to Europe.

According to American nuclear strategy, "centralized command and control" is needed to permit a "flexible response" to any military challenge. For the United States, such a strategy is a means of insuring that American cities are not destroyed in a thermonuclear war originating against our will; since the Soviet Union can now destroy us even after having been the target of a nuclear attack, our self-interest requires the coordinated use of NATO military forces according to a centrally conceived strategy (over which Washington maintains a veto). This nuclear strategy has, however, political implications which radically differ in the eyes of the various members of the Atlantic alliance.[1]

For France—and also Great Britain—our conception of a "flexible response" suggests that in some situations the United States might reject European requests for nuclear protection; demands that our European allies build up their conventional forces only seem to reinforce this argument. Washington's declarations of an inviolable commitment to Western Europe are thus contradicted by American strategic thinking, for the latter concentrates explicitly on the circumstances in which we would not use nuclear weapons in defense of Europe (for fear that we would be needlessly destroyed as a consequence).

For Germany, the most exposed member of the alliance and the only one that has formally divested itself of the right to acquire nuclear weapons, this situation creates a particular problem. Bonn is forced to bind itself ever more closely to

---

[1] Henry A. Kissinger: *The Troubled Partnership* (New York: McGraw-Hill; 1965), Ch. i-v. Unfortunately, Kissinger's proposals in the concluding chapters are subject to many of the criticisms he himself raises against past American policies; despite this fact, his book is a good introduction to the problems now besetting NATO. For a more recent statement, see his "For a New Atlantic Alliance," *The Reporter* (July 14, 1966), pp. 18-27.

Washington, if possible by participating in a joint NATO nuclear command such as the frequently postponed Multi-lateral Force (MLF), to insure that the United States could never abandon the Federal Republic. At the same time, however, the West Germans are loath to give up hope of reunification and have justified their participation in NATO as a means to this end.

Unfortunately, however, neither the United States nor the other members of the alliance are willing to use NATO forces to reunite a Germany that twice in this century has led Europe into disastrous war. Moreover, the very existence of West German military units as the backbone of NATO's conventional army—not to mention the possibility of German participation in one or another version of a NATO nuclear force—is perceived by both Russia and her Eastern European allies as a threat to the status quo.

Under these circumstances, the tighter the bonds between Washington and Bonn, the more discomforted is Paris (since the French see the result as an increasing if not perpetual European dependence on a distant ally who may not rise to some future crisis). Conversely, the more isolated the French, the more tempted they are to develop an independent nuclear arsenal, capable of defending Europe should America withdraw—or at least of drawing the United States into war even against our will.

Although our major allies—Great Britain, France, and Germany—all share a desire to increase their participation and control over the American nuclear umbrella, this desire has been manifested in radically contradictory ways. The British sought to retain some degree of nuclear independence even when proposing that their atomic deterrent be nominally committed to an Atlantic force (thereby hoping to restrain any future German aggressiveness by giving Bonn a role in alliance nuclear policy). The Germans have sought a similar NATO nuclear force—or at least a role in strategic planning —for the opposite reason, since they want to force the United States to support them come what may.

In this maze of conflicting intentions, French policy under General de Gaulle has often seemed the sole source of Western dissent, blocking tighter cohesion within the alliance. By insisting on developing a totally autonomous *force de frappe* and withdrawing from military integration within NATO, the French have underlined doubts about our willingness to defend Europe; at the same time, de Gaulle's obstructionism seems to make it impossible to unite all Western nuclear capabilities into a centralized NATO force (be it our original proposal for the MLF or the British Atlantic Nuclear Force).

Current French policy is not merely the result of the stubborn will of one man; it was under the Fourth Republic that the *force de frappe* was begun, and the criticism of America's nuclear hegemony in Europe is widely shared by non-Gaullists (both in France and elsewhere). Having recovered economic stability thanks to American aid, and military security thanks to American predominance, the Europeans have begun to wonder whether they must permanently be our disciples and followers, especially where fundamental national interests conflict. Our NATO allies do not feel committed to American policies in Latin America or Asia, and have come to see that our often rigid anticommunism is costly and militarily unnecessary now that the communist world has begun to fragment. Conversely, American interests do not necessarily demand that we offer our cities as permanent hostages to the Soviet Union, on the assumption that the Europeans would never risk war without our consent.[2]

The root of these issues lies in the fundamental long-range objective of American policy, an objective that has often been obscured by a cloud of verbiage. Our spokesmen often present the noble image of a "grand design" for the West, based on the two "pillars" of a United States of Europe and the United States of America. Especially since the graceful rhetoric of

[2] For a brilliant and provocative presentation of the divergences of interest between the United States and Western Europe, see Ronald Steel: *The End of Alliance: America and the Future of Europe* (New York: Viking; 1964).

President Kennedy enshrined these ideas, we have come to believe that European political unity, like the unity which made our own nation a great power, is the solution to the internecine conflicts that have periodically torn the continent and engulfed the world in war.

Despite the challenge of such goals, the very conception of a "grand design," of whatever sort, now requires re-examination. The French seem committed to sabotage any such construction and to undermine NATO's integrated military structure against our will. Even if many other Europeans did not speak with Gaullist overtones, therefore, we would have to assess the possibility that French interests will never accept the American approach to the Atlantic alliance; without France, it is hard to see how the Europeans could form a supranational or federal political community, and without such a community it is hard to see what the "grand design" really means.

A United States of Europe is not, as has so often been assumed, a natural and inevitable consequence of economic cooperation within the Common Market; a European political community would necessarily have to rest on institutions capable of eliciting support from a broadly divergent population whose interests are far from consistent and whose traditions are hardly identical. Hopes that a United States of Europe would shortly be produced by a virtually automatic process are therefore baseless; even in the American colonies, the formation of a federal government was hotly contested after the experience of a loose confederation that floundered for a decade. In Europe, where national traditions are more distinct and interests not always easily reconcilable, political union could be quickly achieved only on the basis of external fear—and fear of Soviet aggression appears to be declining throughout Europe.[3]

Not only does this imply a great realism in de Gaulle's con-

[3] The political implications of European supranationalism (as well as Gaullism and the American "grand design") have been insightfully analyzed by David Calleo in *Europe's Future: The Grand Alternatives* (New York: Horizon; 1965). For those who are puzzled by de Gaulle's policies, this book is invaluable.

ception of the persisting influence of nationalism, with its corollary immediate goal of a confederal Europe (the so-called *Europe des patries*) instead of a supranational European state; it also suggests that our own alignment with Europe must be reconsidered from a political perspective, and not solely with reference to the presumed needs of nuclear strategy in a bipolar world. If the interests of France and her European partners are sufficiently diverse to preclude the rapid realization of the dream of European unity, can the "grand design" of an alliance with an "equal" European partner really be taken seriously? What is the inevitable consequence of our insistence on the priority of an integrated NATO under these conditions?

Despite the prevailing assumption that the defense of the West is "indivisible," NATO members exhibit sharply conflicting interests. Great Britain owes her "special relationship" with the United States to historical traditions and her nuclear deterrent, but neither prevented the rude shocks of Suez and the cancellation of the Skybolt missile. France has greatly increased her prestige by using an independent nuclear force for exactly the opposite purposes; eschewing a similar special relationship after Washington's rejection of a Franco-Anglo-American directorate in NATO, de Gaulle has set out to show that political "equality" is only possible on the basis of military and political independence, backed up with at least token nuclear forces. Many West Germans still seek a common nuclear force as the only means of acquiring similar nuclear status, while several of our small NATO allies are only too willing to shift responsibility for European defense onto the United States.

To produce common policies among such divergent interests would require a clear recognition of the indivisibility of the Atlantic alliance in political terms, rather than merely in technical or strategic ones. American forces can legitimately be counted upon to defend European cities for the indefinite future only if Berlin, Bonn, Paris, Washington, or Los Angeles are viewed as interchangeable targets. If the "grand design" is to have any sense, it is not as a militarily integrated alliance with a nonexistent European federation but as a supranational Atlantic government to which the United States has surrendered its sovereignty.[4]

Perversely, virtually no American statesman dares to propose such a thoroughgoing revolution to the Congress or the American people. Yet it is contradictory to speak of the "grand design" as the American goal without establishing supranational institutions as an immediate objective; if we do not give an Atlantic federation the highest priority in the short run, attempts to achieve such a community by indirect means will merely destroy NATO and erase the "grand design" as a feasible policy goal. We must see why this is so.

The United States has followed a number of distinct policies, more or less simultaneously, believing that each might contribute to Atlantic or European unity. We have encouraged the British in their belief that a "special relationship" exists between London and Washington (for example by sharing nuclear secrets and selling Polaris missiles); we have increased West Germany's unavoidable dependence on the United States by supporting Bonn's conception of German reunification and establishing close military procurement agreements; and we have pleased small European powers, such as the Dutch, by indicating our preference for supranational institutions as the means of uniting Western Europe (sometimes explicitly, as in our support for the once proposed European Defense Community, and more often tacitly, in the context of our opposition to Gaullist "nationalism"). Paradoxically, each of these policies serves to divide the alliance and make the grand design harder—not easier—to achieve.

Anglo-American relations have often seemed like undue favoritism not only to the French, to whom we have refused to extend the military and technological data offered the British, but to other allies as well. To be sure, common lan-

---

[4] Steel puts the problem of an integrated NATO in a nutshell: "The alliance . . . must develop into a political federation or it must disintegrate." *The End of Alliance*, p. 64.

guage and traditions may go far to explain our policy, but they do not fully justify it; American sympathy for British policies goes far deeper. In part, we share economic interests; under present conditions, the financial solidity of the dollar can not be assured without maintaining the value of the pound (which explains our repeated willingness to protect the pound from devaluation). Ultimately, however, the reasons for our special concern for the English have been political.

Great Britain has most often appeared, in American eyes, as the prototype of an Atlantic ally. Excepting the Suez crisis, we have found it possible to negotiate virtually all outstanding political differences with the English, and if disputes have not always been resolved, at least they have been sufficiently papered over so that we have not lost face. Accustomed to government by compromise and by committee, both Anglo-Saxon nations find each other congenial partners who refrain from posing fundamental threats to each other.

Moreover, from the American viewpoint Great Britain serves a useful function in world politics because of her relationship with the Commonwealth. The military and political commitments that the British have retained from the colonial era permit us to delegate to them part of the responsibility for containing communism and maintaining the peace in the underdeveloped world; in the Near East, Africa, and Malaysia, British interests complement our own and provide the model of an ally whose actions rarely contradict our fundamental policies.

Because Great Britain seems to be so generally reliable as the core of the Atlantic alliance, we must look carefully at the effects of a particularly close Anglo-American tie. By emphasizing directly the British stake in her transatlantic relationship (and indirectly in her Commonwealth responsibilities) the United States necessarily reinforced obstacles to British entry into the Common Market. After Great Britain showed great hesitation and reserve in her prolonged negotiations with the EEC during 1962, Secretary McNamara's cancellation of the Skybolt missile (on which the future of an independent British nuclear force had been based) and the hastily negotiated Nassau agreement (by which we replaced the Skybolt with Polaris missiles) proved conclusively the extent of London's dependence on Washington.

Whether it was this Nassau agreement that caused de Gaulle's brusque veto of the British application to the Common Market may never be truly known, but this incident did indicate the way the Anglo-American "special relationship" undermines European and Atlantic unity.[5] It is not merely a question of the division of Europe into "sixes and sevens," although as long as England remains outside of the Common Market there will be tension between the six signatories of the Treaty of Rome and the seven states that joined the British-sponsored European Free Trading Area. Even within the Common Market itself, Great Britain's absence creates a serious obstacle to unity since the smaller members—Holland, Belgium, Luxembourg, and Italy—would generally prefer a counterweight to a feared Franco-German domination. Hence American policies that increase British reluctance to join the Common Market simultaneously reduce the likelihood of political union among the six EEC members.

Some Gaullists cynically attribute this result to a carefully planned American effort to sabotage European unity by discouraging British cooperation. Be that as it may, there can be little doubt that one major reason for French intransigence, both within the Common Market and in NATO, is frustration with British ambivalence toward the continent. A striking example of this English attitude occurred shortly after Prime Minister Wilson came to power in 1964, for the new Labor government proceeded to call into question the Anglo-French project to build the supersonic "Concorde" jet transport. The French concluded that if London was not certain to honor a signed agreement that promised to save the British aircraft industry from the threat of extinction at the hands of Amer-

[5] For the history of de Gaulle's attitude to British membership in the Common Market, which shifted from encouragement of London's application to the sudden rejection announced on January 13, 1963, see Robert Kleiman: *Atlantic Crisis* (New York: Norton; 1964).

ican competition, there was little hope that Great Britain would ever become a truly European power.

As the tortuous negotiations over the continuation of the "Concorde" reveal, not all sources of Anglo-French tension are due to American policy; on the contrary, the English have long prized their sense of insular independence and are only slowly realizing the inevitability of a choice between membership in a European community and continued dependence on the United States.[6] American policies have, however, reinforced this indecision, for we have encouraged the British to believe that they can still play a great power role on the basis of their limited, postcolonial military and economic power base. In so doing, we may have done our old ally a singular disservice.

It can be argued that Great Britain simply cannot meet its commitments throughout the world, and that the attempt to do so is one of the prime causes of her present economic difficulty. Certainly the enormous effort required to develop and maintain an independent nuclear force has not had any overwhelming advantages, for in such distant areas as Aden and Malaysia, England must still protect her allies with conventional armed forces and a large navy; nuclear weapons were hardly relevant as a means of dealing with the crisis in Rhodesia.

Nor has the respect which seems due Great Britain as a nuclear power produced any political pay-off. While supporting the right of the United States to send troops to South Vietnam and to bomb the North, Wilson has tried to secure a negotiated settlement; such efforts seem doomed to failure, if only because London has not felt free to diverge from Washington to the degree required of a potential mediator. This limited ability to influence United States policy, which is particularly frustrating to the Labor Party rank and file

[6] See George Lichtheim: *The New Europe* (New York: Praeger; 1963). The inability of the Conservative Party to convert its newly pro-European policy into a vital issue during the 1966 British election reveals the deep popular skepticism concerning the necessity and desirability of such a choice.

(skeptical if not openly hostile to the American position in Vietnam) makes one wonder whether the British will not sooner or later discover that their "special relationship" with Washington is useless.

In short, our favored treatment of England has divided Europe (by reducing British desire to join the Common Market and thereby depriving it of a needed balance to France and Germany), undermined NATO (by convincing de Gaulle that the British were totally dependent on the United States and unwilling to seek an independent European policy), and harmed Great Britain itself (by fostering illusions that can never be realized). Faced with this situation, the Wilson government tried to recoup its prestige by proposing the formation of an Atlantic Nuclear Force that could provide West Germany with a nuclear role within NATO, where the United States could veto any German aggressiveness. But our favorable response to such a proposal, which might have replaced the ill-fated MLF, would only worsen the confusion by further alienating the French without fully placating the Germans; given Russian opposition to any scheme giving the Germans a share in a nuclear force, the British themselves appear to be backing away from their own proposal, leaving the Germans politically isolated in the alliance. Wouldn't we be better off seeking other solutions that encourage the British to cast their lot more wholeheartedly with continental Europe?

From a number of points of view, the American attitude toward Germany is historically astonishing. Having insisted on unconditional surrender in World War II, on the assumption that Germany should be so thoroughly defeated that she could never again threaten the peace, we have done our utmost to make Germany a major power; having once considered dividing Germany to insure her impotence, we now find ourselves committed to German reunification. It was insistent pressure from Washington that induced our European allies to tolerate German conventional rearmament, and despite their fears of a reunited Germany, we have steadfastly maintained not only the principle of reunification but also the view that the Oder-Neisse line should not be recognized as the permanent eastern boundary of Germany prior to a formal peace treaty. That is to say, the United States is thoroughly committed to creating again a large and powerful German state at the center of the European continent.

We must consider frankly why this peculiar policy should be adopted and maintained. Until very recently, American statesmen have been reluctant to recognize the Oder-Neisse boundary or to indicate that we find the current division of Germany tolerable for two rather different reasons. Ideologically, we consider communist control over East Germany abnormal, and assume that unification would produce a stable, pro-Western democracy. Politically, and this is perhaps more important, we have been afraid to take positions divergent from those of our West German allies. If the Germans conclude that we will not support them to attain unification, wouldn't Bonn seek an accommodation with Moscow without reference to the Atlantic alliance?

This fear, often described as the threat of a new Rapallo, is paradoxical. If we are afraid that failure to support Bonn fully would produce a Russo-German accommodation under some neutralist formula,[7] we assume that West Germany places her national interest above the interests of the Atlantic alliance as a whole. Yet if we make such an assumption, it is hard to see why a united Germany—perhaps neutralized according to some plan of military disengagement in Europe—

[7] As of January, 1966, a study group at Yale University concluded that the fear of a new Rapallo was unfounded: "Neutralization in exchange for reunification, the only solution which has ever been suggested by the Soviet Union, appears unacceptable to a majority among European leaders and masses alike." Richard L. Merritt, ed.: *Arms Control and European Unity* (mimeographed; New Haven: Yale University Political Science Research Library; 1966), p. 226. But cf. p. 251 n. summarizing West German public opinion polls: "In February 1964, 42 per cent thought neutrality between East and West was to be preferred to friendship with the United States, 49 per cent believed the latter was the more desirable course."

would not be more hostile to the West and more dangerous than the present divided Germany. Certainly there are many Europeans who are quite content with the status quo precisely because they fear a unified German state that would combine the enormous industrial potential of the West with the agricultural resources of the East.

In any event, it can be said that the American policy of supporting German reunification on Bonn's terms has been designed to keep Germany in NATO. Yet this is an internally contradictory goal, for it is unlikely that the Soviet Union would permit the acquisition of East Germany by a reunified German state that would still be a member of the NATO alliance. Hence we seek to keep West Germany within NATO as a means to achieve German unification, despite the fact that any conceivable reunification (except by force) would probably mean that Germany would leave NATO.

This fundamental contradiction in our German policy has not been readily apparent because of the customary American concentration on short-term objectives. Since we have assumed that the Soviets would never acquiesce in German reunification, we have encouraged the Germans to believe that alliance with the West was the only means of attaining this goal; discounting the possibility that the long-range objectives of Bonn could ever be realized, we concentrated on the immediate advantages of securing wholehearted German support in NATO.

In the short run, this policy was undoubtedly wise. Of all the European powers, West Germany is the most exposed to any conceivable communist threat; moreover, German institutions immediately after World War II were fragile. By binding ourselves to the aims of most Germans and making membership in the Western alliance the condition of such support, we reinforced the position of the Adenauer administration and were able to convince the West Germans of our willingness to defend them.

We thus made it clear to Bonn that without American support, both militarily and politically, the West German regime could not hope to achieve its goals. In other words, we established a kind of bargain, giving Bonn assurances of immediate defense and eventual German reunification in return for dependence upon the United States. This policy was particularly useful as a means of reinforcing our commitment to defend Europe, which we demonstrated by placing large conventional forces, and ultimately tactical nuclear weapons, in Germany.

Thus we encouraged the formation of a European Defense Community, so that German military units would be absorbed into and controlled by a Western European military establishment that could check any West German aggressiveness; Secretary of State Dulles even promised an "agonizing reappraisal" of American policy if the EDC were defeated. But after the French rejected this concept, in part as a reaction to our heavy-handed methods, we found ourselves perfectly willing to maintain our prior policy of exchanging an American guarantee for West German security for our blanket approval of Bonn's own long-range goals.

The characteristic vulnerability of this German policy is all too evident when one considers the problems posed by the continued division of West Berlin and the tensions created by the Wall. While it has been easy for Washington to join Bonn in condemning the Berlin Wall as a unilateral abrogation of the Four-Power agreements reached after World War II, we have not opposed West German efforts to reach ad hoc pass agreements with Ulbrecht's regime so that relatives in the divided city can be reunited for short visits; West Germans themselves are increasingly tempted to grant a more or less tacit recognition to the German Democratic Republic, if only to make the unpleasant facts of national disunity more tolerable.

Having fully endorsed reunification on Bonn's terms and opposed the East German regime on ideological grounds, we are in a poor position to restrain our ally from coming to agreements with the communists even should such agreements contradict our own policy. Our commitments to West

Germany have been so unconditional that we may one day be incapable of exercising leverage on Bonn's policies (if only for fear that an open disagreement would destroy NATO).

The ultimate consequence of this policy has been to drive a wedge between the French and the Germans, forcing de Gaulle to attempt to outbid us in order to gain a more secure control over West German policy. American statesmen have assumed that our pledge to defend West Germany is intrinsically permanent and that we should ultimately rely on our own ability to deter Russian advances into Western Europe rather than delegate most of this responsibility to our European allies. But our current nuclear strategy in a way contradicts these assumptions, and many Europeans—particularly the French—have come to wonder whether reliance on the United States places West Germany in a dangerous position.

Even apart from de Gaulle's intransigence, our German policy has played a large role in driving the French out of an integrated NATO. It has done this because we have so fully bound ourselves to Bonn's declared long-range goals, and have so clearly connected German defense with support of American policy that the French cannot see how they could influence American positions within NATO. Given the "special relationship" between the United States and Great Britain and the dependence of Germany on our deterrent, the French perceive that the alignment of Germany, England, and the United States can easily outweigh them as long as Western policies are determined within NATO. And although the interests of Germany and England tend to be contradictory—often preventing the adoption of effective Atlantic alliance policy—the French have seen in this alignment a persistent block to their own policy goals.

Naturally, the French have felt isolated within NATO as a result of our German policy, for one of the principles of our German policy is to isolate the French. It remains to be seen, however, whether this objective makes any sense whatever. Although the usual justification is that, after the passing of General de Gaulle, Paris will be forced to come into line with the rest of the alliance, the contradictory objectives of NATO powers—and France's progress in developing a nuclear deterrent and an autonomous foreign policy—suggest that the tactic of isolating France may, if pushed too far, gravely weaken or destroy NATO. To prevent such an eventuality, American policy-makers have largely relied on the hope that a Western European economic and political union would continue to emerge on the basis of the Common Market; since France is a crucial member of the six, we have assumed that it is by means of supranational political institutions in Europe that French political objections will be overcome. Here again, however, our policy is fundamentally contradictory.

Our support of a supranational Europe is, like our favorite relationship with Great Britain and our strong support of the West Germans, designed to force France to take a more agreeable position over the long run. In effect, our endorsement of a united federal Europe appeals to many individuals who have championed the European idea since the war, both in France and elsewhere. Politically speaking, however, the greatest support for these supranational institutions comes from the Dutch, the Belgians, and other small powers, who fear that otherwise they will be dominated by the economic and military power of West Germany and France. In this sense, the conception of an equal partnership between the United States of America and a United States of Europe is particularly directed to securing the support of the smaller European powers for NATO as a whole.

It has not been fully seen, however, that the price which the smaller European powers ask for European unity is effectively increased by our support—even tacit—for supranational political principles. In particular, our position has led to the paradox that the Dutch pose as the most insistent supporters of supranational institutions and simultaneously as the strongest champions of Great Britain's membership in the Common Market. As the French have bitterly remarked, these two objectives are strictly contradictory, because the British—even if willing to join some form of European community—have firmly refused to surrender national sovereignty.

Such a view on the part of the British flows naturally from their insular traditions and their continuing ties within the Commonwealth. But because we have shown a preference for a supranational Europe without stating our own priorities, we have encouraged the Dutch to ask the impossible. Thus the American attitude toward Europe, while apparently benign (since we officially indicate our willingness to support any institutions the Europeans choose for themselves), has increased European dependence on the United States by leading the French and her Common Market partners to fundamentally conflicting demands. In a real sense, it can be said that our alliance policy is one of "divide and control."

The dynamics of this situation are well illustrated by the recent crises in the European Economic Community. The Common Market Commission, under Walter Hallstein, gambled that the French interest in a common agricultural policy was so great that de Gaulle would tolerate the establishment of a European budget, directly financed from the import duties of the Common Market as a whole. For the smaller members of the Six, this policy was highly attractive as a means of forcing the French to accept supranational institutions. For the French, a common budget supervised by a consultative European assembly in Strasbourg and controlled by the Common Market Commission in Brussels would have opened the resulting European union to American control. Given the contradictory interests of the various European powers and the extent of United States business investment on the continent, this French fear is highly reasonable; it would be entirely possible for the United States to continue to play upon the conflicting interests of the small European powers, the Germans, and even the British, in such a way as to insure that the European community would be politically subservient to American goals within the Atlantic alliance as a whole.

Whether or not the French position is justifiable, it exists as a fact. Nor can French attitudes be dismissed as the personal vanity and stubbornness of one man. Morton Gorden and Daniel Lerner, summarizing extensive interviews of the political elites in key Western European countries, described their findings as follows:

> British and German attachment to the Atlantic Community, and the inclusion of Europe in it, contrast sharply with the French preference for an independent European role between the dominant East-West bloc leaders. This French sentiment antedates de Gaulle, for throughout the years of our studies the French have maintained a European rather than an Atlantic orientation. It is unlikely that this long term preference for European ties will pass with the retirement of de Gaulle.[8]

As such studies of the attitudes of politicians of all parties throughout Western Europe indicate, there are deep and persisting differences of opinion within the Atlantic alliance that reflect strategic and national viewpoints too often ignored by Americans.

In the light of these realities, the effects of our policy toward NATO can be summarized as follows: The more we woo West Germany, encourage Great Britain as our favorite ally, and dream of a supranational Europe, the more we isolate France. The more we isolate France, the more we blame de Gaulle for problems within the alliance. But the more we blame de Gaulle personally, the less we see that even without him the same logic of power will apply and, as a conse-

---

[8] "The Setting for European Arms Controls: Political and Strategic Choices of European Elites," *Journal of Conflict Resolution,* IX (December 1965), 419. Gorden and Lerner document not only the sharp differences between the French political elite and leaders in West Germany and Great Britain, but also the fundamental divergences in outlook between the latter two nations; their analysis shows that the comments in the text reflect perceived attitudes of relatively long standing throughout Europe. For further evidence, see *Arms Control and European Unity,* ed. Merritt, esp. ch. v; and Karl W. Deutsch: "Integration and Arms Control in the European Political Environment: A Summary Report," *American Political Science Review,* LX (June 1966), 354-65.

quence, the less we are prepared to meet the challenges de Gaulle raises and those which will arise after his departure.

The general reaction of frustration, anger, and impatience with which the American press greeted General de Gaulle's announced intention to withdraw France from military integration in NATO is an index of our general lack of understanding of tensions within the alliance. De Gaulle's action could have been predicted long before March 7, 1966, when his handwritten letter to President Johnson announced that NATO bases in France would have to come under national control by April 1, 1967. Before considering the effects of our response to this unilateral action, therefore, we had better understand it.

Throughout the fall and winter of 1965-6, it was no secret that de Gaulle intended to renegotiate France's position in NATO in order to replace those aspects of the alliance's military integration which he has long viewed as "subordination" to American "hegemony." Reliable sources stated that the matter was not pressing, however, and that there would be plenty of time to negotiate the issue prior to 1969, when the NATO treaty can be denounced by its members. Suddenly, the General reversed his policy, apparently without even notifying some of his collaborators. Why this sudden change?

In assessing de Gaulle's strategy from a distance, it is only possible to make conjectures, but his explicit statements and past actions are helpful guides to an interpretation. Four broad foreign-policy aims can be suggested in his decision to upset the NATO applecart:[9] first, to force the United States

[9] It should be added that de Gaulle's move had, especially with respect to its timing, equally important domestic implications: by setting April 1, 1967, as the deadline after which military installations in France must be under French control, de Gaulle could hope to create a *fait accompli* prior to the French legislative elections of 1967. Since de Gaulle's opposition to an integrated NATO divides many Socialists (who claim he has moved too rapidly) from the French Communist party (which tacitly supports this policy), the French president has tried to split the alliance between these two parties established during the 1965 presidential campaign of François Mitterrand.

to negotiate with France as a major nuclear power (rather than to treat her merely as another member of the alliance); second, to make other NATO powers aware of the danger of excessive reliance on the United States; third, to insure a long-range development of NATO in line with de Gaulle's own view of the future; and fourth, to make it possible for France to mediate between the superpowers (not merely in Southeast Asia, but also and primarily in Europe). Each of these aims deserves calm consideration.

At first glance, it will seem absurd that de Gaulle's abrupt rejection of negotiations concerning NATO was intended to produce negotiation, but the General has frequently taken one step backward in order to advance two steps (or even two steps backward to take one forward). Since Americans tend to stand pat when they cannot advance—a procedure that often leaves us empty-handed in times of change—an effort is required even to understand the French maneuver.

Having realized that the administration was not disposed to make any fundamental reorientation in its European policy, de Gaulle saw little advantage in awaiting a spontaneous change in our attitude toward NATO. With Johnson's preoccupation with the Vietnamese war, a crisis within the alliance probably seemed the only way of forcing us to take France seriously as an independent nuclear power equal to Great Britain in status.

A unilateral demand that all American or NATO installations on France's soil come under her military command created a suitable crisis because it required removal of NATO headquarters (not to mention reorganization of NATO forces in Germany together with their logistics). At the same time, American bases existing in France under bilateral treaties had to be disposed of; even against our will, therefore, we were forced to negotiate with the French (which has been de Gaulle's continuing aim since he first proposed a NATO directorate composed of Britain, France, and the United States).

The French president was obviously aware that the other

members of NATO would criticize his action (just as the other Common Market nations criticized his policy of an "empty chair" in Brussels). It could not have been a surprise in Paris when the remaining fourteen nations in NATO immediately responded, in a statement laboriously drafted with State Department prodding, that the alliance's integrated structure is still necessary. On the contrary, this may have been exactly what de Gaulle hoped would happen.

Here we must consider the second apparent objective of the French policy. De Gaulle's isolation in the alliance forced him to look for indirect means of persuading other European statesmen that total strategic dependence on the United States is unwise. A traditional French tactic in such circumstances is called the *levée de l'hypothèque;* one convinces others that a policy must be abandoned by allowing the objectionable alternative to be adopted under conditions of almost certain failure.

Under the Fourth Republic, for example, politicians would openly support a parliamentary coalition they privately sought to defeat, knowing full well that the coalition would fall apart due to internal conflicts, thereby leaving the way open to a more satisfactory solution. As Nathan Leites described these maneuvers, they "show a given policy, imagined by some, is not possible"; as a consequence, "the road will be 'cleared' to follow that in favor of which the operation was undertaken."[1]

In this perspective, de Gaulle is attempting to dissuade other Europeans—and notably the Germans—from placing their primary reliance on the United States. As he put this lesson in his news conference of February 21, 1966: "While the prospects of a world war breaking out on account of Europe are dissipating, conflicts in which America engages in other parts of the world—as the day before yesterday in Korea, yesterday in Cuba, today in Vietnam—risk, by virtue of that famous escalation, being extended so that the result could be a general conflagration. In that case Europe—whose

[1] *Du Malaise Politique en France* (Paris: Plon; 1958), pp. 62-3.

strategy is, within NATO, that of America—would be automatically involved in the struggle, even when it would not have so desired."

European fears of a world war arising out of our commitment in Vietnam reflect a basic conflict between our Asian strategy and our goals in NATO. The administration has sought to strengthen the integrated aspects of the Atlantic alliance while pursuing a policy of isolating China that our allies do not support as enthusiastically as Washington desires. Secretary of State Rusk's criticism of German participation in financing and constructing a steel mill in China is a perfect example: in Bonn, part of the price of our defense of Germany through NATO seems an American attempt to veto Western policies and trade with the Chinese.

De Gaulle is well aware that the Germans—and other Europeans—will not long remain oblivious of the extent to which Washington demands support for its Asian policy from NATO members. At the same time, he expects that our desire for an antiproliferation treaty will alienate those Germans who see in it a device for permanently relegating Bonn to the status of a second-rate power; in particular, there have been fears that we might accept the Soviet proposal to prohibit the use of nuclear weapons on the territory of non-nuclear powers, a seemingly innocuous agreement that would effectively outlaw NATO's strategy of using tactical nuclear weapons to counter a major Russian attack in central Europe. As Franz Josef Strauss (former German Defense Minister) asked Robert Kennedy in a televised discussion, the Germans would like to know whether we will give priority "to NATO or to Geneva."

In other words, de Gaulle is trying to force our NATO allies into closer dependence on the United States so that they will be more fully aware of France's decisive position in the alliance. This lesson was not long lost on the West Germans, who were forced to support Washington's general position while trying to keep two French divisions in their territory on a bilateral basis after France removed her troops from

NATO control.[2] Secretary of Defense McNamara conveniently strengthened de Gaulle's hand in this respect by announcing the "temporary" withdrawal of 15,000 specialized American troops assigned to our NATO forces in Germany, thereby underlining the contradiction between our commitments in Europe and our involvement in Vietnam (concerning which NATO had no say). Any further reductions of American forces in Europe will only strengthen the French and increase German doubts of our reliability.

With time, therefore, de Gaulle could hope that negotiations within the alliance would lead to an increased appreciation for his position and broader demands for an independent European viewpoint in alliance planning. Since his strategy of leaving an empty chair in Common Market negotiations had this effect, superficial declarations of unanimity by the remaining fourteen members of NATO could not mask the fact that the French are decisive members of the alliance. Indeed, President Johnson was soon forced to realize that it would be folly to push a policy of isolating the French as far as some State Department officials desired, for to do so would compel Bonn to make a choice between Washington and Paris—a choice that the West Germans seek to avoid if at all possible.

Besides the long-range goal of establishing a favorable situation in which to press for French goals, de Gaulle had a more immediate objective in showing increased independence from American policy. As the Western nuclear power least subservient to Washington, France can pose as the most likely mediator between East and West. Despite de Gaulle's offers to assist in finding a settlement in Vietnam when the "time is ripe," the crucial area in this respect is Germany (for it is here that de Gaulle ultimately hopes to offer Bonn something that Washington, despite its nuclear power, cannot obtain from Moscow).

From this perspective, de Gaulle's flirtation with Moscow may be primarily of symbolic importance. Even if he were to

[2] See Philip Ben: "The Sense of Insecurity in West Germany," *New Republic* (April 30, 1966), p. 10.

sign a nonaggression treaty with the Soviet Union (despite denials of such an intent), the consequence would not be France's withdrawal from the Atlantic alliance; de Gaulle still seeks and enjoys the comfort of the American nuclear umbrella and has repeatedly insisted that some form of alliance with the United States is necessary. But by showing his ability to bargain with both superpowers, he can offer to lead a stronger Europe, not totally dependent on the United States, toward a solution of the German problem that is acceptable to the Russians.

De Gaulle's views are often denounced as an archaic, right-wing nationalism (despite the irony that his position on Vietnam has long been to the "left" of many American liberals). All the more important, therefore, to ponder the following passage in his February, 1966, press conference: "The union of the Six, once achieved—and all the more if it comes to be supplemented then by new European memberships and associations—can and must be, toward the United States, a valid partner in all areas, I mean powerful and independent. The union of the Six can and must also be one of the piers on which will gradually be built first the equilibrium, then the cooperation and then, perhaps one day, the union of all of Europe, which would enable our continent to settle its own problems peacefully, particularly that of Germany, including its reunification. . . ." Such a view does not seem to be against the position, expressed by some in Washington, that the Atlantic alliance should ultimately be composed of two pillars —the United States and a united Europe; it does, however, insist on a different route to this goal.

The American reaction to de Gaulle's admittedly brutal (if handwritten) diplomatic procedures is unfortunate because it rests on a failure to understand his objectives and how far we ourselves have contributed to his policies. As the influential French paper *Le Monde* (certainly not an unquestioning supporter of de Gaulle) put it in an editorial soon after the opening of the NATO crisis:

In limiting itself to the strictly legal and military questions, the United States once again avoids the true problem. Moreover, this problem—which is above all political—is not limited (as is generally believed) to the French desire for independence from the United States. The uneasiness within the alliance comes just as much from the fact that the United States, which solidly supports its allies against the menace of aggression in Europe (in which the peoples concerned believe less and less), is so little united with them outside of Europe, where it is a question of settling the major problems on which the maintenance or reestablishment of peace truly depends: the place of China in the world, the war in Vietnam, the division of nuclear responsibilities, etc.[3]

This underlying problem of the disunity within the Western alliance, which de Gaulle has merely brought to the surface, must be faced directly as a political crisis; in so doing, it would be fatal to attribute all blame to others on the assumption that the alliance is essentially united except for the obstinacy of the French.

American policy toward Western Europe in the immediate future will depend on our response to the French withdrawal from an integrated NATO command. Any attempt to defend continental Europe in the absence of French participation would gravely weaken NATO's logistics and strategic position. At worst, the attempt to isolate France totally might even lead to the collapse of the Common Market, bringing with it the danger of severe economic repercussions throughout Europe. Even without such an outcome, the strategic logic of European defense, combined with the German commitment to a common NATO nuclear planning, forces us to implement some form of common nuclear control, be it the MLF, the Atlantic Nuclear Force proposed by Britain, or a nuclear directorate within the alliance.

Such means of tying the wounded alliance together again

[3] *Le Monde,* April 14, 1966, p. 1.

seem necessary because joint nuclear control would be the only way of increasing the credibility of our European commitments under the difficult circumstance of French nonparticipation. A NATO nuclear force or directorate is also politically advisable, as otherwise European states might begin to wonder whether an American deterrent in which they had little voice was any more reliable than an uncontrolled French deterrent. After all, at least France is in Europe and has a national interest in preventing communist forces from advancing to the Rhine. Since the United States is viewed as a distant power, American abandonment of her previous proposals for alliance nuclear forces (especially if combined with transfers of American troops out of Europe) would seem to be the foretaste of an ultimate American withdrawal.

But if we are forced to proceed with nuclear cooperation in a NATO alliance without the French, we must be clear about the consequences. The MLF or similar arrangement, without French participation, appears largely as a means of giving West Germany a form of participation and control in nuclear matters. If we were to implement our original proposal to create the MLF, the West Germans, owning up to 40 per cent of a common-alliance nuclear force and participating in alliance decision-making, would acquire the technology and habits of a quasi-nuclear power.

Such a development would make it virtually certain that at the first major conflict between Washington and Bonn— or even at the sign of fundamental divergences of interest—the West Germans would consider acquiring their own nuclear forces. Clearly both the Russians and the French fear this, so that proceeding in the direction of the MLF in a truncated alliance without France would almost certainly produce a further Franco-Russian rapprochement if not a formal alliance.

We could still control the remainder of the Atlantic alliance, especially by dividing Europe between the French and the other powers, playing on the conflict of interests between Great Britain and Germany, and maintaining American troops in Europe. The real question, however, is whether such a divided Europe, in which the West Germans will increasingly be tempted to develop their own nuclear weapons should they doubt the reliability of the American alliance, is in our national interest.

Despite formal statements of unity by the fourteen members of an integrated NATO, we must ultimately face the question whether we believe in European unity in some form. If we do, then it has to be admitted that a European community will sooner or later be independent of the United States. The grand design of an equal partnership between Europe and the United States could operate only if the partners were truly equal, and an ally is equal only if he can break the alliance without leaving himself open to disaster. An alliance between the United States and Europe must depend upon common interests, and not institutions, to keep the West together.

This is not merely the Gaullist position, for the most thoughtful supporters of European union, whether in supranational or confederal form, are generally agreed that the consequence of such a community would be an independent Europe, whose policies are not dictated by Washington and are supported by an independent nuclear capability. This was the view of Jean Monnet, and is widely held by anti-Gaullist planners throughout Europe. If we believe in Western European unity as a means of ending the perpetual danger of war on the continent, then we must deal with the power relations as they face us.

Since these power relations include a France hostile to what it considers subservience to the United States, and since American control of our allies depends on our playing upon their contradictory national interests, we must consider an alternative to the maintenance of an integrated NATO as an end in itself. If the United States is forced to choose between a hobbled NATO without France, perpetuating American presence in Europe at the cost of European division and weakness, and an allied but independent European union with parallel interests in most but not all circumstances, the latter is surely preferable.

There is an additional and quite practical reason for abandoning our attempts to isolate the French in order to force them to return to an integrated NATO. The status of the 70,000 French troops formerly assigned to West Germany under NATO commands became a focus of concern after de Gaulle's denunciation of the alliance's supranational command structure in February, 1966. The negotiations on the status of these troops during the following summer therefore reveal the costs involved in forcing Paris to choose between national isolation and military integration within NATO.

This issue provides another example of our tendency to confront the West Germans with the option between France and the United States as a preferred alliance partner; given this choice, Bonn must (in the short run) choose an American alliance, thereby weakening European unity. Perhaps more important, this crisis reflects our habit of giving priority to technical and institutional formulas rather than political realities. Is the removal of French troops from Germany, because Paris rejects any form of integration with NATO forces, actually desirable? There is ground for doubt, even on the assumption that the remaining American, British, and German forces would be sufficient to guarantee the security of the Bonn regime.

While the fourteen NATO members other than France have been willing to endorse continued military integration in public statements, many consider that it is at least as important—if not more so—to maintain French troops east of the Rhine. In the first place, French presence in West Germany, if it can be negotiated, is the best guarantee that Paris will not opt for neutrality in any future crisis; however useful integrated military commands may be from a technical point of view, both political symbolism and the logic of self-defense are prior concerns for the Europeans.

Second, it is feared that the withdrawal of the 70,000 French troops would leave Bonn dangerously exposed within the alliance. Immediately following the June, 1966, meeting of the NATO Council of Ministers, the French tried to warn other Europeans to this effect by announcing that some air-force units would be withdrawn from German soil in any event. Since escalation in Vietnam threatens to require further "transfers" of trained American troops now in Germany—and since the British are increasingly tempted to reduce their forces for economic reasons—the consequence of pushing the French to withdraw could be a larger *Bundeswehr* (which is not as popular in Europe as it is in the Pentagon).

The principal danger of these developments does not lie in a resurgence of German nationalism and aggressiveness (though this is a possibility of great concern to the Russians and all Europeans alike). Rather, there is the risk that Bonn, feeling insufficiently protected by the American nuclear umbrella (should NATO ground forces be reduced), would be tempted to opt for some form of neutralist disengagement that gave promise of reunification. This solution may seem attractive elsewhere on the continent should an integrated NATO be viewed as an invitation to probing actions or misunderstandings that might result in a major war.

The possibility of a *détente* based on the simultaneous abolition of NATO and the Warsaw Pact has received increased attention in Europe, especially now that the Rumanians have proposed a withdrawal of Russian and American military forces from the center of Europe. French diplomacy, by no means limited to de Gaulle's trip to Russia, may well encourage this orientation. In the face of this ferment, Washington's attempts to do business as usual may result in the collapse of NATO should our allies opt for disengagement (if only to avoid involvement lest the war in Vietnam escalate out of control).

In one sense, disengagement in Europe and the end of the NATO and Warsaw Pact alliance system may not seem undesirable; many point out that the absence of American troops on the continent would be quite acceptable if the Soviet Union ceased to pose any kind of threat to Western Europe. Such an optimistic view ignores, however, the continuing importance of the ideological difference between communism and Western democracy (a theme to which I will turn in the next chapter). Even more serious, schemes for European neutralization and disengagement do not take into consideration the inescapable realities of the balance of power.

For many, a disengaged, neutral Europe implies the reunification of Germany, but the Germans are too powerful to remain simply neutral. Either they would come to dominate the center of the continent (thereby threatening the states of Eastern Europe), or Europe would come to be unified, to one degree or another, as an independent—hence hardly neutral —factor in world politics. On the other hand, if Germany were to remain divided in a neutralized Europe that was disengaged from alliance with the superpowers, one would return to the condition of Balkanization that led to World Wars I and II. Insofar as our traditional approach to NATO makes disengagement seem more attractive in Europe, therefore, we may unwittingly create long-term risks, and above all the possibility that Western Europe may one day reject all forms of alliance with the United States.

Given the ultimate dead end of American attempts to force the notion of an integrated NATO on an unwilling French ally, we must consider an alternative policy. Having failed to unite the West by means of pleasing every European power except France, perhaps we should adopt what could be called a pro-French policy. The outlines of such an approach can be stated as follows: the United States would abandon the notion of a multilateral force or indeed any Atlantic nuclear force connected with NATO; Washington would make it clear that we do not intend to give West Germany nuclear weapons in any form. These two objectives already have large support throughout many of our NATO allies, and would be strongly opposed only by Bonn.[4] In place of our reliance upon an inte-

---

[4] Recent surveys of West German opinion indicate, however, that "there is strong opposition in Germany to the acquisition of national nuclear weapons, and there is no strong positive desire for any German share in a nuclear weapons system through some multilateral arrangement, such as the MLF project." Deutsch: "Integration and Arms Control in the European Political Environment," p. 364.

grated—hence hegemonic—alliance as the means of defending Europe, we would support the emergence of the most fully cohesive form of European union possible at present, namely, a confederation defended by Anglo-French nuclear forces, allied with the United States without common military command.

Since a NATO nuclear force may founder on the differences of interest among our allies, this consequence may occur anyway; recent British reluctance to press for the Atlantic Nuclear Force they once proposed, based on fears of alienating the Soviet Union and undermining a treaty against nuclear proliferation, indicates this possibility. The ultimate problem is to insure that West Germany has an overwhelming national interest in tying its military defense and political aims to those of other Western European powers. Only in this way can we be assured that Bonn will never attempt to change the status quo by force or to re-enact Rapallo by leaving the Western camp for a feeble neutralism as the price of reunification.

The way of showing the Germans that it is their permanent interest to orient their policies toward the West lies in a radical reversal of our policy toward de Gaulle. The key would seem to be acceptance of France's independent nuclear striking force as a reality, just as we have accepted Britain's nuclear status. This means not merely the formal admission that we welcome the French as a nuclear ally, but also the explicit decision to share nuclear secrets with France on the same basis as with Great Britain. Our failure to do so to date has established an invidious distinction between the French and British as allies, and has cost the French great financial sacrifice to reproduce, on their own, technological processes and weapons systems like those of Great Britain and the United States.

It will be immediately objected that such a move would legitimize nuclear dissemination, encouraging the Germans to follow the French example. Without underestimating the dangers of certain forms of nuclear dissemination, however, we should not deceive ourselves on this point; as the French and

Chinese have shown, nuclear proliferation is a fact of the age that cannot be avoided by pious hopes, or even by treaties that cannot be enforced. The only possibility of preventing the Germans from developing their own nuclear weapons is to show Bonn that it has a greater interest in casting its lot with a European confederation armed with nuclear weapons, over which it may have considerable political control even if it does not itself possess them.

In the long run, independently controlled nuclear forces on the continent are the only solution to fears that the United States may one day refuse to defend Europe. It follows that the only realistic check on nuclear dissemination in Europe is the existence of a common nuclear force, based on present British and French capabilities, which is sufficiently independent of the United States so that even if we failed to come to our allies' defense, a European deterrent would be credible against Russia (not to mention other powers).

Our current policies thus unwittingly contradict the objective of limiting nuclear diffusion. Paradoxically, our willingness to grant nuclear assistance to the French can have great utility in furthering this aim, for the *force de frappe*, like the British nuclear force, already exists; the creation of an independent European nuclear capability, composed of these existing units, would ultimately reduce the number of nuclear powers in the world from five to four. We can prevent further development of autonomous national capabilities in Western Europe only by seeing to it that existing nuclear arsenals satisfy the strategic needs of those who are tempted to acquire their own nuclear weapons.

States act only when they have an interest in doing so; therefore we could tie our nuclear assistance to France to the French willingness to put forth again the Fouchet plan or a similar device for a confederation between European states—including Great Britain—that would be ultimately capable of acting on a common foreign policy distinct from that made in Washington. A recent French proposal for reorganizing NATO, apparently formulated by leading French strategists, would provide a good starting point for negotiations within the alliance.[5] Our support for such a solution would therefore be consistent with French interests, and this is the main condition for developing any sane European policy.

It will be argued that the Germans, as well as the Dutch and other smaller powers, would be radically opposed to the end of NATO as now organized because they fear French hegemony on the continent. The only possible basis for avoiding such a danger is to bring the British into the Western European community, for only their presence could assure lesser powers that they would not be totally dependent on France. But since the British can only be expected to join European institutions which are confederal (at least at the outset), a clearly stated American preference for the French proposals is the condition for bringing Great Britain into Europe.

Such a European construction, based on the unavoidable fact that European nationalism is not yet sufficiently well developed to support supranational political institutions, is the only available alternative at present. Moreover—and this is decisive—confederal institutions in Europe show promise of satisfying the interests and needs of each of the European powers. This may not seem to be the case at the moment, but dispassionate analysis indicates that events are moving in this direction.

For the Benelux countries and Italy, a Europe in which Great Britain participates would seem to be the only means of counterbalancing French or Franco-German hegemony. Since no British politicians will support a total surrender of national sovereignty, a confederal "Europe of States" is the only way of reconciling the interests of the European powers who fear France. Yet such a solution would clearly be the only one consistent with French interests, and hence the only one that will not drive France from the Western alliance.

[5] "Faut-il réformer l'Alliance atlantique?" *Politique Étrangère,* XXX (1965), 230-44. For a more detailed presentation, see General André Beaufre: *NATO and Europe* (New York: Knopf; 1966).

For West Germany, a European confederation in which her security and her desire for reunification could be supported by the dual nuclear forces of Britain and France—with the residual deterrent of an alliance with American nuclear power—would have great advantages for several reasons. West Germany has the potential of utilizing her special ties with France and her economic dominance within the Common Market to play a major role in the resulting European community. Moreover, German reunification is only conceivable as the adherence of a quasi-communist East German regime in a confederal Europe which is no longer the member of an integrated alliance ultimately controlled in Washington.

As one West German has written and more of his countrymen are coming to realize, "It is probable that a reunited Germany will have to renounce membership in NATO" because the Soviet Union could hardly tolerate the addition of a united German state to existing American power (unless militarily forced to do so). The commentator just quoted went on to say that "the two objectives—European unification and German reunification—are not in my view irreconcilable"; in other words, German reunification and European unity are both possible, but only at the cost of the demise of an integrated NATO.[6]

This argument deserves more attention than it has received in the United States, for General de Gaulle has clearly understood the incompatibility of an integrated Atlantic alliance and any resolution of the current division of Europe. A European community in which national diversity is tolerated, and whose common policies are independent of those determined by American interests, can appeal to the Soviet Union for a German settlement—and perhaps an ultimate relaxation of the satellite condition of increasingly nationalist East European states; even though a combined Anglo-French nuclear force would be weaker than the Soviet deterrent (or rather,

[6] Ferdinand Friedensburg: "L'unité européene et la reunification de l'Allemagne," *Politique Étrangère*, XXX (1965), 134, 137.

for this very reason), a *Europe des patries* no longer militarily integrated into NATO could resolve the tensions produced by the division of Germany without posing a life-or-death threat to Moscow.

What is needed, in other words, is the transference of our current special relationship with Great Britain to a similar relationship with a confederal Western Europe which includes Britain. As this analogy implies, strategic or political arguments against our support of an independent confederal Europe with its own nuclear weapons can equally be raised against the present relationship with England (with the proviso that our present relationship with England serves to divide the West and undermine NATO).

A word should be added concerning the arguments that have led American policy-makers to insist on military integration, and especially centralized nuclear control in the Western alliance. Our strategic thinkers have usually considered nuclear diffusion as a so-called Nth country problem, without reference to the specific powers that have nuclear weapons. They have also tended to perceive nuclear strategy as a two-person game, largely confined to the calculation of deterrence between the United States and the Soviet Union.

Strategists on the continent, and especially in France, do not always share the prevailing American assumptions. For example, General André Beaufre, a French military planner, has insisted on the importance of the political characteristics of the specific nations holding nuclear weapons.[7] Beaufre's argument deserves attention because it is representative of current French nuclear strategy, and subtler than the more widely publicized views of General Gallois (who seems to overstate the deterrent capacity of the nuclear forces being developed by France).

[7] See especially his *Strategy and Deterrence*. For a somewhat more pro-American view, see Raymond Aron: *The Great Debate* (Garden City, N. Y.: Doubleday; 1965).

General Beaufre admits from the outset that French nuclear capabilities—and the argument would apply equally well to a combined Anglo-French force—will be of secondary status by comparison to the nuclear power of the United States and Russia (at least for the immediate future). His argument, however, is that such secondary nuclear forces, if they are independent, actually increase nuclear deterrence throughout the world as a whole. This is so, according to Beaufre, because these independent nuclear forces are not centrally controlled by the major partner in the Atlantic alliance, i.e., the United States.

A secondary force, itself incapable of deterring the Soviet Union, nevertheless increases the West's ability to deter aggression because it makes the consequences of conventional (or for that matter nuclear) adventures by the Soviet Union more uncertain. Since nuclear deterrence depends on the Russian belief that the United States will use its atomic weapons, even at the cost of the destruction of American cities, minor provocations might now seem to lie outside of the American nuclear umbrella. Should the lines of communication with West Berlin be cut, for example, the threat of an immediate American nuclear attack on Russia is of decreasing credibility to the Soviet Union; in this view, it is the presence of American troops in West Germany and the risk of uncontrolled escalation that now restrains the USSR.

Whereas the calculation of America's willingness to use its deterrent may be relatively favorable to marginal Russian provocations, the existence of secondary but quite independent nuclear forces complicates things. Even assuming that the French are no more willing than we to have their society destroyed in order to preserve West Berlin, the Russians must predict the reaction to their provocation in both Paris and Washington. But insofar as the French determination of vital national interests is different from that in Washington, or at least has a high risk of being different, the Russians have to calculate the credibility of a French intervention as well as of an American one.

Moreover, a French intervention would pose the risk that

although the United States did not respond with nuclear weapons over the original provocation in Berlin, a Russo-French nuclear exchange would trigger American participation. Studies of this type of situation by the Australian strategist Arthur Lee Burns have suggested that even a relatively minor nuclear capability in a country like Sweden might effectively deter a nuclear superpower like the Soviet Union.[8] Thus the French strategic position is hardly absurd.

As General Beaufre suggests, the acquisition of secondary but independent nuclear forces by an ally can have the effect of transferring the vital interests of the weaker ally to his stronger nuclear partner. In this view, French nuclear forces effectively transform all those interests for which Paris is willing to sacrifice French society into vital American interests as well. Whereas an alliance based on centralized command and control in Washington is vulnerable to the tension between the interests of its allies (who may feel that a marginal provocation is effectively vital to them) and the interests of the American nuclear superpower (who may prefer an accommodation in a minor skirmish to nuclear destruction), the development of independent but allied nuclear forces could actually reinforce alliance.

This argument is borne out by the relationship between each of the two nuclear superpowers and its allies who have acquired nuclear weapons. The clearest case, of course, is that of Great Britain, which has developed a nuclear capability, a close tie with the United States, and as a result a kind of extension of the American nuclear umbrella to those interests for which the English are willing to commit themselves by using their nuclear forces independently.

Despite the Sino-Soviet split, this logic has even worked to a limited extent in the relationship between Russia and China (whose defensive alliance is still legally in force). By making it a decisive Chinese interest that the United States not destroy North Vietnam, China as a nuclear power has

---

[8] Arthur Lee Burns: "Power Politics and the Growing Nuclear Club," *Policy Memorandum Number 20* (Princeton University, Center of International Studies; 1959).

in effect transferred this national interest to the Soviet Union; as a result, the Russians have been forced to aid Ho Chi Minh, despite fears of a confrontation with the United States. Even the possibility of a Sino-American war cannot be totally gratifying to Moscow; since the Russians could fail to respond to an American nuclear attack on China only at the cost of a considerable loss of control within the rest of the Communist world, it is in the Soviet interest to bring her deterrence to bear on the United States in Southeast Asia.

It would appear, therefore, that defensive alliances between a superpower and a nominal ally with a less impressive array of nuclear weapons can persist and even, in a sense, be strengthened with respect to the ultimate decisions of total nuclear war. Short of such decisions, however, these alignments presuppose considerable flexibility because the secondary ally, because of its weakness, can adopt positions different from the allied superpower. The superpower cannot enforce its will on a weaker nuclear ally, yet at the same time is forced to defend—or to threaten to defend—its independent ally in time of crisis. Certainly the costs of not doing so, be they for the United States or Russia, would be serious (unless the weaker nuclear ally took such aggressive positions as to be easily disavowed).

These considerations of nuclear strategy suggest that the development of confederal European institutions, backed by an Anglo-French nuclear force that would be independent although coordinated with the American nuclear forces, would strengthen the position of the West in an era of disintegrating bipolarity. Should we fail to encourage our European allies to develop political integration based on independent military power, the probable consequence will be a further proliferation of isolated national nuclear forces over the next twenty-five to fifty years. This proliferation would occur either within a truncated Atlantic alliance, of which France might cease to be a member, or by isolated nations.

Although it could be argued that the Russians would find a unified European deterrent, based on Anglo-French capabilities, a great threat, certainly they consider the MLF or

Atlantic Nuclear Force proposals (not to mention an autonomous German nuclear capability) an even greater threat. In the case of a confederal Europe, there would be the possibility of a negotiated settlement between the USSR and the Europeans, even should this solution be unsatisfactory to the United States. It is no accident that General de Gaulle has frequently hinted at the connection between his autonomous European policy and a purely European solution to the German question that someday would end the persisting instability in Europe.

This possibility of a European settlement behind our backs is one of the central arguments against a pro-French policy in Washington. Nonetheless, it is just this factor that would be the most attractive aspect of what has been called a pro-French European policy for the United States. De Gaulle has made it quite clear in recent statements that what he seeks is an independent Europe, more responsible for its own defense. By an independent or "European Europe," de Gaulle does not mean anti-American, but simply a confederal European community which can make its own decisions and therefore differ with the United States.

In fact, a Russo-European settlement is in our own best interests, for American commitments in Asia and Latin America will increasingly demand that we have more flexibility of policy than is possible in the context of a totally integrated Atlantic alliance. Just as we do not wish the Europeans to be able to veto moves, such as in the Dominican Republic or Vietnam, which are in our national interest, so the Europeans are increasingly dubious of giving the United States a permanent veto over their vital concerns. Only by recognizing the growing vitality and independence of our European allies can we maintain the common interests that still bind the West together.

The ill-fated grand design, based on an integration of the Atlantic community over which Washington would directly preside, is bound to fail, both because of fundamental differences in outlook between the United States and our European allies and because of our own unwillingness to institute supranational Atlantic institutions to which American sovereignty would be surrendered. Under these circumstances, continuation of our past policies only covers the disarray of the Atlantic alliance with a façade of military integration, thereby giving the Russians an advantage in their dealings with Europe.

By recognizing the autonomy of our European allies, based on independent nuclear forces (coordinated but not integrated with our own), we can strengthen the West immeasurably. In the long run, after all, this policy presents the communist world with two major Western political and economic communities, both of which are armed with nuclear weapons, and both of which are devoted to the principles of Western civilization. If we take seriously our own profession to favor supranational political institutions in Europe, it is only by means of first establishing a confederation capable of adopting its own foreign policies, arising from a consensus in Europe, that such a United States of Europe could be formed.

It is well that we bear in mind the example of our own founding, for the establishment of a strong federal government in the United States did not come at one stroke. Since pressing for supranational institutions as an immediate goal is, whether we like it or not, a means of dividing Europe and maintaining our own hegemony there, a serious attempt to develop a truly united Europe, the stated goal of so many Europeans and Americans alike, would seem to require our acceptance and active support of French policies toward that end.

To be sure, it may be impossible to secure the agreement of our NATO allies for a reform of the alliance that increases European autonomy on the basis of a continental confederation. Some would argue, for example, that we should accept such a change in NATO if it is proposed and widely supported by our partners, but that it is folly for the United States to take the lead in this direction. While consistent with the American habit of responding to crises on a short-range basis, this negative approach is exceedingly dangerous for a major power involved in a delicate and changing global balance of power.

Our allies might resist an apparently pro-French policy (presumably out of fear of French domination, although this fear would not be justified if a more autonomous European confederation included both Britain and Germany), but such a policy is in their own long-range interests. More important, allied reluctance to alter the character of NATO has been due, in large part, to American failure to show the slightest interest in serious negotiations with General de Gaulle prior to the NATO crisis he touched off in February, 1966. Aware of the utility of the American nuclear umbrella, European statesmen, even if they find merit in Gaullist arguments, understandably express verbal support for Washington's policy—if only because they secretly share de Gaulle's fear that one day we might return to an isolationist policy.

Whereas attempts by this country to impose unity and integration on the Atlantic alliance as a whole are bound to weaken the ties that join us to the other Western European countries, the development of autonomous European policies, both with respect to the underdeveloped areas of the world and the Soviet bloc, would make it more likely that the common interests remaining throughout the West could be realized in political terms. In an era of revolutionary change, Western positions will doubtless continue to be challenged, often simultaneously, in the Middle East, Asia, Latin America, and Africa. These threats could easily exceed the single power and will of the United States—or an integrated NATO—to intervene decisively everywhere. Hence we could only gain by encouraging our European friends to adopt their own positions, coordinated with ours as closely as possible, in order to maintain international stability.

It will be at once asked, what of the future of NATO? At first glance, the degree of European independence required for the policy here proposed seems to contradict a formal alliance like NATO, not to mention the continued presence of American troops in West Germany. This conclusion follows, however, only if NATO is equated with the forms of military integration adopted within the alliance over the last twenty years.

While Americans have persistently seen NATO in such institutional terms, de Gaulle's entire policy rests on the premise that the alliance itself can be distinguished from the formal organization of common military forces. This approach is tenable because a defensive alliance between a nuclear superpower and a somewhat weaker nuclear partner can be effective without integrated military commands; as long as NATO does not plan to wage an aggressive war, permanent military integration does not seem to be required for the persistence of an Atlantic alliance.

American military experts admit that the integrated NATO structure is primarily a contingency command in case of Soviet attack in Europe. As the risk of such a war declines, so does the absolute necessity of having a ready-made version of the interallied military structure developed during World War II; it is far more important to secure agreement within the West on over-all strategic aims than to establish formally centralized institutions that lack a solid and lasting political basis.

In addition, no one expects that a West European confederation with an independent foreign policy will emerge overnight, nor that such a union will be able to conclude a European settlement with Moscow in the short run. As de Gaulle has persistently said, the evolution of policies and institutions in Europe will take place slowly, and in this process the Atlantic alliance has a vital role to play. Assuming, therefore, that the United States adopts a position such as that outlined here, NATO would continue to serve a number of functions.

First, in the immediate future it may be necessary to maintain some form of the NATO military commands, to which member states could be attached on a purely voluntary basis.

In this way, those NATO powers that are not within an emerging West European confederation could coordinate their military planning with that of the United States (thereby maintaining their security without feeling the need to develop national nuclear forces).

Second, as the Anglo-French nuclear forces were developed into a more coordinated European deterrent, consultation between the latter and American military planners could take place within the alliance. While formal integration, which implies a common command in wartime, would be abandoned, it need not follow that joint consultation would cease. Considering that Secretary of Defense McNamara altered NATO's fundamental strategy without even consulting our allies, one might even wonder whether the quality of cooperation would be improved by abandoning the fiction of collective decision-making.

Third, the maintenance of NATO as a formal defense alliance would provide a legitimate basis for the continued presence of American troops in West Germany. As long as a European confederation has not been fully established, our commitment to defend Bonn must be maintained (for to do otherwise would invite the Germans to embark on their own nuclear weapons program). Only when asked to withdraw our troops by the Europeans themselves should we consider such a move; once asked, we would be perverse not to comply.

Finally, NATO could have a lasting function even after the emergence of an independent *Europe des patries*. Since some form of defensive alliance would be desired by a West European confederation, it is to be hoped that our commitments to Europe would not be exclusively bilateral; the confederation could then become one member of a reformed alliance that included other associated states as well. In this way, for example, the defense of Greece or Turkey might be assured by both a Western European and an American deterrent, whose use in case of enemy aggression could be coordinated precisely because the allied nuclear forces were not under a single commander.

In other words, NATO would become a more cooperative enterprise by virtue of the autonomy of a European component that would feel less dependent on the United States. Differences of opinion could be openly stated instead of hidden in the ambiguities of joint communiqués. The mystique of a common attachment to collective security would be undermined, but this may be the prerequisite to continued cooperation (not an obstacle to be avoided).

Only by abandoning the fetish of military integration can the unity of the democracies that ring the North Atlantic be maintained. The desirability of such an evolution is indicated by West European fears that our commitment in South Vietnam could escalate into a global war and cause their destruction. Since valid differences of interest exist within the alliance, cooperation cannot be based on a refusal to admit differing interpretations of challenges to world peace. While American opposition to communist aggression has often been justified in terms of the image of Munich, some of our allies think—perhaps more correctly—that the appropriate analogy is Sarajevo.

CHAPTER SIX

The Soviet Union and the Communist World

WHEN WE SPEAK of the iron curtain, the cold war, or the two superpowers, we commonly refer to the rivalry between the United States and the Soviet Union that has dominated world politics since 1945. Although many commentators have discussed the possibility of relaxing the hostility between Moscow and Washington, very real dangers of a direct confrontation remain; even if bipolarity has declined somewhat over the last few years and will probably decline further, these risks are not about to disappear completely. On the contrary, the signs of Russo-American *détente* (symbolized by the hotline and test-ban agreements between Kennedy and Khrushchev) have been recently counterbalanced, especially by the tensions arising from the war in Vietnam.

To reassess our attitude toward the Soviet Union, it is first necessary to consider in some detail the nature of communism. Americans assume that the principles of communism were effectively developed by Marx, Lenin, and Stalin, and are more or less realized today by Mao Tse-tung and the Soviet leadership. Such a view reflects the extent to which we take communist propaganda at its own word, for in fact the writings of Marx do not necessarily justify international communism as we see it; although both the Soviet and Chinese leaders have an interest in asserting that Lenin was Marx's only true heir, the very conception of "Marxism-Leninism" has been attacked as a travesty of the original teachings of Karl Marx, especially by anticommunist Marxists in Europe.

Marxism originated in Germany, France, and England a half century before its emergence in the Soviet Union; despite prevalent beliefs, Lenin was not the principal disciple of Karl Marx. Although socialist ideas and political parties did not flourish in the United States for reasons peculiar to our historical situation, Marxism was widely attractive in other Western nations undergoing the industrial revolution. Marxist parties usually called themselves "Social Democrats" until the second decade of the twentieth century, when the German party split into two distinct parts—one of which took the name "Communist." After the so-called Bolshevik wing of the Russian Social Democratic party took power in October, 1917, it adopted the Communist title as a reflection of its divergence from the less revolutionary European Marxists, who retained the "Socialist" or Social Democratic label.

According to the main thrust of Marx's thought, all history can be described as conflict between the classes created by particular economic systems. To gain power, the capitalist class had been forced to overthrow the aristocracy (as in the French Revolution), but Marx thought this victory would be short-lived because industrial production necessarily generated intense conflict between the owners of property and the labor force they "exploited" to secure bigger profits. Since economic factors determine political life, the conflict between the proletariat and the bourgeoisie was inevitable in all industrial societies. And since the progress of industrialization would lead to ever greater hostility between the property owners and a growing, increasingly miserable working class, the proletariat would inevitably revolt and gain control over industrial society, just as the middle classes had revolted against aristocratic society.

This summary of Marx's principles, though oversimplified, should indicate that he expected the proletarian revolution to take place in the most highly developed industrial nations. To be sure, Marx allowed for the possibility that the first revolution might begin in a relatively backward state that was undergoing industrialization in an effort to catch up with its more fully developed neighbors; in the 1840's he wrote that German workers might revolt before those of France or England. But Marx assumed that the first proletarian victory would be the signal for a general overthrow of the capitalist order in the more advanced nations; since the national state was the product of the capitalist revolution and reflected the interests of the property-owning class, the working class would have no interest in supporting its own state in a war against a newly established Marxist regime.

Marx's historical predictions have not been borne out; by a perverse twist of fate, Marxist regimes have come to power in backward or nonindustrialized societies, not in the highly developed nations of Western Europe. The working class in capitalist states has not shown the massive support of the communist revolutions required to trigger a worldwide chain of revolutions; on the contrary, Marxist movements have generally failed in both the United States and Britain. Even where Western European workers have been more receptive to Marxism, as in France and Italy, the most characteristic response has been a split between Communist and Socialist parties, both of which claim to be Marxist but only one of which admits the legitimacy of Russian or Chinese communism.

The failure of proletarian revolutions in highly developed economic systems deserves special emphasis, for it is related to the persisting tendency of Marxists to be split into radically opposed groups by debates on the extent to which circumstances demand a revolutionary strategy. The radical or extreme left wing tends to seek revolution at any price, while more moderate or cautious elements are willing to capitalize on positions of strength already achieved, deeming that previous gains should be defended even at the cost of postponing revolution.

The rise of Marxism itself in the middle of the nineteenth century was an example of such a split; within a socialist movement popular among the German working class, Marx represented a radical splinter group, originally without great resources, that took a revolutionary stand in opposition to the entire capitalist order. In contrast, leaders like Ferdinand Lassalle were more concerned with the immediate benefits that could be obtained within the existing political order by a militant working-class party. Even where Marx and Lassalle agreed in rhetoric, therefore, considerable differences in analysis, strategy, and emphasis were evident.

The contradiction between Marxian and Lassallean socialism has been repeated frequently in the history of international Marxism. Later in the nineteenth century, differences arose within the German Marxist party (the Social Democrats), opposing orthodox intellectual leaders to the trade-union hierarchy; when Eduard Bernstein, once a leading "orthodox" doctrinaire, proclaimed the necessity of revising Marx's analysis and revolutionary strategy, this split came to the fore. Although his revisionist point of view was formally adopted only by a minority of Social Democrats before the turn of the century, the outbreak of World War I triggered a new crisis; the majority of the German Marxist party abandoned the principle of the international working-class solidarity and voted—along with the pro-governmental parties—for credits to support the Kaiser's war policy. Outraged Marxist intellectuals split from the Social Democratic party on this issue, forming a revolutionary movement that was to be put down by force, after World War I, by a German government that included the Socialists.

The history of other European parties, and especially the early years of the Russian socialist movement, shows that such schisms are endemic to Marxism. Although national traditions in many ways influenced the Russian Marxists, the Bolsheviks split from the more moderate Mensheviks because the latter insisted that the time was not "ripe" for revolution, whereas those who followed Lenin sought the earliest possible revolt, regardless of the risks. Leninism represents the wing of Marxism that characteristically insists on the possibility of immediate revolution, even in a society that is only partially industrialized. The anomaly of this view is striking when compared to the dominant theme of Marxist literature, for the prediction of capitalism's inevitable doom can be interpreted as grounds for postponing the proletarian revolution (at least until the bourgeois class has sown the seeds of its own destruction by establishing a fully industrialized economy).

Since the early twentieth century, therefore, "revisionism" has challenged the necessity of immediate revolution in industrialized nations, whereas Leninism has emphasized the possibility of successful revolution in peasant or backward societies. As a result, it can be said that orthodox Marxism is dead: the simple predictions of Karl Marx have failed in the industrialized societies of the West, and communist regimes have come to power only in the more backward nations of the East. The only industrial nation to become communist in the twentieth century has been Czechoslovakia, where Russian military force and not a popular revolution overthrew an anticommunist regime that lacked sufficient Western protection.[1]

Since the truly "orthodox" interpretation of Marx has been rendered impossible by the events of the last century, a faithful Marxist must now apply the teachings of his ideology to circumstances that were not foreseen by the founder. In the

---

[1] For a careful and sophisticated presentation of the argument hastily sketched here, see George Lichtheim: *Marxism: An Historical and Critical Study* (New York: Praeger; 1961).

process, communists who are out of power or who have little to lose by revolution often proclaim that Marx's doctrine requires violent combat with capitalism at all costs—or, to use communist terminology, a "left" strategy. Marxists or socialists whose position of strength would be threatened by all-out violence insist that the working class can make impressive gains by a more cautious or evolutionary policy—a so-called "right" strategy. Because both strategies can find authority in Marx's own writings, his principles are inevitably used to justify contradictory policies.[2]

The Sino-Soviet split therefore reflects the pervasive tendency of communists to be irreconcilably divided over the "correct" interpretation of Marxian dogma. This does not necessarily mean that the opposed factions within a given party, or within the communist bloc as a whole, do not sincerely believe in the superiority of their ideology; communists in both Russia and China agree on the fundamental objective of overthrowing the capitalist order and establishing a world based solely on Marxist principles. It does mean, however, that it is a grave mistake to treat communism as a monolithic force that pretends to be internally divided only to lure us into error. Communists take their ideology very seriously—so much so that divisions within the various Marxist movements can give the West important leverage in dealing with them.

We can gain a clearer view of American relations with the communist world, and especially with the USSR, if the basic doctrine of "containment," first proposed by George Kennan, is reconsidered in the light of subsequent experience. Kennan

[2] The application of Marxist ideology has thus been subject to a dialectic of contradictions that ironically reflects Marx's own assertion that all history is a dialectical process of contradiction. Stalin himself admitted as much by introducing the doctrine of "non-antagonistic contradictions" within Communist societies (as distinguished from the inherently antagonistic or violent contradictions discovered in capitalist society by Marx). That Socialists or Communists can be subject to "antagonist contradictions" has, of course, been revealed by the Hungarian uprising of 1956 and by the Sino-Soviet split.

identified communism with Russian communism and argued that our goal should be to restrain any further Soviet advances into Western Europe; if Russian communism could be contained within the limits it had reached in 1948, Soviet ideology would "mellow," an accommodation would become possible, and the Russian state would come to approximate that of an industrialized nation in the West (though with significant differences in internal policy).

Although a reduction of Soviet aggressiveness could doubtless be documented in recent years, particularly with reference to Khrushchev's failure to sign a treaty with East Germany (as he threatened), Kennan's prediction has largely failed to materialize; whatever moderation has been shown by Moscow is as much due to the balance of terror and the mutual possession of nuclear missiles as to containment in Europe. Kennan argued that our policy would result in fundamental changes within the Soviet state, and most particularly in a decline in totalitarianism as such. Despite de-Stalinization and an increased attempt to provide a better standard of living, there is little evidence that the Soviet Communist party is willing to allow anything like Western democracy within the USSR.

Some scholars have argued that industrialized societies have an internal logic of their own, so that the United States and Russia will become more and more alike; as Americans realize the need for some degree of central planning, the Soviets admit the need for "prices," "profits," and decentralized decision-making in a complex economic system. This argument, which has a curiously pseudo-Marxist tone of economic determinism, cannot be pressed too far, because on both theoretical and practical grounds the degree of convergence in the internal political systems of communist and capitalist states has decisive limits.[3]

For example, relaxation of rule by terror and cautious "liberalization" in the Soviet Union and some Eastern Euro-

[3] See, for example, Zbigniew Brzezinski and Samuel P. Huntington: *Political Power: USA/USSR* (New York: Viking; 1964), esp. pp. 419-36.

pean satellites have not essentially weakened the political power of the ruling Communist parties. These internal modifications, while making totalitarianism more palatable to the populations under its control, have probably strengthened communist societies; in particular, a lesser reliance on terror and violence, when combined with increased emphasis on technological competence as a requirement for advancement within the party hierarchy, reduces the regime's reliance on the secret police.

The net result would seem to be an evolution of Soviet society toward a highly technocratic order in which the Communist party remains the decisive center of power. Since individuals will reach the highest political offices only if they are capable of managing a complex industrial society, conflicts between the party leaders, the secret police, and the army, would become somewhat less likely; changes of personnel and the decline of the "cult of the personality" would thus reflect bargaining between proponents of different policies, and would be accepted more easily than under the reign of Stalin.

Recent trends of this sort may not continue unchecked, but even if they do, one need not conclude that ideology had ceased to play a decisive role in communist society or that the Soviet Union had come to approximate a Western democracy. On the contrary, the managerial and political elites would have access to power in the USSR only within the Communist party or by its approval; the subterranean character of political infighting would remain, with the corollary that the regime would justify its decisions in agriculture, economic development, or foreign policy in terms of Marxist-Leninist dogma.

We must not mistake an evolution in the character and impact of Marxist ideology, especially in an advanced industrial society, for a disappearance of that ideology itself. Such changes are not unlike the alteration of Christian doctrine associated with the Reformation and Counter Reformation. It might have been possible for a sixteenth-century observer to remark that Luther and Calvin, in attacking the power and supremacy of the Catholic Church, reduced the importance of theology as a guide to political or secular life; this view of the Reformation might have led to the conclusion that the end of Christianity as an effective religion was in sight. As this example shows, adjustments of a body of thought do not always mean that its principles are in the process of disappearing; on the contrary, changes in Marxist ideology (and even an increased toleration of divergent interpretations of its proper application) may represent a reinvigoration of what would otherwise become a hopelessly obsolete teaching.

The opposition between Western democracy and communist ideology, however it may be altered in coming years, cannot be expected to wither away. An extreme solution would be to obliterate all regimes and individuals who believe in Marxism. Apart from the absurdity of viewing the so-called battle for men's minds in this way, it is impossible to base foreign policy on such a crusade; it is neither militarily prudent nor morally defensible to destroy the Soviet Union and other communist societies by brute force.[4] Even if we did so, communism would not disappear—on the contrary, it would probably be strengthened, just as Protestantism was strengthened by the attempts of Catholic rulers to wipe it out.

Assuming, therefore, that a conflict of political principle is highly likely to persist in Russo-American relations, we must assess the specific threat posed by communist ideology. Although some domestic critics of social welfare or big government assert that communist or Marxist influence is implicit in policies they dislike, the weakness of the American Communist party reflects the fact that Marxism has had less effect in the United States than in other industrialized societies; confusion between the challenge of world communism and disagreements in American domestic politics obscure rather than clarify the essential issues.

American foreign policy must be directed to enabling us to cope with a variety of threats arising in world politics, of which aggressive communism is but one. Russian or Chinese

[4] See George Kennan: *On Dealing With the Communist World* (New York: Harper & Row; 1964), esp. Ch. i.

communism represents a way of life that is inimical to American traditions; in particular, rule by Communist parties that claim sole access to the truth contradicts the democratic assumption that no single group should have a monopoly of power or legitimacy. Communism has produced totalitarian regimes in which all spheres of private and public life come under political control in the name of a single principle of justice, concerning which no dissent is legitimate. American statesmen have the right and the duty to oppose such hostile states wherever they directly challenge our own political principles.

The issue of totalitarianism versus democracy is, however, very revealing. Many Americans believe that Nazi Germany and Fascist Italy were the first totalitarian regimes to arise in this century; nothing could be further from the truth. In fact, Hitler and Mussolini rose to power partly as a reaction to the increased importance of the communist movements in Germany and Italy, which took on added significance after Lenin had successfully overthrown the czarist regime in Russia.

When Hitler's challenge to conquer Western Europe became so evident that further neutrality would have resulted in our isolation, we found it necessary to come to the assistance of Great Britain and, after Pearl Harbor, to engage in a major world war to defeat Nazi totalitarianism. Because the enemy of the moment seemed to be the essence of moral evil, we sided willingly with the Soviet Union as a means of defeating Nazi Germany. Such an alliance was obviously in our own interests, but it need not have suggested—as it did to President Roosevelt and many commentators—that the post-World War II world could be governed by amicable agreements between the great powers that had allied against Hitler.

The prevailing American view during the early 1940's was therefore blind to the persisting differences between Soviet communism and Western democracy; ignoring the rivalry in ideology and power that was bound to divide the postwar world, we vainly assumed that cooperation would be possible if only Nazi totalitarianism could be defeated. The sad fate of these dreams of "one world" should be a sobering warning: although the challenge of communist ideology is likely to continue, the belief that it is the sole threat to American democracy—like the view that Nazism was the only enemy— is insufficient as a guide to policy.

Having underestimated the importance of communist ideology in World War II, many Americans have now come to view it as all-important. Some politicians vigorously attacked President Kennedy's efforts to reach minimal agreements with the USSR on the grounds that communists cannot be trusted to keep agreements, even when (as with the hot line or test ban) these accords rested on a real convergence of self-interest. But the opposite extreme seems no more defensible: the existence of the common interests between the United States and Russia need not imply an absence of rivalry and contention between them. Sound American policy requires that both extremes be avoided.

It is frequently said that, since the two superpowers seek to avoid mutual destruction in a nuclear war, agreement to end the cold war is possible; some go so far as to assert that Moscow's fear of Peking could produce a Russo-American alignment against China. Such arguments are based on the assumption that ideology is a secondary factor in Soviet thinking, which is presumably dominated by a rational calculation of Russian power. It would be more realistic to say that the Soviets—and all communists—analyze power relations from the perspective of Marxist ideology; since the Sino-Soviet split itself is characteristic of the internal contradictions of communist doctrine, it is not enough to analyze the hostility between Moscow and Peking in terms of the conflict of interest between two states named China and Russia.

Americans would be ill-advised, therefore, to underestimate the primacy of ideological concerns in the communist bloc. As one acute analyst of the Sino-Soviet split commented:

A Soviet-American alliance directed against China, a subject of occasional speculation in the West, is extremely unlikely. There is no indication whatever at the present time that such a consideration enters Soviet thinking.[5]

No Russian government can openly align itself with the United States at the expense of Marxist principles, for the consequence would be a surrender of Soviet pre-eminence in the communist bloc. Moreover, if Russo-American accommodation were to make China the leader of world communism, it is not even certain that such agreements would be in the American national interest.

Since the Soviet Union, however willing it may be to adopt a moderate or evolutionary strategy to safeguard its gains, is thereby merely following one strand of Marxist thought, the prospect of an imminent resolution of the ideological conflict between communism and Western democracy seems exceedingly doubtful. Soviet leaders do not define Russia's national interests as if they were czarist diplomats, for the very words they use depend on ways of thinking that are impregnated by political principles.

Those Americans who have most strongly insisted on this point have, however, often misunderstood the implications of the conflict between our political principles and those of the communists. All states, regardless of ideology, seek to defend themselves against foreign attack; all societies have a view of the legitimate political order which they seek to protect at home and encourage abroad. The United States and the Soviet Union are no exception. But the preservation —and if possible the spread—of any society's most cherished political ideals greatly depends on a nation's security in world politics; a conquered state can hardly maintain its form of government against the wishes of the conquerer.

The primacy of ideology does not mean that Marxists are impervious to questions of power and self-interest; on the

---

[5] Donald S. Zagoria: *The Sino-Soviet Conflict, 1956-1961* (Princeton, N. J.: Princeton Univ. Press; 1962), p. 385.

contrary, it may only heighten the importance of such considerations as a restraint on Russian policies. Although Soviet calculations of political power are intended to further their communist aims, objective considerations of power can—and, in a sense, must—lead to modifications of ideology.

The most famous example of this phenomenon is Khrushchev's abandonment of the thesis that major war between communist and capitalist societies is an inevitable and necessary step in the movement toward world communism. Khrushchev had to alter Marxist-Leninist teachings on this point once it became clear that a Russo-American thermonuclear war would destroy the USSR as an industrialized society; when the Russians recognized that an exchange of intercontinental missiles would kill communists and capitalists alike, they emphasized a policy of peaceful coexistence and proclaimed that a nonviolent transition to communism in the industrialized countries of the West was possible.

Considerations of power have also been evident in the different responses of Russian and Chinese leaders to the revolution in military technology. Since China is far less developed than the Soviet Union and would not be the prime target of an American nuclear strike on the communist bloc as a whole, Peking has consistently played down the danger of nuclear war; as cynics point out, a mutually destructive missile exchange between the United States and Russia would make China the most powerful communist state and greatly increase its importance as a world power.

As these examples suggest, we can induce communist statesmen to caution because they are aware that failure to understand the implications of new military weapons or economic developments could lead them to disaster. Curiously enough, the more importance one attaches to differences in political principles or ideologies, the more vital become questions of the global balance of power, defined in nonideological terms.

This paradox deserves emphasis. Precisely because the USSR and China view power from the perspective of ideology, the United States can gain leverage on communist states only by policies defined in terms of power. Precisely because the ideological conflict between East and West is not likely to disappear, the United States must frame its foreign-policy goals without reference to ideology.

This argument will seem strange to many, who would prefer to conclude that devotion to democracy requires a persistent crusade against communism; since Marxist doctrines are uncompromisingly opposed to the political principles of the West, must not this difference be the prime consideration in all American policy? The answer is no, and the reason lies in the nature of communist ideology itself. Implacable ideological conflict is in the interest of the communists, for it implies that we accept the Marxist view that there is but one intellectual system providing the truth concerning all questions of political life, both theoretical and practical. The tactics adopted by communist parties, especially when in power, reflect a conception of self-interest that cannot be modified by appeals to Western ideals of peace and justice; only by emphasizing national interest and the balance of power can we check the growth and appeal of Marxist-Leninist ideals.

At the same time, however, we must be aware that communist leaders will necessarily have to justify any accommodations or concessions to the West on ideological grounds; we cannot expect them to admit publicly that their policies are determined by calculations of national interest and power that are not essentially Marxist. Hence we cannot orient our policies toward the establishment of an explicit Russo-American agreement to manage world crises in our mutual self-interest, even though mutual self-interest is the basis on which international stability can be preserved in an ideological confrontation of the two superpowers.

The complex relationship of ideology and power was fully revealed in a generally misunderstood interview between Soviet Premier Kosygin and James Reston of *The New York Times*. When Reston asked whether "the two major powers can work together for world order," Kosygin answered:

"I am not quite clear of your meaning there. Of world order—what does this mean? The United States and the Soviet Union, the two most powerful states, should dictate our wills to other nations? This is a most inappropriate principle. If we should attempt to command other nations, that would be tantamount to fascism."[6]

In other words, the Soviet Union cannot explicitly announce that the interests it shares with the U.S. override its ties to other communist states, for to do so would be self-defeating for Moscow.

Although this comment was taken by many Americans, including Reston himself, as a sign of renewed cold-war hostility, the Soviet position is more subtle. In the interview just cited, Kosygin went on to say:

"From the standpoint of these long-term concepts, the most important thought should be the mustering of forces to oppose war. If you in the U.S. mobilize your own forces, then we mobilize and muster ours. But in what direction? If these are the forces of war, that is one prospect for the future. If they are for developing cooperation and solutions, the prospect would be quite different. But this is not a major topic for us to discuss."[7]

In this remark, Premier Kosygin indicated several points which cannot be fully appreciated unless one is aware that, according to his Marxist-Leninist terminology, the "forces" of the major powers may be either "forces of peace" or "forces of war."

First, the Soviet Premier admitted that the Russians are willing to parallel American moves designed to avoid direct confrontations between the superpowers (as Moscow did in the Suez or Cuban missile crises and the Indo-Pakistani war). This realistic recognition of the common interests shared with

[6] *The New York Times,* December 8, 1965, p. 20.
[7] Ibid.

the United States is a ground for optimism, though the passage was not so interpreted by Reston.

Premier Kosygin tried to make it clear, however, that the Russian leaders operate within definite constraints; in particular, they cannot appear to desire a Russo-American world condominium that ignores ideology and would not be tolerated by other communist states. Since the Soviet Union must, like the United States, demonstrate its willingness to defend allies, the Russians feel impelled, even against their preferences, to parallel American moves that increase tension as well as those that decrease it. If we seek Soviet restraint, we must exercise restraint ourselves.

Finally, Premier Kosygin's interview suggests the need to avoid public discussion of the extent to which the superpowers can tacitly cooperate; because open admission that Soviet national interests qualify her ideology would have serious repercussions within the communist bloc, "this is not a major topic" for discussion with a Western journalist. Although Americans are accustomed to free political discussion, we cannot expect frank and unambiguous dialogue with the Russians.

We can therefore hope to influence the policies of the Soviet Union, or indeed of any communist state, only indirectly and tacitly. Accommodations are possible when they are enforced by mutual self-interest, but they must be limited and cannot be presented as ideological surrenders for either party; ideology will continue to divide the United States and the Soviet Union, although the dangers of conflict can be moderated by astute manipulation of power factors. The process depends decisively, however, on tolerating ambiguity and even hypocrisy, for our rivals cannot say publicly that they are adjusting their Marxist principles to suit national interests.

An extended discussion of the relationship between considerations of power and ideology in dealings with the Soviet Union has seemed necessary in order to avoid errors that are commonly made in talking about American foreign policy.

Turning to broader issues, how does the proposed emphasis on establishing a viable balance of power illuminate the means of restraining communism as a world-wide ideology? Does this approach provide any insight into the proper American attitude toward the Sino-Soviet split and the emergence of "polycentrism" in the communist camp?

It has generally been thought that the disintegration of Stalin's iron control over all Communist parties (whether in or out of power) has been a great advantage to the West. Prior to the mid-1950's, the unity of the Soviet bloc posed a grave threat to the United States and Europe, for it could be assumed that any communist gains would directly benefit the Soviet Union. Since the West had been faced with an enemy that seemed to manipulate loyal followers throughout the world, assertions of national independence that undermined the monolithic character of world communism could only be welcomed as a weakening of Russian power.

No doubt the reduction of Moscow's ability to dictate policies to its allies has been advantageous to the West in some ways. But increased nationalism within the various allies and satellites of the USSR, not to mention the Sino-Soviet split, are not totally inconsistent with Marxist-Leninist ideology; on the contrary, the rise of polycentrism may be a means of overcoming or moderating contradictions of interest without abandoning what is essentially a nineteenth-century ideology. Diffusion of power and the weakening of bipolarity increase the flexibility open to statesmen on both sides of the iron curtain, thereby creating new opportunities for communists as well as for Westerners.

The extent to which Stalinist unity in the communist world occasionally worked to our advantage can best be judged by reference to Russian policy in China prior to 1949. In the 1920's, Stalin concluded that China was not ripe for a communist revolution; he therefore decreed a policy of collaboration with the "bourgeois nationalists" and advised the Chinese Communists to ally with Chiang Kai-shek, who received aid from Moscow in building up the Kuomintang.

Although Stalin's strategy could be defended in Marxist terms and was doubtless in the interest of the Soviet Union, it was disastrous for the Chinese Communists; in 1927, Chiang Kai-shek turned against his Communist partners within the Kuomintang and virtually obliterated them in a bloody purge. Stalin nevertheless repeated his advice that the Chinese Communists ally with Chiang Kai-shek in the mid 1930's; again the nationalists came close to annihilating Mao's forces completely. Astonishingly enough, Stalin proposed exactly the same strategy in the years following World War II, but this time Mao ignored the directives from Moscow and successfully led a communist revolution in China.

The history of Stalin's failures in China is instructive, for it explains to some extent the origins of the Sino-Soviet split. It also indicates that Soviet control over the world communist movement created grave problems for many communist leaders and parties.Stalin's interpretation of Marxist-Leninist ideology was usually consistent with his conception of Russia's interests and power, but tactics that reflected Soviet needs often involved severe losses from the point of view of communists in another country; chances for world revolution were therefore sacrificed in the name of "socialism in one country"—i.e., the USSR.

When Tito and Mao demonstrated that a communist regime could be independent of Moscow, local Communist parties began to adopt a line that primarily reflected the conditions in their own societies. As different national roads to communism became legitimate, party leaders could seek support in one or another major center of communist influence; for example, when Gomulka came to power in Poland in 1956, he at first gained ideological justification from the Chinese as a means of increasing his independence from the Russians. As a result of Mao's subsequent attempt to oust Moscow as the leader of revolutionary world communism, other Communist parties no longer needed to follow blindly policies established by the Russians.

The Sino-Soviet split must be viewed in this perspective,

for Mao's challenge to Khrushchev and his successors has been framed primarily in ideological terms. Given the all-inclusive character of communist ideology, the Chinese offer an alternative to Russian positions not only in dealing with the capitalist world but also concerning internal policies and relations within the communist bloc. Moscow has had to tolerate increasing independence on the part of its European satellites, especially with respect to economic planning, and to bid for the allegiance of communist leaders who might be attracted to a Chinese position.

In domestic affairs, a communist state is therefore more likely to adopt effective policies or to gain desired assistance from the Soviet Union than was the case under Stalin. In foreign policy, those who find an aggressive line in their interests can threaten to support the Chinese view if the Russians do not back them sufficiently. Whereas the Stalinist era was characterized by the impact of Russian national interests on world-wide communism, polycentrism has permitted communist ideology to adapt itself to the specific national interests of many states.

This increasing element of nationalism in communist policies places serious limits on the extent to which the United States can "contain" communism by placing pressure on the Soviet Union. Although it is often suggested that the war in Vietnam can be ended by inducing Moscow to restrain China or North Vietnam,[8] such hopes are based on a misconception of polycentrism and Marxist-Leninist ideology. If we succeed in convincing the Russians of the need for accommodation, we merely tempt a state like North Vietnam to turn to Peking, thereby destroying any ideological leverage that the Soviets might exercise. To avoid this, Moscow is forced to support the North Vietnamese all the more vigorously, both to retain its leadership within the communist camp and to limit the power of China.

Whatever the common interest in avoiding an all-out war

[8] For a representative statement of this view, see Eugene V. Rostow: "Vietnam in the Perspective of the Cold War," *Life,* July 2, 1965.

between the United States and Soviet Russia, direct pressure on Moscow cannot be used as the major way of checking all revolutionary communist movements. If other means of limiting communist advances seem to be failing, the very reasons that tempt American policy-makers to turn to Moscow will lead the Russians to reject our offers. To gain the tacit assistance of the Soviet Union on the side of moderation, we must clearly show that we can establish a tolerable balance of power that restrains aggressive communists; thus we can strengthen the hand of those in the Kremlin who argue that Marxist-Leninist ideology requires a careful avoidance of "adventurist" risks when facing superior capitalist power.

The decline of Soviet hegemony in the communist bloc is important primarily because it represents the capture of Marxist ideology by the national interests of different states. According to Marx himself, this was impossible because the economic factors that determine the inevitable success of communism are international in scope; since Marx viewed the state as an instrument of the bourgeoisie in its repression of the workers, the overthrow of the capitalist order was to produce a world of classless societies with essentially harmonious interests.

The international character of communism was therefore based on the premise that modern economic life would render divergences of national interest an anomaly after communists came to power. The irony of history has been that communism gains much of its appeal from an alliance with nationalist forces, be they opposed to "colonialism" or merely devoted to rapid economic development in peasant economies. As a result, the projected withering away of the state, the ultimate paradise of Marxist theory, has been indefinitely postponed by the use of Marxist ideology as a tool for regimes whose interests conflict with one another.

As long as communist governments do not threaten American or Western interests directly, the mere existence of Marxist or pseudo-Marxist leaderships in backward countries need not be a reason for panic in the United States. Given the probability that polycentrism will continue to develop, the task for American policy is not to contain worldwide communism, but to check any state—communist or not—that threatens the global balance of power.

The essential point is that the legitimacy of a specific communist regime should not be an issue; instead, our intention must be to exercise our limited but real potential to restrain or moderate foreign policies that create the risk of global catastrophe. With the exception of the regime in Peking (whose existence as a state we have denied in the past), this has been the general orientation of recent American policy toward the communist bloc. But since "peaceful coexistence" with communists has been an underlying issue in the United States (as is revealed by congressional and public opposition to increased trade across the iron curtain), China is regarded by many as a symbol of an ideological enemy with whom any accommodation is tantamount to appeasement if not treason.

Now that there is widespread discussion of our policy toward Peking, the implications of accepting communist powers as legitimate participants in the global balance of power need to be spelled out more clearly. Although it is generally recognized that Peking's pretensions to ideological leadership reflect the characteristic stance of left-wing Marxists, a closer look at this commonplace reveals the self-defeating aspect of trying to isolate Peking through a policy of nonrecognition. Actually, nonrecognition and isolation are preferred by the Chinese, just as a self-righteous refusal to enter parliamentary politics was preferred by the radical wing of the German Social Democratic party in the 1890's. Indeed, Mao's strategy can be described as an attempt to create an image of China as "encircled" by a ring of hostile states that includes the USSR.

The dialectical explanation of this apparently "unreasonable" desire to remain isolated can best be seen by comparing the Maoist view of a tacit Russo-American coalition against

China with Stalin's doctrine of "socialism in one country."
A communist elite that claims to maintain revolutionary
orthodoxy after coming to power is faced with the difficulty
that Marxism is, par excellence, the ideology of opposition
to an existing government; when governing a society, a
Marxist must make compromises with unavoidable political
necessities (thereby running the risk of deviating from doc-
trinal purity).

Stalin was faced with this problem when the Soviet revolution did not trigger the world-wide proletarian uprising predicted by Marx. The Russian Communists were therefore
torn by a dilemma: Should they devote their limited resources to hastening a revolution in the West (which would
have been consistent with Marx's teaching but highly dangerous to their own positions of power), or should they isolate
themselves in order to strengthen their own power base?
Stalin justified the latter course, over the objections of Trotsky, by speaking of the need to build "socialism in one country"; by depicting the Soviet Union as an isolated bastion of
Marxism, surrounded by a hostile capitalist world, Stalin was
able to industrialize Russia and make it a world power
without seeming to abandon Marxist ideology in favor of
national self-interest.

The Chinese reaction has been essentially identical. From
this perspective, Peking's rabid anti-Americanism and un-
remitting attacks on Soviet revisionism have the strategic
function of producing a kind of artificial "socialism in one
country." Given the formidable obstacles to industrialization
in China, a continued period of neo-Stalinism, complete with
a recurrence of something like the great Russian purges of
the 1930's, is entirely possible even after the death of Mao;
the recent "cultural revolution" may well be the first stage of
a lengthy process. If we wish to moderate Chinese foreign policies, therefore, it is necessary to begin from the awareness that
a sense of isolation in a hostile world may characterize Peking's
leadership for some time to come.

American refusal to recognize China is therefore unwise

just because this is what Peking prefers. But it is also true that the image of containment has essentially the same practical effects, for such an American policy implies that we do not admit the legitimacy of Chinese pretensions to world-power status. If our hostility is actively sought as the basic justification for a revolutionary Maoist strategy, both isolation and containment suffer the same disadvantage: such policies merely strengthen an ideological position we find most dangerous.

In contrast, a balance-of-power approach counsels a dual policy that will strike many as contradictory: recognition and fundamental acceptance of Peking's legitimacy (thereby depriving China of an easy target of hostility—or at least forcing it to increase its revolutionary strategy to the point of manifest risk to Chinese security), and privately communicated but clear indications that certain forms of Chinese aggression will encounter immediate and massive resistance (by nuclear attack if need be). In short, a policy of general accommodation makes sense, but only if it is clear that beyond a certain point we will retaliate directly, even at the risk of global war.

In this context, it is particularly important to understand Peking's repeated assertions that the United States, despite its nuclear arsenal, is only a "paper tiger." Mao does not mean that the United States lacks military power, but only that in the long run we lack the will to use it effectively to prevent communist advances. Since the United States is deterred from all-out war by Russian nuclear missiles, the Chinese argue that they can defeat the West step by step in a series of localized conflicts that we do not understand and cannot win.

As Mao once put it, in explaining the image of a "paper tiger":

In order to struggle against the enemy, we have formed the concept over a long period, namely, that strategically we should slight all enemies, and tactically we should take full account of them. That is also to say, we might slight the enemy as a whole but take full account of him so far as each and every concrete question is concerned. If we do not slight the enemy as a whole, we shall be committing the mistake of opportunism. . . . But on concrete questions and on questions concerning each and every particular enemy, if we do not take full account of the enemy, we shall be committing the mistake of adverturism. In war, battles can only be fought one by one and the enemy can only be annihilated bit by bit.[9]

Mao "slights" the United States "as a whole" because he is convinced that we will use our superior power as ineffectively as did Chiang Kai-shek, but he insists that communists must "take full account" of our strength in "each and every concrete situation."

Only by checking or avoiding those challenges in which the West can be "annihilated bit by bit" can we show that we are capable of using our power. For this purpose, one necessary American tactic will be a distinction between regional challenges and the global balance of power. Given mutual deterrence between the two superpowers, it is exceedingly risky to treat all communist aggression in identical terms, ignoring the specific impact of defeat in any given state. Our threat to unleash a nuclear war must be credible, and can hardly be believed as a response to minor provocations.[1]

American policy can best respond to communist ideology by quietly but firmly emphasizing the dissent and divergence implicit in the various desires and interests of communist re-

[9] Mao Tse-tung: *Imperialism and All Reactionaries are Paper Tigers* (Peking: Foreign Languages Press; 1958), p. 27; cited in Zagoria: *The Sino-Soviet Conflict*, p. 161.

[1] "By defining an issue in all-or-nothing terms, we tend to make sure that we get nothing unless we are prepared to exert the force required to get all. Having declared that the choice is between communism and freedom, little victories look like compromises with communism. . . . Instead of identifying every issue as a part of a Cold War to be dealt with as a single major conflict, it would seem wiser to insist that each issue, whether or not it reflects basic and fundamental differences, be dealt with independently on its merits." Roger Fisher: "Fractionating Conflict," *Daedalus* (Summer 1964), pp. 938, 940.

gimes throughout the world. Just as Mao proposed a tactic of facing threats "one by one," we must do the same, "slighting" the enemy in global or long-run terms; as long as the West remains economically and militarily strong, we need not fear communist take-over at home and can prevent those enemy advances that truly threaten us. Just as Mao justifies "one step backward" on the expectation that he will subsequently take "two steps forward," we must be aware that tactical retreats need not be disasters.

Communist gains in internally unstable and backward countries may be an uncertain blessing for Moscow or Peking. In Indonesia, overconfidence or haste led to a premature coup that greatly weakened the Indonesian Communist party; in this case, as in Guinea and some other Asian or African states, it was the West that made two steps forward after taking one backward. The Soviets and Chinese may even discover that commitments to communist governments in weak countries are more expensive than they are worth. There are, for example, indications that the cost of supporting Castro has discouraged the Kremlin from attempting to acquire new satellites in South America at the present time.

It follows that the most effective means of manipulating polycentrism to our own advantage lies in minimizing the explicitly anti-communist orientation of our foreign policy. By playing directly and primarily on the national interests of each communist state, we may reach those accommodations that lessen the dangers of major war without thereby encouraging the radical or Maoist interpretation of communist ideology. Avoiding both a self-righteous identification of American traditions with ultimate truth and a flight from all conceivable risks, the United States should base its actions on a realistic and flexible view of the distribution of power in world politics. In particular, we must be very clear about the limits of any possible *détente* with the Soviet Union. A relaxation of cold-war tensions cannot be an end in itself, for signs of an accommodation between Russia and the United States often produce increased conflict elsewhere in the world.

For example, in 1964 there were riots in Panama directed

against the American presence in the Panama Canal Zone; fomented in part by leftists (and perhaps communists), this tension was used by a right-wing president to increase his domestic electoral appeal at the expense of the United States. In a time of maximum cold-war hostility, this tactic would have seemed less attractive to a right-wing Panamanian politician; during the Kennedy-Khrushchev *détente,* the reduced danger of East-West war gave a minor ally more room for maneuver. As is shown by French and Chinese assertions of independence following the hot-line and test-ban agreements, the results of Russo-American accommodation may therefore be unpleasant for both the United States and the Soviet Union.

Because bipolarity is declining somewhat in importance, American policy over the next decades must manage rivalry and avoid all-out war under the most complex circumstances. Sweeping denunciations of communism or equally sweeping demands for peace at any price are therefore highly dangerous, for they create popular expectations within the United States that cannot be satisfied. In order that the public develop greater tolerance of apparently unsatisfactory compromises with communists or an apparent unwillingness to use our nuclear stockpile, our political leaders must discuss foreign-policy alternatives with a dispassionate objectivity that has often been absent in the past. This may seem an impossible requirement, but there are signs that politicians in a democracy can make the calm assessments of international power demanded at the present time.[2]

It should be added that the interests of American business may reinforce the trend away from an ideological approach to communist states. Because Eastern European satellites seek Western markets and manufactured goods (in part as a means of increasing their autonomy from Moscow), the possibilities for trade across the iron curtain have become more attractive. Attempts to limit trade with the communists,

[2] See, for example, Senator Frank Church: "How Many Dominican Republics and Vietnams Can We Take On," *The New York Times Magazine,* November 28, 1965, pp. 44-5, 177-88.

while supported by many in Congress, seem self-defeating **to** businessmen who realize that such a policy merely abandons profitable markets to our less scrupulous allies. Since West Germany is willing to provide Peking with a steel mill **and** Canada trades with Cuba, rigid anticommunism implies a criticism of our NATO allies that must seem unprofitable and unwise to Americans seeking global markets.

Crystallized by dissent over Vietnam, moreover, many intellectuals have become increasingly critical of the legacy of the cold war. Although bitterness over our inability to gain "victory" over revolutionary movements infiltrated or led by communists may inhibit popular realization of the new phase of world politics, domestic debates over foreign policy could also produce a willingness to approach the communist bloc in terms of the balance of power. It would be indeed pessimistic to assume that the American people are incapable of understanding the dangers of making anticommunism the sole goal of United States foreign policy.

Although the threat of communism is often equated with Chinese expansionism (to be analyzed in the next chapter), relations between the United States and the communist states of Eastern Europe pose a major problem for American policy. This area is decisive not merely because of the number of communist regimes it contains, but above all because it is along the iron curtain—and especially in Germany—that the two superpowers face each other most directly. The division of Germany and the proper Western attitude to the East European satellites must therefore be treated jointly, for both arise out of the power situation created at the end of World War II.

American statesmen have repeatedly asserted their desire for German reunification on the basis of free elections, but it is no secret that our public statements have been less than completely candid. It is generally assumed in the West that free all-German elections would result in a defeat for the East

German Communists; on this basis, the American view is tantamount to a demand that the Russians withdraw from a reunited Germany that is explicitly or tacitly aligned with the West.

Communist regimes in Eastern Europe, who fear the reunification of a Germany that unleashed major war twice in this century, would feel threatened by such a solution. In fact, many European and American observers are content with the present division of Germany; despite the precarious situation of West Berlin, the existence of two German states, each tied to a hostile superpower, seems preferable to a united Germany that could threaten the European balance of power. While this view is understandable and especially widespread in both Eastern and Western Europe, the continued existence of the iron curtain creates a perpetual danger of war arising either from a confrontation between the superpowers or from the discontent of the Germans themselves.

Since West Berlin is in the position of a Western hostage in communist hands, the Russians can move to isolate and take over that city in response to American attacks against a communist state elsewhere in the world. As our passive attitude during the construction of the Wall indicated, Western planners have only limited means of countering Soviet probing actions aimed at Berlin; although we can threaten to use our NATO land forces in a conventional war, the risks of escalation are high (especially because these troops have been armed with tactical nuclear weapons).

Although most Western Europeans have come to doubt the possibility of an all-out Soviet attack in Europe, the current sense of security hides unspoken risks of carefully circumscribed, aggressive moves that could easily erupt into major war. These dangers help explain why some Europeans want to acquire independent nuclear capabilities and to dissociate themselves from American policies in Asia and Latin America. They also indicate that the status quo in Europe may not be in the long-range advantage of the United States, if only because it provides the Soviet Union with a relatively vulnerable target. True, Moscow did not move on Berlin during the Cuban missile crisis (as some of President Kennedy's advisers feared), but we have no assurance that such a response will not occur at some future time.

The second long-range danger created by the present division of Europe is the possibility of German dissatisfaction with the status quo. Demands in Bonn for some form of ownership or control of nuclear weapons are considered threatening not only by the Soviet Union, but by Poland (whose borders now include areas claimed by West Germany) and other Eastern European states. Fear that the West Germans would use force to secure unification thus binds the satellites to Moscow, at least for defensive purposes, thereby limiting the extent to which the communist bloc is weakened by polycentrism. It follows that the continued existence of the iron curtain in Europe may serve to strengthen the Soviet Union unnecessarily.

While granting these risks, some will object that there is little that can be done to alter the balance of power in Europe. As our actions during the Hungarian uprising of 1956 made clear, the United States is unwilling to move aggressively in order to detach an Eastern European state from the Soviet bloc even when an anti-Soviet revolt takes place. Since neither superpower can tolerate gains for the other in Europe, the situation seems to be frozen for the indefinite future.

One alternative that is sometimes mentioned is a "disengagement" of Soviet and American forces in central Europe. First proposed by the Polish foreign minister Rapacki, and subsequently suggested by George Kennan among others, this policy calls for parallel troop withdrawals along the iron curtain by both superpowers; some form of "denuclearizing" Germany and central Europe is also usually included in the concept of disengagement.

American leaders correctly rejected such plans on the grounds that disengagement would result in a withdrawal of our troops across the Atlantic, whereas the Russians would merely be withdrawing across a border; as long as the presence of American forces in Germany has seemed necessary to deter the USSR—and this need still exists—any plan for disengagement seems both dangerous and futile. Given the emergence of an autonomous French nuclear capability, however, the strategic balance on the European continent is changing. If the European policy proposed in Chapter v were to be adopted, perhaps the dangers created by the iron curtain could be somewhat mitigated. This possibility deserves more attention.

As an example of the kind of long-range planning required, let us assume that, at some point in the next decade, there emerges in Western Europe a political confederation including both France and Great Britain. Without the existence of a single, supranational government, this confederation would be defended by a more or less integrated military command including British and French nuclear forces (which could also be used independently, much as now is the case within NATO).

It should also be assumed that this Western European confederation would still be allied with the United States, although not necessarily within a tightly integrated NATO. Some American troops would thus still be in Germany, unless the Europeans themselves asked us to withdraw them—an unlikely eventuality since the French and British nuclear and conventional forces will presumably be strategically inferior to those of the Soviet Union.

At that time, the division of Europe might be modified without thereby altering, at least in a decisive way, the power of either the United States or the Soviet Union. Eastern European communists, seeking increased national independence and access to the Common Market area, would probably desire some forms of contact with the Western European confederation; the latter would probably seek closer ties with the Eastern Europeans. Indeed, both trends are already in evidence.

A solution to the divison of Europe might then have two aspects. First, a kind of associate membership in the West

European confederation could be opened to East European states on the principle that domestic regimes would remain untouched. The communist states in Eastern Europe would be tied to the West European confederation by a series of bilateral arrangements approximating treaties of alliance combined with selective economic advantages; a confederal Western Europe would act as one party, whose national members were more closely identified with each other than with any single Eastern European state.

One crucial question in this respect would be the status of East Germany. Although it could be treated like other communist states, such a policy would probably be unacceptable to Bonn, for it would make permanent the division of Germany. An alternative might be to establish loose intergovernmental relations between East and West Germany that paralleled the ties between other East European states and the West European confederation as a whole; in this way the principle of a united Germany could be maintained without threatening the communist regime in Pankow with immediate extinction.

The second element of this hypothetical solution would be a fundamental alteration of the role of the superpowers in Europe. Given the presumed increase in the ability of the West European confederation to defend itself, the presence of American troops in Germany could become negotiable in exchange for the withdrawal of Russian troops from the states of Eastern Europe and the formal abandonment of all vestiges of the Warsaw Pact and NATO. The United States and the Soviet Union could maintain alliances with whatever states in Europe they desired, but the independence of European powers would be recognized and the current division of the continent into those exclusively committed to one or the other superpower would end in its present form.

This proposed solution is, of course, highly speculative; one can imagine many events that could make its realization impossible. It remains true, however, that most alternative projects for increasing the stability of Europe are either highly dangerous (because they envisage an American disengagement without assurances of the security of Western Europe) or certain to fail (because they depend on the actions of one or the other superpower). The integration of Eastern and Western Europe is possible only by reducing the role of the superpowers on the continent, and such a goal is possible only if the European powers can defend themselves and resolve their internal problems.

In order to demonstrate the kind of analysis needed for American policy, it will be useful to consider whether the proposed approach to Eastern Europe is in the interests of all the powers concerned, and whether it would result in a reasonably stable balance of power. While these two criteria are not sufficient to insure that a policy will be adopted successfully, they are a minimum requirement that must be satisfied by any sober proposal.

The Soviet Union has little interest, all other things being equal, in an evolution of Eastern European states away from their present status. Fortunately, all things are not equal, or need not remain so as world politics evolves. If a Western European confederation is successfully achieved, it will pose a very grave risk to the USSR for two reasons: militarily it will represent a second pole of capitalist power, capable of acting independently in opposition to Soviet policies; politically it will strongly attract East Europeans who desire access to Western markets and increased independence from Russian control.

Moscow will therefore have every interest in reducing as far as possible the ties between the United States and a West European confederation. While Washington has no interest in abandoning all forms of alliance with Europe, the mutual withdrawal of the military forces of both superpowers (and the abandonment of the formal institutions of NATO and the Warsaw Pact) could be in our interest so long as it was evident that our European allies were capable of deterring any likely communist threats.

The United States has a further interest in abandoning the dreams of Atlantic union in favor of a European solution that would raise the iron curtain. Since our European allies seek assurance that their security is not endangered by escalation arising out of our global commitments, a tightly integrated NATO may unnecessarily reduce the West's freedom of maneuver. Given the vulnerability of West Berlin, an Atlanticist view of our relations with Europe provides the USSR with easy means of counterescalation should the United States deem it necessary to attack Cuba or any other communist state. Precisely because the balance of terror is relatively effective between the superpowers, we should avoid situations in which the USSR can retaliate on Western positions by conventional means short of all-out war.

In other words, the solution proposed here would permit the United States to create for the Soviet Union the same kind of dilemma that many American strategists have tried to avoid for ourselves—namely, the choice between thermonuclear war and a limited defeat. Because Marxist ideology justifies retreat in the face of superior power, it seems unlikely that the Russians or Chinese would risk destruction by initiating a nuclear war when they could easily withdraw. But if we are to be in a position to engage communists in localized wars that we can win, and if we seek to prevent Soviet escalation as a means of retaliation, it is necessary to disassociate our global commitments from those of the Europeans.

Within Europe itself, is the proposed means of reducing East-West tension viable? Many Western Europeans earnestly desire a reduced reliance on American defense, if coupled with the means of deterring Russian attack and measures that establish peaceful links with Eastern Europe. For the West Germans, this policy would be a way of eventually reuniting their country without resorting to war; in particular, Bonn would not have to choose between a reunified Germany which is impotent and neutralized and a continued association with Western Europe which is economically beneficial.

For the East German regime, this policy seems about the only means to achieve both a measure of unification without giving up power and a kind of recognition making possible more effective economic development. It would, moreover, permit the East Germans to reduce their dependence on the Soviet Union without the risk of immediate isolation; since the ties between East and West Germany would be paralleled by a series of bilateral agreements between the other East European states and the West European confederation, the principle of limited collaboration between communist and democratic regimes would become tolerable to the superpowers without being dangerous for the participants.

The foregoing policy is proposed with the utmost hesitation. In many respects, it seems purely utopian. Nonetheless it is suggested as an example of the kind of rethinking that is necessary if American policy is to emerge from a dangerously frozen stance. Such fundamental revisions are particularly important because communist advances are far more likely on other continents than in Western Europe. This does not mean that we should abandon our allies, but we must also consider the great risks of basing American policy on the image of a united Atlantic alliance as the sole method of dealing with the communist world. The rise of polycentrism implies that rigid bipolarity is or soon will be a thing of the past.

Basic revision in our attitude to communism, and particularly to the Soviet Union, is paramount because our European allies doubt the necessity of some American commitments, like that in Vietnam. Moreover, on such issues as trading with the Soviet bloc, there is more often rivalry within the Atlantic alliance than agreement on policy goals or the means of achieving them. Trade with communist states is perhaps a fitting issue with which to conclude this examination of the relationship of the United States to the communist world.

One characteristic of highly industrialized societies is that they increasingly trade with each other; in contrast to the

Leninist thesis that capitalism, in its highest stages, depends on commerce with underdeveloped or colonial economies (as a means of exploiting the backward and purchasing raw materials at low prices), such trade has actually played a decreasing role. As a consequence, communist nations, especially if economically advanced, are more and more desirous of trading with the developed nations of the West. Although the United States may be opposed to this trade, our allies need not agree; American refusals to trade with the communist bloc have often been effectively negated by our allies' willingness to gain new markets.

We must therefore reconsider the argument that our trade with communist states should be limited. The usual reasoning is that trade strengthens the enemy, so that our self-restraint will ultimately lead to the weakening or downfall of communist economies. There is little evidence, however, that this will happen, both because our allies are often willing to trade and because communist economic development is to some degree independent of foreign trade.

In fact, one could make exactly the opposite argument: leaving aside military goods that could be used directly for hostile purposes, exports of capital investment, manufactured goods, and raw materials (especially food, fertilizers, and feed for livestock) may be more in our national interest than trying to isolate the communists ever could be. Of these three forms of trade, the communists are least likely to seek capital investment from private sources in the West. Because the acceptance of capitalist forms of economic activity is ideologically suspect to Marxists, opportunities to extend private investment to communist states, particularly where an effort is being made to increase economic independence from the USSR, are highly desirable; no single act could have greater significance in undermining Marxist ideology than the construction of a steel mill in China by private firms from Western Europe.

Moreover, evidences of successful Western investment in the communist world would be beneficial because they would strengthen the economies of regimes that are otherwise forced to depend totally on their ties with other communist powers. It is this last point that is the most difficult for many Americans to believe, yet a persuasive case can be made for our encouragement of economic development in the communist bloc. The characteristic splits within Marxist ideology have always been created by the distinction between those who seek to maintain existing positions of strength and those with little or nothing to lose. Insofar as the United States can profit from the growth of polycentrism, our leverage is increased by the economic stability of communist states (which are thereby induced to consider factors of political and economic advantage with less ideological rigidity).

The same arguments can be made with respect to trade in manufactured goods and food. There is no reason to believe that starving or ill-clothed communists are easier to deal with than those who are well-fed and comfortable. Communist regimes can remain in power during periods of famine and economic dislocation more easily than democratic governments. Totalitarian controls can be justified in the name of ideology, centralized planning can be used to equalize as far as possible the sacrifices required, and Marxist principles can be used to unite the populace on the basis of aggressive policies. Economic isolation has never yet led to the collapse of a communist regime, though at various times both the Soviet Union and China have been faced with severe economic difficulties.

Whereas it seems improbable that communist states can be isolated into submission to the West, trade has on occasion led to a weakening of ties within the communist bloc. Overly much cannot be expected, of course; Tito has not become a Western democrat. But it is enough for American and European purposes if a communist state becomes sufficiently nationalist that it can proclaim its place among the "uncommitted nations." As Khrushchev's attempts to woo Tito back into the communist camp showed, such defections are indeed galling to the Soviet Union.

We cannot hope that communism will cease to exist in the next fifty years, and we should not attempt massive destruction of all enemy peoples. But the United States can and should realize that communism has passed out of the phase when it is necessarily a tightly unified, international movement directed solely from Moscow. As national interests come to dominate more and more the policies of each communist regime, the flexibility open to American policy-makers also increases.

From this perspective, the possibility that new communist regimes may come to power in backward lands, especially in Asia, should not terrify us. On the contrary, communist states infected with conflicting national interests may well check each other more effectively than the United States could do by direct action.[3] For example, in recent years the Sino-Soviet split has been one of the strongest restraints on Russian aggressiveness (forcing Moscow to recognize the interests it shares with Washington).

Only by focusing decisively on questions of the balance of power, therefore, can the United States come to grips with the ideological challenge posed by Marxist-Leninist principles. It will be exceedingly difficult for Americans to reverse the habits of thought that characterized our emergence as a world power; it will be exceedingly tragic if we are led either to world war or greatly reduced power because we were unable to make the intellectual effort required.

[3] "Even if additional Communist regimes were to arise in some parts of Asia, we need not be indefinitely paralyzed or driven into further and ever costlier military adventures. The nationalization of Communism—even within the restrictive perimeter of Russia's satellite empire—is by now too well established a fact for us to believe that Communism in Asia could somehow abolish or cancel out human experience." Harry J. Benda, "Reflections on Asian Communism," *The Yale Review*, LVI (Autumn, 1966), p. 16. tions on Asian Communism," *The Yale Review*, LVI (Autumn, 1966), p. 16. Benda's article is a brilliant analysis of the origins and causes of Marxism's attractiveness in backward societies.

CHAPTER SEVEN

Asia and the
Rising Power of China

IT HAS BEEN PROPOSED that the United States adopt a foreign-policy objective of establishing and maintaining a balance of power based on continental-scale superpowers. To see how such a goal would influence events in Asia, it is first necessary to consider Southeast Asia, the scene of the most important armed conflict between communist and American power in the 1960's. Yet so much has been written on the strategic and political situation in Vietnam that one almost hesitates to add to the debate.

Discussion is difficult because facts have often been distorted by military or political figures attempting to justify—or reverse—our policy. Moreover, circumstances can change rapidly, making a particular argument obsolete overnight. It will be useful, therefore, to focus on the general nature of the situation, considering the American commitment as coolly as possible.

If it is true, as has been argued, that the choice of long-range goals is of primary importance for American foreign policy, an examination of the controversial issues created by our intervention in Vietnam must begin with our aims. Let us assume that the problem must be analyzed in terms of rivalry for power, without primary reference to the ideological conflict between communism and democracy. What then is the objective of our commitment to support Saigon against the Vietcong and North Vietnamese?

According to one popular view, American intervention to prevent a communist take-over in South Vietnam is required by the "theory of the falling dominoes." It is widely argued that loss of South Vietnam would bring about communist control of all Southeast Asia, if not of Asia more broadly defined. By implication, this would lead to communist hegemony throughout the world. In a bipolar world, it is natural to believe that an American setback anywhere is tantamount to defeat, for when international politics is characterized by only two well-defined power blocs, all gains for one seem to represent losses for the other. It follows that the end of bipolarity (as marked by the Sino-Soviet split, among other things) undermines if not destroys the logic of falling dominoes.[1]

Some will object that the logic behind the American commitment in Vietnam was derived primarily from the lessons of history, and not from the characteristics of the bipolar world as such. In particular, the experience of the West when faced with Hitler's expansionism seems to indicate that "appeasement," symbolized by Munich, is futile.

[1] It is hard to know whether the popular belief in the disastrous consequences of a defeat in Vietnam has been reinforced by the use of the theory of two-person games by American military strategists. Since the most unambiguous games of this sort, from the theoretical point of view, are "zero-sum games" in which all losses of one are gains for the other (see pp. 56-7, notes 7-8), decision-makers may have been unintentionally influenced by that part of game theory that seems most immediately relevant to a bipolar world. In fairness, it should be added that some strategists have explicitly attacked the conclusion that might be drawn from such an approach. For example, Herman Kahn concludes that "there is no inevitable domino effect from Communist aggression." *On Escalation* (New York: Praeger; 1965), p. 103.

This objection deserves serious consideration, for throughout history aggressive powers have sought to expand, and in countless cases have been checked only by military action. Moreover, many statesmen have followed the maxim that it is wise to fight an inevitable war before the probable enemy has reached the height of his power. As Machiavelli put it: "The Romans, sensing trouble from afar, always found a remedy; and they never allowed it to develop in order to avoid going to war, because they knew that war cannot be avoided but only postponed to the advantage of others." (*The Prince*, Ch. iii).

In power politics, Machiavelli's maxim is not the only lesson presented by the history of international relations. Machiavelli himself elsewhere wrote: "When any evil arises within a republic or threatens it from without, . . . the more certain remedy by far is to temporize with it, rather than to attempt to extirpate it" (*Discourses on Titus Livy*, I, xxxiii). Which lesson of history, then, is most appropriate to the conflict in Southeast Asia?[2]

Hitler's expansion in Europe, like that of Napoleon, created a direct confrontation between the major powers on a single continent; under these conditions, an aggressor who absorbs minor powers must be immediately checked lest its ever-increasing appetite lead other states into total conflict. In other words, where major powers (such as France and England) are in close proximity to an expansionist or revolutionary state (like Nazi Germany), the hope of buying time by agreements is often illusory.

If it could be shown definitively that the situation in South Vietnam is identical to that in Europe in the 1930's, this historical precedent would be compelling as a policy guide. In fact, however, the differences between the confrontation

[2] Those interested in Machiavelli's own suggestion as to the appropriate policy would have to consider, among other passages in his works, Book II, Chapter xii, of the *Discourses* ("Whether it is better, when apprehending an attack, to await it at home, or to carry the war into the enemy's country"). While the adequacy of Machiavelli's theory can properly be questioned, it is not without interest that his conclusions would probably be equally unpopular with hawks and doves in the United States.

in Southeast Asia today and the problems posed by Hitler's demands for *Lebensraum* are as striking as the similarities. Southeast Asia is a marginal and highly unstable area, close to one major power and defended by a distant source of even greater strength. Moreover, the Chinese did not directly launch a war of conquest, but rather support a revolutionary move-ment in the weakest portion of the former French empire in Indochina.

If one seeks historical precedents, it is perhaps more realistic to consider the mid-nineteenth-century conflicts in the Balkans (particularly the Crimean War), which occurred as a conse-quence of the internal instability of the Ottoman Empire and the desires of czarist Russia to expand its influence. As in Vietnam, Turkey—itself highly unstable—was defended by dis-tant major powers (England and France) who were stronger than the aggressive local power trying to expand (Russia). And as in Vietnam, the Ottoman Empire was apparently incapable of political organization or military power enabling it to preserve itself without foreign assistance against Russian encroachment.

The similarities go further. In both cases, during the war "expectations of defeat proved as unfounded as earlier ex-pectations of success"; strategically speaking, all that seemed objectively possible was "military deadlock." The English commitment in the Crimean War, like the American one in Vietnam, suffered from a lack of clear, long-range policy ob-jectives; in both cases, "neutralization" through negotiation was posed as the basis of a settlement that would check an aggressive enemy. It should be added that when superior Anglo-French naval power led to military success in 1855, "the allies were as far as ever from knowing what to do with their victory"; the peace settlement of 1856, while apparently a defeat for Russia, was but the prelude to a series of extensive changes in the European balance of power (which had the ultimate result of radically reducing English power on the continent).[3]

[3] See A. J. P. Taylor: *The Struggle for Mastery in Europe, 1848-1918* (Oxford: Clarendon Press; 1954), esp. pp. 68, 77.

Of course, no historical parallel is fully identical to a present event (for example, Russia was ideologically conservative in the 1850's; China is revolutionary).[4] The analogy suggested has, nonetheless, two implications. First, just as a Russian victory over Turkey—or even a Russian occupation of the entire Ottoman Empire—could not by itself have undermined the strategic position of England and France (which rested on a solid military and political base distant from the scene of operations), so Chinese control of the Southeast Asian subcontinent would not necessarily involve hegemony over the United States or Western Europe in their own areas. In itself, this analogy suggests that the problem in Southeast Asia concerns relative gains of power, not an absolute question of life and death.

The second lesson suggested by the analogy between the Crimean War and the conflict in Vietnam concerns the long-range dangers of highly unstable areas near a major expansionist power. The Balkans remained a source of international friction long after the Crimean War and ultimately served as the point from which World War I erupted. As this analogy indicates, moreover, the immediate source of conflict in an unstable area need not be the state that ultimately poses the greatest threat to peace; although Russia was the enemy in the Crimean War, it was the Germans who, sixty years later, caused a world war by exploiting tensions in the Balkans.

A catastrophic war was not prevented by establishing nominally independent states (such as Rumania), which supposedly served as buffers between major European powers. Since history shows that such a solution is insufficient if not based on a mutually recognized, stable balance of power and divison of influence, partisans of negotiation in Vietnam must explain how any proposed settlement can provide a lasting solution. Under intrinsically unstable conditions, a so-called "inde-

[4] Even this difference should not be overestimated. Both Russia in the 1850's and China in the 1960's had the status of a large but not fully developed state, trying to convert a massive population into increased international power; both adopted, with national peculiarities, an ideology characteristic of a more developed major power.

pendent" South Vietnam, based on a return to the Geneva agreements of 1954, does not provide assurance of peace in Asia.

Historical analogy is therefore hardly comforting. Whether we gain a military victory in Vietnam (as did the Anglo-French in the Crimea) or achieve essentially the same results by negotiation, the long-range prospects for peace seem dim. It is insufficient to argue, as Secretary of State Rusk has done, that stability will be assured once the "aggressors" have been "taught" that violence does not pay; statesmen have not drawn this lesson from military defeat in the past. The peace can be maintained only if the power configuration is such that wars seem unpromising before they start. Since international stability depends on the self-interest of potentially hostile states, who must find moderation desirable because other means of increasing power are too risky or too unprofitable, it is unwise to hope that hostile nations will one day become peaceful and danger will disappear.

Two questions must be answered in the affirmative if our commitment in Vietnam is to be successful. First, can an anticommunist, pro-American regime in South Vietnam be defended and maintained under present conditions? And second, even if the Vietcong have been defeated or a peace negotiated, will the result be a stable and lasting balance of power in Asia? Both questions must be considered dispassionately, without assuming that America's military and economic power enable us to impose our will at any point in the globe.

Despite the escalation of the war, the first question depends primarily on conditions within South Vietnam itself. Whatever the origins of the communist insurgency—and it is hard to believe that it can be described entirely as an act of aggression by one sovereign state upon another—the Vietcong gained control over the largest part of the land territory of South Vietnam. Ground communications between major South Vietnamese cities have often been either completely broken or conducted only with the tacit permission of the Vietcong itself; movements of American or South Vietnamese personnel or goods have frequently been permitted by the communists only in return for "tax" payments. Insecurity within the South is marked by the ability of the Vietcong to harass governmental forces within a few miles of Saigon.

Since political factors are ultimately decisive in guerrilla warfare, military power is not enough to gain and keep control over the countryside; it is even more important to obtain the allegiance of the peasantry. To this end, "pacification" campaigns of reconstruction and indoctrination as well as thoroughgoing political reforms must complement strictly military action against Vietcong troop units. Despite programs announced with high hopes, there are many obstacles to total victory in South Vietnam—some military, some political, some economic.[5]

Militarily, it is not at all certain that even radically increased American commitments on the ground in South Vietnam could lead to victory in the guerrilla war. This is not simply a question of the will to win, nor of the ability of superior firepower to achieve decisive military gains in direct combat. The experience of guerrilla warfare, from the battles of Lexington and Concord to the French struggle in Algeria,

[5] The most useful summary of the strategic situation we face in Vietnam is General André Beaufre's analysis of the general problem of "indirect aggression"; see his *Introduction to Strategy* (New York: Praeger; 1965), Ch. iv. Because Beaufre is not involved in the American debate over Vietnam—and writes on the basis of a broad experience with similar conflicts elsewhere in the world—his conclusions are sobering: "It must always be remembered that in this type of warfare it is an exception for the defense to be successful; . . . this has only happened when there were no bases outside but adjacent to the theatre of operations from which the guerrillas could be supplied. An attempt to respond to an indirect strategy [i.e., guerrilla warfare] by direct defense is as foolish as the bull charging the red cloak rather than the toreador. It is the toreador, in other words the 'exterior maneuvre' [i.e., global political, psychological, military strategy as it indirectly influences the scene of hostilities], which must be our target" (p. 127). While some have argued that the successful defeat of Communist insurgents in Malaya is a model that can be followed in Vietnam, careful comparison of the two situations shows many crucial differences. See Robert O. Tilman: "The Non-lessons of the Malayan Emergency," *Asian Survey*, VI (August 1966), 407-19.

shows how difficult it is for a foreign power to intervene decisively and permanently when domestic rebels can gain security in the countryside among a potentially (or actively) hostile population. Although some observers have spoken of the possibility that the Vietcong might simply fade away, as did the Malayan insurgents, this is probably not the most relevant historical example.

The failure of the French, with an army of 500,000 men and a very short supply line, to eradicate the Algerian nationalists is particularly instructive with reference to the problem of assistance and infiltration from North Vietnam into the South. Because the North Vietnamese have sent major military units across the 17th parallel to counterbalance our increased troop commitments, it is widely believed that the war in the South can be won by convincing Hanoi to desist from "aggression." Should massive American forces defeat the organized combat units of the communists, the Vietcong could still resort to the kind of terror that forced de Gaulle to abandon the goal of an *Algérie française*. Even if we succeeded in sealing the borders of South Vietnam, as the French sealed the borders of Algeria (and in Vietnam this is almost out of the question), total victory may be impossible.

The disadvantage of the American combat position is not merely military. On the contrary, our military actions have political consequences which may in turn make a military victory unlikely. American military tactics, relying on superior firepower (including napalm raids and large-scale bombing) inadvertently destroy civilian targets and thus make it more difficult to secure total support from the South Vietnamese population. The peasantry may show at least passive obedience toward the winning side, but if the military victories required are only made possible by the commitment of ever-increasing numbers of American troops, the government of Saigon may be preserved at the cost of appearing to be a puppet of the United States. For example, it is said that the Honolulu conference between President Johnson and Premier Ky, originally intended to show the strength of American support for

Saigon, triggered the Buddhist unrest that paralyzed the South Vietnamese war effort in the spring of 1966.

We would be blind to ignore the loss of prestige produced by the frequent *coups d'état,* palace intrigues, and personal rivalries that have often rendered South Vietnamese politics inexplicable and frustrating to American advisers. More important, the religious controversy between Catholics and Buddhists, constantly in the background of this governmental instability, makes the establishment of a truly democratic and stable government in South Vietnam questionable, at least in the near future. Since an elected government in Saigon seems unlikely to be effective, a repressive military regime may be the only political solution at present; yet the history of rivalries between Vietnamese generals makes even this remedy, however distasteful, of doubtful reliability.

We must also consider whether it is possible for the United States to contribute to or create a stable economy in South Vietnam. One of the consequences of the American commitment to check the Vietcong has been a complete dislocation of the South Vietnamese economy. Some of the major economic resources, and especially the large rubber plantations, have been extensively damaged if not completely destroyed. Even more important, the sudden injection of huge quantities of American money into the Vietnamese economy, while needed to finance military operations, has a destabilizing effect. In addition to undermining the value of domestic currency, our intervention has caused increased wealth in largely non-productive sectors of the South Vietnamese economy: speculators, those who work for the American mission, and those who serve it (be they hotel-keepers or prostitutes). These sectors do not invest their newly gained wealth in productive economic ventures: on the contrary, abnormal profits tend to support a high standard of living, to permit further financial speculation, or to be exported for safety.

The resultant dislocation of the Vietnamese economy, together with the persisting political problems that would remain if the Vietcong disappeared tomorrow, force us to admit that South Vietnam would probably not be a stable society even if our military efforts were completely victorious. There are numerous examples of regimes throughout the world which, despite considerable American economic aid, have not achieved a truly stable internal economic and political system; Greece, the Dominican Republic, and other South American countries come to mind (not to mention pre-Castro Cuba). Where such countries lie in a zone of great-power contest, our limited ability to buy stability with foreign aid deserves great attention; an intrinsically unstable nation can be a liability to the power dominating it, whether communist or democratic.

While circumstances within South Vietnam do not incline the observer to optimism, it need not be concluded that we face inevitable defeat; as long as the United States is willing to devote sufficient manpower and resources to the battle, the strategic situation seems rather one of a stalemate. One side or the other could conceivably be victorious, but it is also possible for the war to continue over a number of years. Since frustration with this prospect has led to demands within the United States that we "win or get out," it is in this context that we must consider the problem of escalation and the role of China in Southeast Asian politics generally.

The notion that escalation or an expansion of hostilities can produce a mutually acceptable negotiated settlement is by no means ridiculous. This strategy arose from the realization that an all-out exchange between Russian and American nuclear forces would be self-defeating for both superpowers; hence less destructive means of employing military force had to be discovered in order to convince one's enemy of a will to defend vital positions by all means. The awareness of this problem dates essentially from the 1950's, and most specifically from Henry Kissinger's *Nuclear Weapons and Foreign Policy* (1957), which convincingly demonstrated the necessity for limited warfare where the alternatives are unacceptable defeat or a mutually disastrous nuclear war between the United States and Russia.

As originally developed, however, escalation was a strategy for dealing with a more or less direct confrontation between nuclear superpowers. It was not presumed that escalation would necessarily operate in the same fashion should the West be challenged by guerrilla war or by a minor power allied with (or acting as the proxy of) a communist nuclear power. On the contrary, the fundamental logic of escalation is that the increasing threat of mutual destruction would lead Russia and the United States to negotiate a settlement explicitly or by tacit understanding. Just that happened in the Cuban missile crisis.

This model does not necessarily apply in Southeast Asia for a number of reasons. In Vietnam, we have dealt with revolutionary local forces aided principally by second- and third-level powers—that is, North Vietnam and Communist China—under circumstances in which China has tried to expose the lack of revolutionary fervor of the Soviet Union. Unlike the Cuban missile crisis, this has not been a direct Russo-American confrontation; even if the Russians so desired, it is not clear whether they could force the Vietcong to accept a negotiated settlement.

The Soviet Union is still bound by treaty commitments, which they must insist they will honor before the fact, to defend communist states—including China—in case of American attack. Consequently, the threat of an all-out nuclear war produced by escalation in Southeast Asia is most strongly felt by the Russians, who are naturally induced to greater caution than either the Chinese or the Vietnamese. Yet this is precisely the position in which the Chinese wish to place the Russians, for by making the Soviet Union appear less revolutionary, Peking can hope to increase its influence in Vietnam and weaken the Russian leadership in the communist world.

Since the Sino-Soviet split limits Moscow's freedom of maneuver, the Russians could openly seek negotiations only at the cost of an enormous loss of prestige in the communist world. Even if the Soviet Union is restrained from direct intervention in Vietnam by fears of a nuclear exchange with the

United States, the risks of escalation do not prevent military and technical assistance. In the early 1960's, President Kennedy tried to use this kind of indirect commitment in order to avoid the risk of sending American troops into a ground war that our Vietnamese allies were losing. Our decision to bomb North Vietnam therefore forced the Russians to increase their aid to Hanoi, just as the latter's increased assistance to the Vietcong forced President Johnson to commit American forces directly.

In other words, the process of escalation in Vietnam has worked somewhat differently than the escalation strategy originally proposed to deal with direct Russo-American confrontations. Rather than produce a desire for negotiation between the principal combatants, each superpower has had to increase its assistance to a local ally, thereby making a protracted conflict more likely. Because an "erosion strategy" has been successfully used in the past by Asian Communists, Hanoi and Peking may be willing to suffer considerable losses in the hopes that they can force the superpowers (albeit unwillingly) to underwrite a lengthy test of strength.

It follows that the Russians are unlikely to force their nominal allies to the negotiating table as the result of American bombing of North Vietnam; this strategy can only produce immediate results if the direct victims of escalation decide that further conflict is dangerous. Yet there are several reasons why escalation need not force the Vietnamese and Chinese to negotiate. The first is a purely psychological factor that has unfortunately been omitted from much American strategic thinking: the bombing of military or civilian targets in an enemy society does not necessarily make negotiations more likely. Remember the response of the English to Hitler's bombardments in the 1940's. Under foreign attack, any society instinctively unites and increases its opposition to the enemy. This was how Americans responded to Pearl Harbor, and it has been—predictably enough—the response of the North Vietnamese.[6]

[6] See especially Robert Ardrey: *The Territorial Imperative* (New York: Atheneum; 1966), Ch. vii, viii.

Second, in a curious way the escalation strategy, as it has been applied in Southeast Asia, may have been less effective than a threat of massive retaliation. Agrarian countries like North Vietnam or China do not fear aerial attack, whether with conventional or nuclear weapons, to the same degree as industrialized societies which offer more vulnerable targets; our restraint in bombing North Vietnam may therefore have been taken as a sign that we are unwilling to run the risks of all-out war. If so, the adoption of an escalation strategy will have merely convinced most of the North Vietnamese and Chinese that they can survive when under attack by admittedly superior American airpower. In contrast, a massive attack destroying all of the major urban centers of North Vietnam or China would demonstrate that Asian communist states can be seriously hurt by our firepower. When faced with a state lacking its own operational nuclear weapons, the threat of a massive destruction of cities might well have greater psychological effect than a policy of escalation in which military targets are selectively attacked, even if the latter policy ultimately resulted in escalation that destroyed cities and industrial targets.

Some argue, however, that escalation is needed to reduce the flow of supplies and men from North Vietnam into the South; in their view, the predominant factor is strictly military (rather than psychological or political). It is dangerous to grant primacy to such narrowly defined objectives as cutting supply lines, however, for when one technique fails it becomes logical to turn to another—regardless of the likely responses of one's rival. If bombing has failed to reduce the rate of enemy infiltration, new measures (like mining Hanoi harbor or cutting the Ho Chi Minh trail by a land invasion north of the 17th parallel) become attractive. Yet such measures could increase the commitment of Russia and China even should their immediate objectives be achieved.

Escalation was not originally conceived as an essentially military device for defeating the enemy's armed forces; unlike earlier strategies, the concept of a staged response was intended to persuade aggressors to negotiate (and therefore depends decisively on the psychological response to our use of force). But since the Vietcong, the North Vietnamese, and the Chinese do not view strategy in the same terms as the Pentagon or the Kremlin, their reaction to military defeats may be quite different from the Russian response to the threat of war over Berlin or Cuba.

If the strategy of escalation does not operate as expected in Southeast Asia, attacks on North Vietnam or China cannot be considered as a panacea for inducing these powers to restrain the Vietcong and negotiate a mutually acceptable settlement in South Vietnam. Should we be unable to achieve a decisive victory on the ground in South Vietnam, attacks on the North short of an all-out counter-city strike may only increase the stubbornness of communist resistance, and an all-out strike, especially with nuclear weapons, would pose grave risks of a third world war.

Since total military victory seems both difficult to achieve and unsatisfactory as a policy goal, many have proposed negotiations as a means of ending the war in Vietnam. President Johnson has repeatedly insisted that the objective of our escalation is a negotiated settlement, not conquest. Since the foregoing analysis could conceivably be proved incorrect by events, let us assume that American escalation forces the North Vietnamese and Vietcong to negotiate a settlement. What are the chances for successful negotiations, and will mutually acceptable compromise be stable over the long run?

In any negotiations, the communist *sine qua non* will doubtless be the removal of American troops from South Vietnam. Our negotiating position would therefore depend on our response to this demand, and most particularly on our willingness to see the Vietcong participate in a South Vietnamese government (be it directly or in the form of a reunified government controlling both the North and the South).

In a broad sense, the United States will have two options

at a peace conference: either we could accept the Vietcong as a legitimate political force within South Vietnam (as Senator Robert Kennedy has long proposed), or insist that American troops will not leave the country unless a stable government is established without communist participation. But since the latter solution will be unsatisfactory to the Vietcong as long as they believe they can win a protracted war, the second option will be open only if we have totally defeated the enemy. And even in this unlikely case, the Vietcong might rise from the ashes to resume guerrilla activity, much as the Chinese communist party twice survived virtual annihilation before coming to power.

Short of an immediate and decisive military victory that seems almost beyond hope, a true willingness to negotiate a settlement implies that the United States would accept a South Vietnamese government that included the Vietcong. It will be immediately objected that such a regime in Saigon, even if originally committed to a neutralist policy, would rapidly become communist as soon as American troops left the country. This fear is not totally irrational (though it does raise questions about the strength of our allies in South Vietnam), for it can hardly be expected that communists who now control the largest part of South Vietnamese territory would enter a nominally neutralist government in such a way as to lose, in peace, positions of strength they gained by violence.

The consequences of a communist regime in Saigon should not, however, be overstated. Despite the religious, ethnic, and political obstacles to unity, which would face the Vietcong just as they have faced other South Vietnamese governments, let us assume that the communists were to gain control over the entire populace. Would the resulting regime necessarily become a satellite of Peking (or even, assuming that North and South Vietnam remained separate states, a satellite of Hanoi)? A nominally independent South Vietnam, without the support of American troops, would probably be forced to seek an accommodation with China—as have Burma and

Cambodia, not to mention Pakistan. But this need not mean that the South Vietnamese, even if governed solely by the Vietcong, would be mere tools of Peking.

Vietnamese nationalism and the tradition of opposition to the Chinese might be counted upon to limit the ability of any single foreign power to control Saigon completely; even the United States, despite the presence of a large army, has not always been able to dictate to the South Vietnamese (and indeed has often been manipulated by the government of the moment). These constraints on Chinese influence would be multiplied by the increased Soviet interest in counterbalancing Peking throughout Asia; just as both North Korea and North Vietnam are now wooed by both Peking and Moscow, a communist South Vietnam would be able to play the two major communist powers against each other to its own advantage. A stable Titoist regime in Saigon might well be a greater limit on Chinese aggressiveness than an impotent anti-communist government.

We need not, however, assume that the Vietcong would emerge as the sole political force in South Vietnam; short of a military disaster that virtually annihilated all pro-American forces, it is more likely that negotiations would produce a supposedly neutralist coalition in Saigon (including the Vietcong but not totally controlled by it). Under these circumstances, we should not ignore our own ability to manipulate the situation and dissuade the Chinese from attempting to turn South Vietnam into a satellite. As long as Peking does not totally dominate all of Southeast Asia, we would have bases from which a guerrilla action in reverse could be mounted whenever the Vietcong tried to take a strongly pro-Chinese line. And since Vietnamese nationalism (not to mention religious particularism) will persist regardless of other international factors, we have the means—provided we have the will—to limit the effective control that China could exercise in South Vietnam.

In other words, a neutralist or even Titoist South Vietnam would be, over the next decade, a tolerable solution for the

United States provided that it could be achieved without the appearance of a major American defeat. Granted that unilateral withdrawal of American forces could be highly dangerous, if only as a sign of our failure to defend those to whom we had become committed, a negotiated settlement need not be a disaster. But the corollary is that a negotiated settlement would also not be a "solution": on the contrary, it would be a means of continuing the political rivalry in Southeast Asia by less violent, and hence less dangerous, means than a large-scale ground war.

Although Laos has often appeared to be an example of a "failure" to eradicate communism and establish a stable, free government, such a confusing and shifting political situation may well be the most satisfactory outcome that we can seek in the short run. This means that an agreement in South Vietnam should not be viewed as a policy goal, but rather merely as a step in a persisting process of power politics. We might agree to withdraw our troops, only to find ourselves supporting a guerrilla movement directed against Saigon; certainly the threat of such a tactic might be as useful as American bases in a country we cannot control. A coalition government in Saigon that included the Vietcong could be in our interests not because it permitted the United States to forget about Southeast Asia but because it might give us greater room for maneuver.

We are led to conclude that neither total military victory in South Vietnam nor a negotiated settlement will be easy to achieve or sufficient as a policy goal. We must then consider the real problem in Southeast Asia, namely, our policy toward China. It is clearly Chinese power and intransigence that are the major threat to the United States, and unless this threat is adequately countered, even victory in South Vietnam will not bring peace and stability to the area (especially since the communists could violate any agreement forced upon them). Without this regional focus, American policy in Vietnam will be impotent.

As the fifth nuclear power in the world, China is committed to a program of nuclear-weapons development that has proceeded somewhat more rapidly than many Western experts predicted (China's first nuclear device having been produced with enriched uranium instead of plutonium). There is nothing to indicate that the Chinese lack either the theoretical knowledge—for China has first-rate physicists and mathematicians—or the industrial capacity to create an effective nuclear capability within the next ten to twenty years.

Sooner or later, the Chinese will be able to produce their own missiles, for the technological know-how needed to build such delivery systems is being diffused along with nuclear technology. Advances in weapons technology will probably permit the Chinese to avoid the expensive stage of developing intercontinental bombers in their quest for a nuclear force that can attack distant enemies. Unless subjected to a preventive war of annihilation, China will become a major nuclear power if not a full-fleged superpower.[7]

The present American attitude toward China consists in refusal to recognize communist control on the mainland and an attempt to isolate the Red Chinese. This approach, which was tried without success toward Russian communism, is intrinsically self-defeating, for we are faced with a revolutionary nation that finds the greatest freedom of maneuver in the isolation we pretend to impose on it. Non-recognition is not a long-range solution to our Asian policy because it encourages the belief that the communist regime in China is only temporary.

We need a conscious policy toward Peking, for attempts to bring Russian influence to bear on China are not likely to be effective and the Chinese will presumably limit their aggressiveness only when it is in their self-interest to do so. Sooner or later, we must either admit that the government in Peking is a legitimate participant in international politics

---

[7] See Lewis A. Frank: "Nuclear Weapons Development in China," *Bulletin of the Atomic Scientists,* XXII (January 1966), 12-15. China's successful test of a nuclear-tipped missile in October, 1966, indicated that the above predictions were overly conservative.

or wage a preventive nuclear war aimed at destroying China. Before considering other possible approaches, therefore, let us consider whether the United States should attempt to reduce China to helpless impotence as a means of preventing her emergence as a nuclear superpower in the coming century.

Most Americans recoil from preventive war, but it is an alternative that must be soberly considered. Whatever the moral arguments against killing 700 million people—and such arguments would have to be considered by any sane statesman —let us here indicate only the main political and military points relevant to this policy.

A preventive war would be strategically valid only if, under conditions of imminent danger, the United States could be assured of destroying the capacity of the enemy to become a great power, and if this could be achieved without subjecting the United States itself to a crippling nuclear attack. An attack that left the victim in a condition to rearm and gain revenge against us in ten to twenty years would be absurdly shortsighted (as we discovered after World War I); an adventure that brought about our own destruction would be simply stupid. Assuming—though it would be questioned by some— that the Chinese pose a sufficiently grave threat, to what extent do we meet these two criteria for justifying a preventive war?

It is apparently within our power, at least in 1967, to render the Chinese communists militarily and politically impotent by means of an extensive strike by bombers of Strategic Air Command, using large and "dirty" nuclear warheads. Later, this capacity will not be readily assured, because an attack using missiles alone, while well suited to pinpointing military targets and destroying cities, would not sufficiently damage the rural areas of China, in which approximately 90 per cent of the Chinese live.[8] Hence, if we are to launch an all-out preventive nuclear war, we would have to do so in the next few years to achieve the desired objectives.

What, then, would be the risks to the United States of a preventive war? Many observers discount the willingness of

[8] See the article by Ralph Lapp in *Life Magazine*, May 28, 1965, pp. 86-97.

the Soviet Union to engage in a thermonuclear exchange with the United States merely to defend the Chinese. Others suggest that Russian leaders would feel compelled to intervene in case of an American nuclear attack on China (regardless of the tension between Peking and Moscow). Since we can never predict the Russian response with certainty, we can only say that the likelihood of Soviet retaliation is increased by considerations of prestige and fears of American power.

To calculate more objectively the dangers involved, it is healthy to remember that the same doubts arise in Russian minds when they consider whether the United States would risk its own destruction to defend Western Europe. Given the parallel between the Sino-Soviet split and the French assertion of independence from the United States, can we presume that Russian reluctance to defend China is radically greater than our reluctance to defend Western Europe? To put it the other way around, if we could attack China and "get away with it," would not the Soviet Union be tempted to do the same in Germany (where our position in Berlin is militarily vulnerable)?

After an all-out nuclear attack on China, the Soviet Union would be faced with a choice between some sort of nuclear attack on the United States (be it an extensive strike or "limited strategic retaliation"), and some other response. In the first hypothesis, the consequences of a preventive war against China would be the devastation of part if not all of the American homeland—a price few would be willing to pay. In the second, the United States itself would be uninjured, but at the price of greatly exposing pro-Western positions, since the Russians might be tempted to "save face" by a move on Berlin (where they could retaliate with conventional weapons and hence at minimum risk to themselves) or by attacking Strategic Air Command bases in allied countries.

While the exact consequences of a preventive war are difficult to predict, it could easily boomerang. Since a war of annihilation against China might produce either a reverse in Europe or a direct Russo-American nuclear exchange, the costs of this policy are greater than its proponents admit. Yet the results of a preventive war, even if militarily successful, may not even be consistent with American interests. Aside from the opprobrium attached to genocide by world opinion (or the corrosive effects of such action on our own morality), we would still face other challenges to American power after the destruction of Communist China.

Although there would be a great risk of serious repercussions in Europe (perhaps including the rupture of the Atlantic alliance), the decisive point is that a power vacuum would thereby be created in Asia. The Soviet Union would probably try to secure any available remnants of Chinese productive capacity (e.g., Manchuria), and would in any event be led to play a larger role in Asian politics. The same logic now used against China would soon apply equally well against any state that moved to increase its power as a result of the obliteration of the Chinese. Can we embark on a policy of simply annihilating every country that poses a revolutionary danger? One of the greatest frustrations of the nuclear era is that much of our tremendous military power cannot be actually employed (not only against the USSR but against other hostile nations as well). However useful the threat of a nuclear attack may be as a deterrent, carrying one out is exceedingly dangerous.

Since preventive war seems to be an unpromising policy, the main alternative left the United States in Asia is some form of accommodation with Communist China. Despite the widespread opposition to such an approach, let us consider whether recognition of Communist China, her admission to the UN, and even treaty agreements with her can be justified as means of establishing a stable balance of power. Though this may seem absurd to many, such an American policy would in fact produce grave problems for Mao Tse-tung or his successors.

Take first the question of Chinese admission to the UN: should Peking be offered admission to the United Nations with the full power allotted China in the Charter, including a permanent seat in the Security Council? At present, Peking's exclusion fits perfectly the needs of Maoist policy, which seems to require isolation. Since it is likely that a majority of the members of the UN will vote to seat Peking sooner or later (and since the present distribution of power in the Security Council fails to serve the purposes for which it was intended), the United States should gain the advantage of taking the initiative.

By so doing, we would place the Chinese before the embarrassing alternative of accepting their status as a great power within the UN or formally rejecting membership in the UN. In the former case, Peking's claim to serve as the core of a "true" or more revolutionary international organization (like the now defunct Conference of the New Emerging Forces) would become impractical; by that very token, some of the radical implications of Chinese policy would be restrained. On the other hand, Chinese refusal to enter the UN would be a further blow to their prestige among Asian and African countries that believe the existing international organization is the primary means by which minor states can influence the nuclear superpowers. Because such a refusal would be treated by other nations as a declaration of hostilities toward the UN and its principles, China would isolate itself more effectively than we can do by refusing to recognize her formally or voting against her admission to the UN.

If the Chinese should persist in refusing to join the UN as one of the permanent members of the Security Council, a proposal to amend the Charter by giving India the seat currently allotted to China would reflect America's insistence on achieving a balance of forces in Asia. Indeed, such a proposal—even without any other changes in current American policy in Asia—might be a highly useful step, not only to show our determination to counterbalance Chinese hegemony in Asia but to escape from our totally unrealistic commitment to the nationalist Chinese as if they effectively controlled the mainland.

There are other reasons why a prompt American decision to

support admission of Peking to the UN is in our own interest. It seems only a matter of time before the General Assembly decides that the effective government of China is not led by Chiang Kai-shek; this fiction seems especially ridiculous at a time when the United States is preoccupied with the aggressive intentions of Peking. The argument that China should not be allowed to shoot her way into the UN is unconvincing to statesmen who believe that a regime must be formally recognized if the international community is to restrain it.

Unless the United States moves rapidly to propose that Peking's admission should coincide with the independence and autonomy of Taiwan (Formosa), the seating of Communist China will probably imply the expulsion of Taiwan from the UN. It is true that Chiang Kai-shek has opposed the so-called "two Chinas" policy as strongly as Mao, for both claim to be the sole, legitimate rulers of all China. But it is not in America's interest to underwrite the identity of Taiwan and mainland China for several reasons: first, it would effectively cost the West a vote in the UN if Peking was seated; second, it would establish the precedent that one segment of a divided nation may legitimately claim to represent the entire country (a dangerous principle if applied to other divided nations like Germany and Korea); finally, it would force Peking to choose between maintaining maximum, aggressive demands like Taiwan's expulsion from the UN (at the cost of alienating noncommitted states) and making concessions which reflect toleration of the status quo.

While we need not abandon the existing government on Taiwan, therefore, our entire Asian policy should not be mortgaged to a military regime devoted to the reconquest of mainland China (under circumstances in which American participation in an unwanted major war might be unavoidable).[9] When succession to the present leadership of Chiang Kai-shek

[9] For a variant of the "two Chinas" policy, in which Taiwan's autonomy —but not its sovereign independence—would be recognized, see John K. Fairbank: "Taiwan: Myth, Dream and Nightmare," *New Republic* (February 6, 1966), pp. 11-13.

becomes an issue, it may be absolutely necessary to isolate Taiwan from interference by mainland China. If we fail to do so, we run the risk that the Kuomintang will prefer an alliance with Peking to a loss of control to the Formosans— a shift that would result in an undesirable expansion of Chinese power to include an island whose industrial and agricultural output would best be denied to Peking.

If we do not desire a preventive war against China, any American policy in Asia must ultimately be based on the assumption that China will be a major nuclear power that must be brought into the play of international affairs explicitly and directly. Peking is aggressive, but so are many other states with whom we have diplomatic relations; the Chinese cannot be expected to keep any agreements against their own interests, but neither will any other power. Proposals for a treaty forbidding the diffusion of nuclear weapons illustrate the necessity of the fundamental choice between preventive war and a Sino-American accommodation; since any such treaty would be useless (if not dangerous) without Chinese participation, we must eventually recognize China explicitly if we admit the impropriety of obliterating her.

That the Chinese have been recognized or have signed a treaty does not mean that they will cease to be a threat to the peace, but they can be expected to seek their own interests with a modicum of hard-headed intelligence (as Peking has done to date). The entire problem, therefore, can be reduced to the question of whether we can confront China with situations in which it is to her own interest to keep agreements or refrain from aggression.

It is characteristic of American attitude toward foreign policy that we regard the keeping of international treaties as a purely moral question. In fact, this attitude does not even describe American behavior, since the United States has violated agreements (such as our treaties with American Indians) when this was clearly in our own interest. Any power that sees an immediate and compelling reason to ignore its treaty obligations will do so, for in the absence of a world government there is no way of punishing rulers who show "bad faith." The essential point is to achieve agreements based on mutual interest, be they informal understandings or written treaties, which no major power is tempted to violate. There is no reason to believe that this logic does not apply to the Chinese, for Peking has not more radically violated the Korean truce agreement than has the United States: both sides have ignored specific stipulations with reference to forces north and south of the 38th parallel, but neither has contested that dividing line.

The question then is whether some self-enforcing agreements, explicit or tacit, can be reached with Peking. One possibility is an agreement by all major powers not to give nuclear weapons to secondary powers who have not developed them themselves.[1] It is hard to conceive why it would be in the interests of the Chinese to provide such weapons to the North Koreans, the North Vietnamese, the Indonesians, or indeed to any other state whose use of nuclear arms might not be controlled by China; elsewhere in the world, states acquiring nuclear weapons (with the possible exception of Britain) have been thereby encouraged to take a more independent foreign-policy line, and the Chinese are certainly capable of applying this lesson to their own interests.

If an agreement against diffusion includes a prohibition on the development of new weapons (including nuclear tests and the building of missiles), it would not be in the interest of the Chinese (or the French) as long as they still lack a fully operational nuclear capacity. Only when a power is a full-fledged member of the nuclear club does it appear to see its own interest in limiting and stabilizing the nuclear arms race. In contrast, a minimal agreement prohibiting the gift or sale of warheads (and perhaps missiles) might soon be feasible.

The United States could easily demonstrate to Peking that

[1] See the general discussion of this possibility in Ch. iii (pp. 62-3).

it shares our interest in a treaty prohibiting diffusion by indicating in advance that without Chinese participation we would offer nuclear weapons to India. Questions of ideology would take a secondary role as soon as the Chinese realize that, as a nuclear power, they have a selfish interest in keeping potential Asian rivals from getting such weapons; when national survival is at stake, the Chinese will act according to the rules of power politics, just as the Russians have done.

A second kind of explicit treaty that has been officially proposed in recent months is an agreement not to initiate the use of nuclear weapons. At first glance, such a treaty seems even more promising than a prohibition on nuclear diffusion. The Chinese have declared that their strategy excludes the initial use of nuclear weapons; even assuming they develop intercontinental missiles within the next ten years, a nuclear attack by China seems less likely than is sometimes supposed.

Nuclear war is not well suited to further Chinese power in Southeast Asia: Vietnam seems hardly worth the risk as long as the Vietcong has a good chance to take power over the long run, Taiwan is effectively neutralized as a base for a possible attack on the mainland (and is ultimately worth more to the Chinese intact than in ruins), and most of the remaining states (Burma, Pakistan, Cambodia, North Vietnam) carefully avoid a hostile attitude to the Chinese. Thailand and India represent the most likely targets for Chinese war efforts, the former being unsuited as a target for nuclear war whereas the latter, if given nuclear weapons, may be the best source of restraint on Peking.

That China would probably observe an agreement not to initiate the use of nuclear weapons makes one wonder, however, whether a formal treaty is desirable on this point. As was suggested in the general analysis of such proposals, there is good reason to believe that tacit understandings not to initiate nuclear warfare are superior to explicit treaties (which may increase the danger of conventional war by undermining nuclear deterrence).[2]

[2] See Ch. iii, pp. 63-9.

It takes but little reflection to see that without a treaty, the restraints of nuclear deterrence will apply to China as well as to other atomic powers. Mao's profession of indifference at the threat of an American nuclear strike, like similar Russian statements in the early years of the cold war, is intended to deter our attack by denying its effectiveness. We need not succumb to such a psychological gambit, especially since Mao's reasoning assumes that the United States would have to attack China and Russia simultaneously (which need not be the case).

The risks of a crippling counterattack on China, however minimized at present by Chinese spokesmen, are much greater as retaliation for a nuclear strike than they would be in response to conventional or guerrilla war; if Peking initiated nuclear warfare, Moscow would probably dissociate itself from the Chinese. The current Chinese attitude toward nuclear war is, after all, based on the premise that Russia and the United States would be the major losers in any nuclear exchange—much to Peking's advantage. As the Chinese develop an operational nuclear capability, the Russians will find it easier to stand aloof from overly risky moves of their former ally; as a result, the Chinese will then have to consider the possibility of a Sino-American nuclear exchange to which neither Western Europe nor Russia would be a party. Such calculations can be counted upon to sober the Chinese, who have never been totally convinced that the Russians would defend them, and who in any event are not willing to sacrifice their own power for the sake of the Soviet Union.

The foregoing arguments may be contested on the ground that an expansionist power like China will not alter its goals even if it does not launch a nuclear war after acquiring nuclear weapons. Moreover, it can be argued that such limited moderation would not necessarily occur in the case of the Chinese because of their ideological commitment to world revolution. Although the evidence is that the Chinese have always been cautious when faced with risks of defeat, at this point it is necessary to introduce the effects of communist ideology.

The previous chapter has shown how Marxism from its very beginning has been split by ideological disputes concerning the strategy most likely to produce a Communist world. In this context, the Sino-Soviet rift appears to be something more than a calculation of national power (although this factor has its role). While it may be true that China is traditionally expansionist, Peking's rejection of Russian leadership in the world communist movement is also the reaction of Marxists who have little to lose and prefer revolutionary purity even at the cost of isolation.

This approach to the Sino-Soviet split suggests the advantages of recognizing the inevitability of the rise of communist China to the status of a world power. Although many will deny that the possession of nuclear weapons would induce the Chinese to a certain moderation, historical evidence as well as the dynamics of communist ideology indicate that the greater the power and industrialization of Red China, the more wary Peking will be of "adventurist" policies. The same process that has operated throughout all communist parties and that has marked the development of Russian communism since 1917 will probably operate in China as well.

Some observers have pressed this argument to the extreme, suggesting that after the death of Mao a new generation of Chinese leaders will emerge that will be more willing to compromise with the West. Such a radical shift over the short run, however, is less likely than a hardening of the party line, combined with massive purges of a neo-Stalinist type; this process has apparently begun as second-level party leaders jockey for positions of power in expectation of Mao's passing.

Moreover, if Chinese leaders feel compelled to reach a limited accommodation with the United States (for example, in Vietnam), their response could well be an increase in totalitarian terror within China itself. Given the enormity of the obstacles facing Chinese industrialization, ideological rigidity will probably serve the next generation of Peking's leadership as it did Stalin throughout his reign. Thus the recent "cultural revolution," by giving China's rulers greater control, could even facilitate compromise with the West (much as Stalin's purges made possible the ill-fated Nazi-Soviet Pact).

Because the internal dialectic of rapid communist industrialization creates a tendency to self-imposed isolation (in China as in Stalinist Russia), neither hawks nor doves have recognized that there is little the United States can do to prevent such communist isolationism (so different from American isolationism because of the ideology involved). Demands for signs of Chinese "good faith" as the prerequisite for a *détente* reveal a lack of understanding of the problem; a shift away from the policy of isolation or containment seems justifiable at present because it will be rejected by Peking under circumstances favorable to the United States.

The main objective of a reversal of our China policy would be to increase the cost Peking must pay for the isolation it finds so useful. By avoiding American commitments that make China's revolutionary strategy in any way plausible to communists and uncommitted nations, Chinese demands will seem more extreme; hence we would make it easier for Moscow to dissociate itself from Peking. Our policy of accommodation could be subtly reinforced by the privately conveyed threat that, should China attack her neighbors, we might retaliate (even with nuclear weapons) in a way that would minimize the risk to ourselves of any Russian intervention.

A policy of orienting American actions and strategies toward the ultimate emergence of a small number of continental superpowers, including China, need not be undermined because the Chinese are hardly likely to become peace-loving in the immediate future. In the short run, we can hope to force Peking to isolate itself, counting on self-interest to teach other national leaders (as it did the Indonesian army) that they have little to gain from an ally who will subvert them whenever possible. Over the longer run, there is rather good evidence for assuming that the greater the power of communist China, the more susceptible she would be to restraints imposed by an international system of superpowers; once the Chinese attain universally recognized great-power standing, the possibility of restraint imposed by their own selfishness—the only reliable means of checking any power—becomes greater. The weaker the Chinese, paradoxically, the more dangerous they may be as a source for revolutionary change in the world.

It is therefore possible that the rise of China to the status of a superpower would contribute to global stability. If so, we may unwittingly share certain interests with Peking (such as the limitation of Soviet power in Asia). Among other things, this possibility implies that a Sino-Soviet war arising out of border disputes or ideological hostility would not be an unmixed blessing for the United States, for a Russian victory over China (like an American one) could create a dangerous power vacuum.

In this perspective, American trade and even economic assistance to all Asian communist states, including China, might be an astute policy. Peking would be virtually certain to reject all American offers, but this rebuff would be, like Stalin's rejection of Marshall Plan aid to Russia and the Eastern European satellites, a source of embarrassment forcing the Chinese to offer an alternative not only for their own people but for their Asian allies. The justification for American aid to Poland and Yugoslavia (which, even when not producing immediate political dividends, effectively weakened the Russian hold over her satellites) could thus apply to North Korea or North Vietnam as well.

This argument would apply with even greater force should American offers of aid be accepted by China. Although American assistance to China would not be very effective as a direct restraint on Peking's ambitions—one need only recall our experience with Sukarno, who told the United States "to hell with your aid" as soon as we tried to restrain his aggressive policy toward Malaysia—the acceptance of American aid would indirectly reduce Peking's revolutionary attractiveness and undermine its claims to leadership in the underdeveloped and anticolonial world.

This reasoning is reinforced by the interrelation between foreign and domestic policy in a backward country trying to industrialize rapidly under a single-party totalitarian regime. With the prospect or reality of foreign economic aid, the Chinese would be tempted to increase the development of the industrial sector of their economy, with the result (found in all modern societies) that the urbanization of their predominantly peasant society would be accelerated. But this stage of economic development, as the Russian example indicates, absorbs the energies of a backward society in domestic affairs, leaves less time for foreign adventure, and provides more vulnerable targets for enemy attack in case of major war.

To be sure, we would then have to face, perhaps somewhat sooner, the challenge of China as a major industrial power, but this is inevitable unless we wage a preventive war of annihilation. At no time was the Soviet Union more expansionist than in the years immediately following World War II, during which Russian industrial and even military potential had been greatly reduced by the devastation of war with the Nazis; if the analogy holds, the period immediately preceding the full-fledged attainment of nuclear superpower status is the most risky one in a major communist nation. It might therefore be in the interest of the United States to shorten this period as much as possible. The analogy of Soviet expansionism in the late 1940's indicates, moreover, the danger of a preventive war against China which does not completely annihilate her population; whatever the appeal of the strategic theory of escalation, as a guide to preventive war the limitation of our attacks is foolhardy, for it would leave the Chinese in the status of a radically aggressive power.

It has been argued that the United States can best contribute to the stability of Asia by adopting a long-range policy goal of establishing a world balance of power dominated by nuclear continent-states, regardless of their ideology. This objective is desirable not only as a response to Chinese communism; as a result of the unquestioned acceptance of the idea of containment, Americans have often been oddly blind to other threats to the peace from powers not openly communist.

As Robert O. Tilman, specialist on the area at Yale University, has put it: "Nasty little wars can break out on almost any given day in Southeast Asia which could have little or nothing to do with the United States, the People's Republic of China, or the USSR. There is a very good chance that Vietnam would still be in turmoil even if China were powerless today and had little prospect of becoming powerful in the foreseeable future. Cambodia has a long-standing dispute with the people of South Vietnam and Thailand that has nothing whatever to do with the cold war. Malaysian-Indonesian-Philippine relations are probably going to be more influenced by domestic politics than by Sino-American relations. If the Malay nationalists have their way and link up politically with their fellow Malays in Indonesia, there might be a new civil war in the Malayan peninsula (which, although opposing Chinese and Malays, would be produced largely by domestic issues rather than by China's attempt to extend its influence)."

Confronted by the likelihood of such violence, it is extremely dangerous for the United States to assume that the major powers are the only participants in the politics of Southern Asia. Since local rulers may act for reasons that have little to do with global power politics, we must orient our policy to limiting the repercussions of conflicts that otherwise could lead to unnecessary American involvement. It is impossible to analyze every possible problem, but let us consider two major ones; the tension between India and Pakistan, and the recently muted but still very real ambitions of Indonesia.

The war between India and Pakistan over Kashmir is clear

evidence that an American-sponsored mutual security pact, such as SEATO, is insufficient to maintain peace in Asia over the long run. It was our nominal ally, Pakistan, that used American military equipment to break the status quo in an attempt to force the major powers (as well as India) to settle the Kashmir dispute. The implications of such unilateral use of force can be made clear by an analogy: a similar situation might occur if West Germany resorted to military attack as a means of changing the unsatisfactory status quo in Berlin. As this hypothetical example shows, alliances directed against communism are not a perpetual guarantee against adventures by a second- or third-level power seeking to alter circumstances tolerable to the superpowers.

Indeed, the American policy of alliances directed against the threat of communism may have increased instability in South Asia. While our military assistance to Pakistan seemed threatening to India, the Pakistanis were frustrated by our refusal to support their demands concerning Kashmir. Because the Chinese were willing to support Karachi on the one issue that really mattered to Pakistan, the result was a tacit alignment that led to violence. If we are to stabilize the region, it must be by encouraging the emergence of countervailing powers, not by formal alliances that ignore the difference between our concerns and those of our allies.[3]

In South Asia, the danger arises largely from the relative weakness of India, faced by a more effectively organized China and embroiled with a restive Pakistan. In the long run, the risk of an unchecked Sino-Pakistani alliance, serving their mutual interests without regard to ideology, is plain; China's threat to invade India in 1965 (as well as the claim that her ultimatum was met) were clearly timed to show the potency of such a combination. Equally dangerous, however, would be a radical increase of Soviet influence in New Delhi and Karachi (patterned on Russia's successful mediation at Tash-

---

[3] On the argument that our alliance ties to Pakistan have outlived their usefulness and should be abandoned, see Selig S. Harrison: "America, India, and Pakistan," *Harper's Magazine* (July 1966), pp. 56-68.

kent). To preclude or restrain such alignments, it is insufficient to preach the virtues of peace to all parties concerned; given the existing power relationship, India can be the only loser in such a case.

Assuming that formal alliance with any single state is an ineffective and unsatisfactory policy, the United States has two main options in South Asia: we could seek a tacit agreement with Moscow to minimize the arms build-up of both India and Pakistan (in the hopes that neither would attack the other and that both together could, with the support of the superpowers, restrain China), or we could encourage India's emergence as a nuclear counterweight to Peking (preferably by indirect means, such as the expansion of economic assistance). The first of these strategies may seem more advantageous because it would permit us to counter the Soviet attempt to remove all American influence in both New Delhi and Karachi; it is, however, the more difficult policy to execute, for it is almost impossible to please local rivals simultaneously. If forced to choose, therefore, we should be prepared to accept the development of nuclear weapons by India, for in this way New Delhi would insure its own defense without calling upon one or the other of the superpowers.[4]

Although the Indian government has long been reluctant to embark on nuclear-weapons development, such a program has been proposed by some influential leaders; the continued threat of Chinese attack may convince New Delhi of the necessity of such a course, especially if (as is likely) the superpowers fail to agree to general nuclear disarmament. Moreover, some observers have pointed out that the emergence of India as a nuclear power could reinforce the unity of that

[4] In the article just cited, Selig Harrison defends the first of these options; for the case in favor of the second, see Leland Hazard: "Strong Medicine for India," *The Atlantic* (December 1965), pp. 43-8; and George Lichtheim: "Vacuum Diplomacy," *Commentary* (January 1966), pp. 49-53. Lichtheim concludes: "If China is to be 'contained' it can only be done through Russia and India, not by propping up comic-opera regimes in Laos and points further east."

still fragile nation as well as maintaining the Asian balance of power.

Since both the United States and the Soviet Union share an interest in enhancing India's military power to the point where it would balance that of China, insistence on pro-American policies in New Delhi (if not formal alliance) as a condition for aid is self-defeating; we are best served by Indian nonalignment if backed up by autonomous strength. Without American support, India would either be forced to turn to Moscow or to be militarily and politically isolated. Under these circumstances, the Russians would be highly tempted to increase their influence in New Delhi.

Although China's implicit threat to join the Pakistanis in fighting India may have been an effort to dissuade Moscow from such a policy, the Russians might be willing to tolerate a Sino-Pakistani alignment that destroyed our alliance with Pakistan and proved that the Chinese were more interested in their national power than in ideological purity. We have no interest in abandoning South Asia to Soviet and Chinese influence, especially since American initiatives to strengthen India would maintain the latter's noncommitment and exacerbate the Sino-Soviet split, while reducing the danger of a major defeat of India—a defeat that would open all of Asia to a greatly increased threat of Chinese hegemony.[5]

Some will argue that the Pakistani position is legally more defensible than that of India, and that our alliance commitments with Karachi preclude massive aid to India. An equally good claim could be made, however, that Pakistan's resort to force violated the UN Charter, that her tacit alignment with China was a hostile act, and that her use of American weapons against India violated explicit treaty

[5] As Arthur Lee Burns has put it: "Though without regional support, India remains the cornerstone of Southern Asia, so that the power structure of the whole region would be transformed were India to join either the Russian or the Chinese camp. . . ." "The Nth Country Problem, Mutual Deterrence, and International Stability," in *International Stability*, ed. Dale Hekhuis, Charles G. McClintock, and Arthur L. Burns (New York: Wiley; 1964), p. 131.

agreements. Since moral or legal arguments can be made on both sides, the ultimate question concerns the relative balance of forces most conducive to American interests and international stability.

From this perspective, the subtle encouragement of nuclear-weapons development in India would be a potent means of convincing the Chinese to act with restraint. Chinese awareness of the potential threat of Indian power is proven by Peking's willingness to use military force along the Himalayan frontier. It is not sufficiently recognized that the Sino-Indian border conflict was far from being a merely legal question or an opportunity of increasing Chinese prestige; the Chinese objective was apparently to gain control of the mountain passes through which they could move troops and material. By gaining this objective, the Chinese simultaneously insured their defensive perimeter and put themselves in a position to launch an offensive against India whenever this was feasible and desirable.

China's concern with her potential rivalry with India (which could also be demonstrated by other diplomatic and political moves) indicates that the threat or reality of American nuclear aid to the Indians would necessarily affect Peking's policies. As soon as the Chinese discover that our objective is to oppose to them powers of equal military potential in their own area, they will be forced to adopt a different attitude than at present. Whereas in South Vietnam the Chinese are convinced that their allies will win in the long run—a conviction which is not entirely implausible—they are obviously concerned with the challenge that would be posed by an industrialized India armed with a nuclear striking force.

It will be objected that the policy here sketched, since it would make of India a major threat to Pakistan (especially should the former become a nuclear power) would force the Pakistanis into alliance with Peking. This need not be the consequence, for we could attempt to convince both Indians and Pakistanis that their common interests require close cooperation. While seemingly impossible at present, one could hope that the two nations, being recent creations, might resolve the tension over Kashmir and cooperate closely.

American pressure cannot be expected, however, to overcome local rivalries that are deeply rooted in popular opinion. Efforts to bring New Delhi and Karachi closer together may founder regardless of the inducements offered by Washington (or Moscow). Conversely, a solution in Kashmir—if not the reunification of the Indian subcontinent—might one day occur by force, under circumstances in which the great powers preferred noninvolvement.

Even if a Sino-Pakistani alliance were to result from India's development of nuclear weapons, however, the result need not be as disastrous as first appears. If China is to gain allies in Asia, it is surely to our advantage that she be tempted to choose a domestically anti-communist military regime, for by so doing we can undercut the Chinese claim to act solely on ideological, revolutionary grounds. Moreover, Chinese influence over Pakistan would probably be limited by ideological and national differences, since it is not in the interest of Ayub Khan to become a mere tool in the hands of Peking.

We have much to gain from forcing the world to see communist China as a national power seeking national gains under the cloak of a presumably scientific and international ideology. In so doing, we increase the chance that Russia can dissociate herself from Chinese aggressiveness, while revealing to other Asian and African powers—and especially to other communist parties—that Peking's offers of support are hardly disinterested. By treating these problems in terms of the power of nations (instead of ideology), we have the greatest chance of showing the Pakistanis that their interests would not best be served by becoming a Chinese satellite, since Pakistan might then be faced with a Russo-Indian alliance with the United States as a potential or actual third partner. Only if India emerges as a truly major power, armed with nuclear weapons, is there any long-range hope of restraining China from supporting other Asian states that seek to overturn the status quo by force.

If Pakistan is an obvious example of the danger of our fixation on anti-communist alliances, Indonesia is no less significant. Prior to the abortive pro-Chinese coup of 1965, which resulted in a bloody purge of the Indonesian Communist Party, Sukarno threatened to destroy the Malaysian Federation. Besides conducting armed (if intermittent) hostilities toward a neighbor, the Indonesians announced their readiness to develop nuclear weapons and missiles capable of reinforcing this aggressive intention. Although the United States took the attitude that this conflict was not primarily an American concern (perhaps because the British had committed themselves to the defense of Malaysia), the "Crush Malaysia" campaign illustrates the dangers of considering communist aggression as the sole threat to peace.

The American tendency to underestimate the importance of Sukarno's "Crush Malaysia" campaign was shortsighted, for we took exactly the same attitude during the French war in Indochina in the 1950's, and now find ourselves committed in the same area as was France, except in worse conditions; our refusal to bomb Vietnamese troop concentrations at Dien Bien Phu is generally considered in France as the cause for the communist victory in North Vietnam (and indeed goes far to explain current French disenchantment with the American policy in Southeast Asia).

Had the Indonesian Communist Party not blundered by attempting to take direct control, thereby triggering a vigorous reaction by the Indonesian army, our preoccupation with Vietnam might have been more immediately disastrous than is usually admitted. Whatever the role of the CIA in supporting the Indonesian army's reaction to the abortive coup, the radical reduction in Sukarno's power must be considered as a windfall largely due to circumstances beyond our control. And while the American attitude of late has been one of complacent relief, on the assumption that the defeat of both Sukarno and Indonesian communism is permanent, such optimism may be unwise.

His relative eclipse did not prevent Sukarno from retaining a considerable personal following (especially in central Java); it is conceivable that the Indonesian communists, like those in China, will one day rise from the ashes to take over a large, chaotic, and largely peasant society whose unity and development seem impossible to achieve under military rule or democratic government. Even should the Indonesian Communist Party be permanently defeated, moreover, it would be incorrect to assume that the military regime in Jakarta (or a non-communist successor) will be either pro-American or indefinitely peaceful. As we take a long-range view, a renewed Sino-Indonesian alignment appears as a threat that, like a Sino-Pakistani alignment, must be either prevented or counterbalanced.

Indonesia's military potential deserves mention, not only because of the size of its armed forces, but because of the population and natural resources of this archipelago. To be sure, Indonesia often appears to be barely a state, with its heterogeneous population, its economic instability, and its precarious political order. Yet these very indications of weakness may make foreign adventure appealing to future rulers, who might view war as the sole means of cementing their internal control.

To limit the aggressive potentiality of Indonesia and China, there are two somewhat complementary means open to the United States. First is the encouragement of other powers in the area, notably Australia and India; second, measures which could increase the tension between China and Indonesia. It is in this direction, rather than in the defense of any single position in Southeast Asia, that the United States must go if it is to prevent major world war from breaking out there.

In this context, a recognition of the inevitable dominance of the Chinese in the Southeast Asian subcontinent does not necessarily imply universal Chinese hegemony. On the contrary, the closer the confrontation of Indonesia and China, the more likely they will see the potential contradictions between their interests. It is apparent, for example, that Chinese membership in the UN could exacerbate the split between Indonesia and China, for American recognition of Chinese status as a continental superpower might in itself tarnish the desirability of an alignment between an independent Indonesia and a much more powerful China. Increased hostility between Indonesia and China might also enhance the unity of Indonesia itself without at the same time encouraging aggressive actions that would destabilize the Asian region.

It is by such means, rather than in the form of direct commitments of American troops, that aggression by Peking can be deterred. Whereas American intervention in Asia produces tensions that are partly anticolonial, partly racial, and partly xenophobic (with the result that our so-called allies often become needlessly anti-American), indirect support for Asian states that seek to counterbalance China is at least strongly rooted in the sense of national pride and the desire for self-preservation shared by all governments—even those that are strongly anti-American.

Hence American recognition of China could serve to increase the Asian awareness of the Chinese threat; we may restrain Peking much more effectively by reaching a limited accommodation with her than by posing as the sole bulwark against Chinese expansionism. The less we promise to intervene directly, the more fully the Indonesians—and other Asians—will be forced to protect themselves; because the appearance of a reduced American counterweight to China might lead Peking to aggressive moves, the likely result will be more pronounced opposition to the Chinese (as was so in India and Indonesia).

Another reason for the approach proposed above is that it would permit the Japanese to develop economic contacts with Peking without destroying the shared interests between Tokyo and Washington. As long as we speak of containment, the Japanese left can demand improved relations with China as a sign of independence from American imperialism; influential Japanese businessmen (the so-called "New Right"), aware of the advantage of securing Chinese markets, may find common ground with the left in such an anti-American policy. After all, it is argued in Tokyo that we would be forced to react to a Chinese attack on Japan even without the mutual security treaty, which could then be abandoned because it interferes unnecessarily with Japanese trade.

Xenophobia may grow as the Japanese become more confident of their power as a successfully industrialized state; present policies may be an invitation to future anti-Americanism. Reliance on direct treaty commitments as a means of preventing possible Chinese aggression would no longer be necessary if Asian powers such as Japan and India were encouraged to play a larger role in counterbalancing Peking; in this case, national pride could work in favor of American interests instead of against them.

Sooner or later the Japanese may be forced to reconsider the demilitarization imposed on them at the end of World War II; just as West Germany has been rearmed as a means of increasing international stability, so Japan may feel it both desirable and necessary to take greater responsibility for its own defense. Already, some Japanese speak of acquiring nuclear weapons unless the superpowers agree to a sweeping disarmament treaty. Such a policy will probably seem most attractive at any time when Japanese industry finds difficulty in securing foreign markets; if so, it may be preferable to outline a program for acceptable Japanese rearmament before a crisis imposes such a decision on us unwillingly.

The most salutary possibility lies in the emergence of closer ties between Asian powers themselves; just as German rearmament was accepted within the context of the Western European Union (and ultimately NATO and the Common Market), so the development of Japanese military forces would be most tolerable if it coincided with the emergence of an Asian confederation, not unlike the *Europe des patries*, centered on Tokyo, Manila, Jakarta, and New Delhi.

However, recent and still very tentative steps in this direction—such as the Asian and Pacific Council, or ASPAC (composed of Japan, South Korea, Taiwan, the Philippines, Thailand, Malaysia, Australia, New Zealand and South Vietnam) —need not bear fruit. An Asian defense community or common market seems so far in the future that any discussion must be extremely hypothetical. Moreover, an Asian approximation of a European confederation—or even a multilateral security pact—could only be the result of a convergence of interest in the states involved; institutions of this sort can hardly be imposed or even proposed from without and still maintain their true meaning. But should China's rising power create a common interest in cooperation (as the threat of Soviet power was a great catalyst in the original movement toward a European community), developments in this direction are not totally impossible.

All that need be added, therefore, is that American policy should not be so designed as to inhibit Asian powers from taking upon themselves a larger role in the preservation of the balance of power. In contrast to the popularly held view that the United States, as a world power, has a direct responsibility in the containment of the Chinese, we ought to make it clear that we seek a reduction of American commitments (including the abandonment of formal treaties) wherever this can be done without too great a risk.

Formal American alliance with anti-communist powers in this part of the world, such as the SEATO pact, has revealed itself to be radically insufficient, especially because of India's desire to remain to some extent nonaligned in the ideological struggle between East and West. If it is explicitly and repeatedly stated that the American goal in Asia is the emergence of a stable balance of power, without prime emphasis on ideology, we may find means of checking Chinese expansionism without having to make commitments that involve us in persisting guerrilla warfare thousands of miles from our shores.

CHAPTER EIGHT

Economic Development and International Organizations

AMERICAN foreign policy cannot be based on the assumption that there is a universally applicable solution to the problem of economic backwardness. It is sometimes argued that since the gap between the poor and rich nations is increasing and becoming a dominant theme in world politics, the United States and other Western powers have a moral commitment to ensure worldwide economic development with massive foreign assistance.[1] Although this is a noble aim, it is questionable whether developed societies can or should undertake such a global obligation.

In moral terms, it seems more accurate to say that the United States realizes humanitarian objectives best by main-

[1] Barbara Ward: *The Rich Nations and the Poor Nations* (New York: Norton; 1962) is a clear and well-known statement of this view.

taining our own economic strength and achieving our domestic political ideals; only insofar as American prosperity and power are protected, consistent with the best traditions of a free and just society, could we be in a position to help those foreign nations that seek to profit from our example, our economic assistance, or our political influence. An American commitment to global economic development that cannot be met or that results in domestic pressures undermining our own democracy is in the interest of neither the United States nor the poorer nations.

We cannot achieve an ethical ideal of treating all men and societies in exactly equal terms, for any foreign policy requires choices and a selective use of resources. Each situation demands different responses, and these responses can never be totally divorced from considerations of political power. This is not to say that the United States should define its national interests narrowly or aggressively, nor that we should ignore the needs and desires of backward societies; since a diffusion of power and the tension between rich and poor nations will characterize international politics in coming decades, a coherent American policy toward the underdeveloped parts of the world is politically and morally necessary. But we must be aware that only by careful appreciation of the possible—which includes an understanding of the imperatives of politics—can the United States hope to contribute to the betterment of mankind.[2]

Because economic development seems to be a process that everywhere proceeds through essentially identical stages, many believe that properly conceived policies could in time lead to industrialization throughout the world.[3] But if, as was argued in Chapter ii, economic development in the fullest

[2] On the argument that rich nations have a moral duty toward underdeveloped societies, see Joseph Cropsey: "The Right of Foreign Aid," in *Why Foreign Aid?*, ed. Robert A. Goldwin (Chicago: Rand McNally; 1963), pp. 109-30.

[3] See, for example, W. W. Rostow: *The Stages of Economic Growth* (Cambridge Univ. Press; 1960). In all fairness, it should be added that

sense is becoming more and more difficult for backward societies, even massive foreign assistance may fail to achieve the desired ends. Political decisions beyond our control will frequently determine whether economic development proceeds in one direction or another—or not at all; given endemic political instability and serious economic obstacles, violence or corruption that negates the effect of our aid may be unavoidable. This suggests that it would be dangerous for the United States to assume responsibility, even implicitly, for achieving economic development in situations where we cannot assure success.

Several summary conclusions follow concerning the general policies that the United States should adopt. Regarding economic assistance, it would be unwise for America to appear to make a commitment to industrialization. But even if a nation fails to industrialize, it will need to feed its expanding population; aid in education, agriculture, and population planning should therefore be preferred to industrial investment. This would make it possible for the most favorably situated backward countries to achieve the industrial development of which they are capable, while at the same time satisfying the most pressing needs of stagnant economies.[4]

Even where successful, however, economic assistance does not insure the United States that developing countries will be internally stable or peaceful; on the contrary, there is every likelihood that the underdeveloped world will be shaken by both domestic and inter-state violence in the years ahead. In political terms, this means that we should minimize our commitments to specific regimes in Asia, Latin America, and

---

Rostow himself was aware of many qualifications to the notion of "stages" of economic development (e.g., pp. 1, 46, 57). Nonetheless he—and still more, those who adopt his views—seem overly optimistic in the belief that "the tricks of growth are not all that difficult" (p. 166) and hence can be learned universally.

[4] Fortunately, population control, agricultural development, and education are increasingly recognized as key sectors toward which American resources should be devoted in backward societies. See in particular President Johnson's Foreign Aid Message to Congress for 1966 (excerpts from which were published in *The New York Times*, February 28, 1966, p. 4).

Africa; since we lack the means to preserve every government we favor, there may be no way of preventing military regimes —or communists—from taking power whenever they are the only alternative to chaos or corruption. The alternative is the risk of perpetual involvement in conflicts over which we have little control, with ruling elites appealing to the United States as a means of using our power to support their privileges.

This does not mean that we should totally ignore the problems of the developing nations, but it does call for a great deal of restraint and circumspection. It is unwise to view the underdeveloped world in the perspective of the bipolar contest between democracy and communism, for the constraints on a major power aiding a weak state apply regardless of ideology; the Soviet Union has encountered difficulties in dealing with Yugoslavia (not to mention Albania), and the Chinese apparently felt that short of a direct communist take-over they could not be assured of influence in Indonesia. Only by relying on the self-interest of the rulers of underdeveloped states (whose intense nationalism is an obstacle to their becoming satellites of any great power) can we hope to encourage global stability.

Discussion of American policies toward every foreign country is neither feasible nor necessary in a book of this sort; details will in any event be highly variable, depending not only on specific circumstances but on the changing political and military relationships between major powers. Since American responsibilities toward specific underdeveloped nations seem so risky and unpromising, it will be more useful to concentrate on the role of multilateral devices and institutions, whether regional or global in extent, in dealing with problems of economic development. The omission of a more detailed treatment of our bilateral policies toward various underdeveloped nations should not be too serious a fault, for a balance-of-power approach to American foreign policy has already been illustrated in three specific areas of the world.

Our limited ability to secure weak countries from internal or external attack has led some to hope that regional and international organizations can play a major role in maintaining a stable balance of power. In the Korean War and the Congo crisis, the United States has relied on the UN as a means for checking communist aggression or limiting violence in underdeveloped areas; in condemning Cuba and intervening in the Dominican Republic we have preferred to work through a regional organization, the Organization of American States. Since these two kinds of international organization are quite different, it is necessary to treat them separately.

On the regional level, the conception of collective self-defense against alien forces tends to contradict the idea of a geographical community of interest in which local conflicts can be regulated without interference by the great powers. The United States has tended to view the OAS primarily as an institution that can mobilize regional support against advances by world communism, and insofar as other Latin-American governments share an interest in preventing revolutions in their own countries, this orientation rests on a common interest. But within the Western Hemisphere there is also considerable resentment against American power and domination; it often seems that the United States is more concerned with the preservation of right-wing regimes that protect American investments than in responding to the desires of weaker states in the OAS.

In other regions, similar contradictions exist between the presumed common interests of most states and the conflicts between local rivals; most African countries can unite in opposition to South Africa and Southern Rhodesia, just as most Arab states are opposed to Israel, but implementation of common programs is inhibited by local jealousies and the contrary interests of neighboring states. Since regional organizations seem to be most easily united on the basis of hostility to a common enemy, they may be ineffective both as institutions for economic development and as a means of keeping the peace between local powers.

For example, the use of the OAS to contain Castro and prevent a left-wing regime in the Dominican Republic entails the risk that the regional organization will appear to be merely an instrument of American power. The tradition of anti-Americanism south of the border will often be manifested by demands that the OAS become an association of equals in which intervention in the domestic affairs of any member is untenable. Since many liberal Latin Americans believe that radical domestic reforms are necessary and desirable, American insistence on the primacy of a communist danger could split Latin America into those who use nationalist and reformist principles to undermine American dominance and those whose professions of fidelity are intended to commit American power in defense of their own domestic self-interest.

To counteract these dangers, we could encourage a regional sense of responsibility in affairs that do not directly involve the basic interests of a major power. Whereas at present the OAS is undermined by fears that it is a tool of the United States, Latin-American nations could be invited to find means of moderating their own disputes without primary reference to our interests; exceptions to this principle would then be dealt with by the United States more directly. In this way, a sense of regional community might be furthered without requiring American approval of each specific action of the OAS, so that the regional organization could mediate conflicts between members without risking the involvement of the superpowers.

American proposals to strengthen the authority of OAS have, however, been coolly received, in part because such power for the regional organization seems a device for increasing American hegemony and in part because many governments do not want to prejudice their claims against local rivals. Although the first of these objections could be met if it became clear that the United States would not try to use the OAS to further its own national policies, the second objection is likely to remain. Only if states had a greater self-interest in cooperating with each other, through an OAS capable of acting independently of American wishes or interests, could the organization develop autonomous peace-keeping functions.

One means of increasing regional cooperation between Latin-American states would be the development of common institutions to channel economic assistance (such as a regional common market or the Latin American Bank for Development). Unfortunately, however, the common interests of underdeveloped nations in the Western Hemisphere are often largely defined in opposition to the economic power of the United States. Hence in economic matters, as in peace-keeping, increased regional cohesion seems largely possible only insofar as American influence within regional organizations is reduced if not openly opposed.

As a consequence, the development of regional organizations does not represent an unambiguous advantage from the point of view of American interest. To make the OAS effective as a peace-keeping agency that could resolve quarrels between Latin-American states, the United States would have to be willing to take sole responsibility in those cases where our political intervention seems strategically unavoidable. In so doing, we would face cries of protest not only from Latin-American countries but also from liberals within the United States (who will condemn unilateral intervention as blatant and immoral power politics). To minimize this danger, it will be necessary to act with restraint and a full awareness of the long-range disadvantages of overly direct military involvement in backward societies.

By emphasizing indirect means of intervention, prior to crises, we can come closest to serving our own national interest (which indicates the undesirability of communist regimes in the Caribbean) while avoiding the onus of blatant interference in the domestic politics of small nations. In this sense, our role in defeating the communist insurrection in Guatemala is a better example than either the Bay of Pigs (where we used a feasible device—indirect intervention—under unfavorable conditions) or the Dominican Republic (where we used a risky method—direct interference covered by OAS authorization—under favorable conditions).

These considerations suggest that we should be extremely hesitant before deciding that our interests require even indirect actions that would prevent hostile regimes from taking power. But where unavoidable, we should be willing to bear the onus of superpower status and should emphasize counter-subversive activity through governments in power (rather than allowing situations to develop in which sending American troops or mobilization of the OAS seems necessary). Only as a last resort should we make a military commitment, but in such extremes our intervention should be sufficiently decisive and effective to permit us to retain control, without having to rely on other Latin Americans whose domestic vulnerability may be increased if they are forced to act as our auxiliaries.

The role of regional organizations in other areas will be subject to limits similar to those confronting the OAS. The Arab League, for example, seems to be primarily united by hostility to Israel; hence in the Middle East it would be impossible to utilize this regional organization to prevent violence between Israel and its neighbors. Note, however, that the very existence of the Arab League may well restrain Egypt and Syria in their hostility toward the Israelis; paradoxically, the assumption that the Arab states should act in concert, given the deep divisions of interest between them, may lead members of the Arab League to jockey for power and influence among themselves.

Should a regional organization like the Arab League (or the Organization of African Unity) remain a loose and largely impotent association of states with conflicting interests and differing objectives, the organization may serve as a reasonably healthy outlet for aggressive rhetoric precisely because it is incapable of effective action. Governments can maintain the image of anticolonialist vigor which they have used to gain domestic support, while at the same time failing to attack the targets of their hostility (or doing so in limited and tolerable ways). In this sense, further development of the unity of regional organizations might be dangerous, for it would permit underdeveloped nations to pool their resources in adventures into which the major powers might be drawn against their will.

The United States must therefore be willing to tolerate

situations that are less than ideal for nations we support. For example, it can be argued that the long-range interests of Israel were best served, along with the American desire to avoid entanglement in a major war in the Middle East, by the tacit Russo-American agreement to stop the Anglo-French-Israeli forces short of a total defeat of Egypt in 1956. Had the United States not sided with the Soviet Union in condemning the Suez expedition, the Israelis might have gained more of their immediate objectives (such as free use of the Suez Canal and better port access to the Red Sea). But the long-range consequence might well have been an exacerbation of Arab nationalism that could have overcome the internecine conflicts of interest in the Middle East; thus the Arab League might have become sufficiently united to wage a holy war against Israel, forcing the United States to intervene militarily or resulting in the defeat of the Israelis.

As this example indicates, there will often be a very narrow line between policies that limit the extent of violence and a timidity that results in unfavorable alterations in a local balance of power. The most that can be hoped for is that, by a diffusion of power due to the weakening of bipolarity, the costs of error will be reduced. Such dangers can be further minimized by a consistent policy of maintaining rough military parity between third- or fourth-level powers in any region, dampening wherever possible arms races between rival states.

This task is by no means easy to achieve. The abandonment of programs of direct military aid would be useful, for it would force rulers to pay for their armed forces out of resources that could otherwise serve peaceful uses. Even where we seek an arms build-up (to balance that of an aggressive local rival), the United States should finance it indirectly by larger economic assistance rather than through specifically military arrangements. In this way, the recipient government —and not the United States—must take responsibility for using funds to buy arms.

In some areas, it may be possible to reinforce stability by international agreements (whether through the UN or regional organizations). The crucial consideration is that weaker states must be persuaded that their own self-interest counsels restraint in expanding their armed forces. In particular, the major powers must convince ambitious developing nations not to acquire nuclear weapons even should they become inexpensive to buy or produce.

Russian Premier Kosygin's proposal that the use of nuclear weapons on the territory of any nonnuclear state be forbidden is a good example of an agreement creating a self-interest in avoiding arms races. While one reason for this idea was to undermine NATO's strategy (which contemplates the use of tactical nuclear weapons in Germany), the proposal has evident advantages in Asia, Africa, and Latin America. In effect, such a provision means that the acquisition of nuclear weapons increases a society's vulnerability. Since the offensive value of nuclear weapons would be reduced if all local rivals possessed them, the loss of security implicit in becoming a legitimate target for nuclear attack (especially from a superpower) might effectively deter proliferation to minor powers.

Nuclear-free zones in Africa, the Middle East, and Latin America would therefore seem highly desirable. They would provide a means of achieving much the same end as Kosygin's proposal in the areas where international agreement is least prevented by the pressing and contradictory interests of the superpowers. Whereas universally applicable treaties may be impossible to establish, both local minor powers and those now having nuclear weapons might accept less inclusive agreements (especially if supported and enforced by the superpowers).

Although such international agreements would not stop nuclear proliferation or conventional arms races in all cases, the possibility of creating a self-interested desire of underdeveloped states to limit the size of their armies deserves further exploration. In this respect, however, it would seem that regional organizations may have less of a role to play than would the UN, for it is in the latter that the major powers could bring their pressure to bear on the weaker states.

Whereas regional institutions are split by local rivalries and most easily united in hostility to a common rival, the UN may be most useful in disputes between underdeveloped countries (and not, as is often thought, as a forum in which the underdeveloped countries mediate and limit conflicts between the major powers).

Since neither direct American aid nor the development of regional cooperation will assure even agricultural self-sufficiency and political stability (not to mention industrial development) in backward societies, there are good reasons for insulating American policy from failures in regimes that we have supported. Direct, bilateral programs of economic assistance may be undesirable because they will, at least implicitly, commit the United States to specific rulers. While one means of avoiding this danger may be private or quasi-official economic assistance,[5] the most promising alternative is multilateral aid, which simultaneously shares the financial burdens and reduces the responsibility of the donor nations.

Without underemphasizing the broad range of assistance conducted by agencies like the International Bank of Reconstruction and Development, the United Nations Special Fund, or the International Monetary Fund, perhaps the most important area for multilateral action lies in the stabilization of world commodity prices. Many underdeveloped countries are exporters of food or raw materials subject to wide price fluctuation (copper ore, coffee, etc.), so that a sharp fall in prices can radically reduce the foreign capital earned by these exports. One of the most effective means of helping those who

[5] The Peace Corps is an example of an official program that operates at a grass-roots, nongovernmental level, but it involves formal arrangements between states that are most completely avoided by strictly private initiatives (such as those of the International Development Foundation or the Rural Development Associates). See, for example, *The National Observer*, July 8, 1963, p. 12; *New Republic*, June 18, 1966, p. 21. Although beneficial, such private programs do not seem to have a sufficiently great impact to be, in themselves, a solution to the problems of economic assistance.

can help themselves, without the United States taking responsibility, lies in assuring price stability in world-wide commodity markets.

The findings of the United Nations Conference on Trade and Development (UNCTAD), held in 1964, indicate the importance of such measures. Whereas the developing countries had a surplus of exports over imports in 1950, by 1962 their imports were $2.3 billion greater than exports. Since "the gap between the import requirements of developing countries and their export earnings has been widening," the Conference concluded that "the realization of economic and social development plans of the developing countries necessitates an appropriate change in the present structure of international trade in such a way as to afford them the opportunity of earning adequate and stable supplies of foreign exchange."[6]

Although many other measures are needed, it seems particularly important to insure the underdeveloped countries that their earnings from the export of primary products will not be wiped out by falling world prices. In the words of General Principle Seven adopted in 1964 by UNCTAD, "All countries should cooperate through suitable international arrangements on an orderly basis in implementing measures designed to increase and stabilize primary commodity export earnings, particularly of developing countries, at equitable and remunerative prices and to maintain a mutually acceptable relationship between the prices of manufactured goods and those of primary products." Unfortunately, the American representative voted against this principle, which was endorsed by a vote of 87 to 8 (with 19 abstentions).[7]

[6] UN Conference on Trade and Development, *Final Act* (UN Document E/Conf. 46/28; 16 June 1964), pp. 9, 10.

[7] Ibid., Annex A, p. 10. See also Special Principle Seven, against which our representative voted. It is discouraging to note that of the fifteen General Principles adopted at the UNCTAD meetings, the U.S. voted against nine and abstained from two more. In fact, the United States cast the only negative vote on four of these principles, one of which reads: "Economic relations between countries, including trade relations, shall be based on respect for the principle of sovereign equality of states, self-determination of peoples, and non-interference in the internal affairs of other countries."

Implementation of the principle endorsed by UNCTAD is not easy, for it implies a direct cost to the governments undertaking price stabilization and higher prices for the private importers of foods and raw materials. Although these factors may explain the reluctance of industrialized states to take strong action that would support world prices, some form of international price supports for the basic raw materials exported by underdeveloped countries seems a valid and perhaps less expensive means of foreign aid than more direct capital assistance.[8]

The principle is not unlike that of agricultural price supports within the United States. In a freely competitive market composed of many producers, increased output sometimes results in falling prices for all—and hence in a lowered net income even with higher production; where direct governmental assistance seems undesirable, price supports can usefully encourage expansion of output and simultaneously increase the income of producers. As in domestic agriculture, it is necessary to limit the amount of production that would be supported. Such arrangements give rise to serious conflicts between various states that produce any given commodity, but the basic idea of stabilizing world prices is attractive because it would permit industrialized nations like the United States to assist developing societies without being committed to the particular regime in power. By insuring that exports would earn a reliable return in hard currencies, a backward country would be encouraged to use its own capital for development (just as American farms have become highly mechanized in part due to the security provided by price controls).

American opposition to multilateral efforts to improve the status of underdeveloped countries in world trade is perhaps the most serious example of a policy which appears to be devoted to maximizing the short run profits of American industry, even at the cost of serious international repercussions.

[8] It is even possible that high prices for primary commodities are actually beneficial to the developed economies; see Rostow: *Stages of Economic Growth*, p. 89. For an example of domestic opposition to United States participation in commodity price stabilization, see the discussion of the International Coffee Agreement, *The New York Times*, Feb. 26, 1964, p. 44; March 1, 1964, pp. F-1, 7; May 25, 1965, p. 57.

More effective world commodity agreements to stabilize prices are not a panacea, however. They would not insure that earned capital be invested in productive ways because the backward country might instead use its resources for military equipment, higher salaries for governmental officials, or programs that benefit the wealthy. But since political control over aid recipients is difficult to maintain anyhow, the advantage of less direct assistance lies in its reduction of our formal commitment to the receiving state; rulers whose policies are ineffective or aggressive should be made to take sole responsibility on themselves. Given the inherent instability of the underdeveloped world, this responsibility may be the most effective check on unwise policies that can be hoped for.

Other forms of multilateral assistance are also promising, for the limited but real success of the International Monetary Fund, International Bank for Reconstruction and Development, and UN Special Fund indicates that such agencies can approach problems beyond the political capacity of any single nation. Moreover, multilateral aid is a means of sharing the financial costs of economic assistance while avoiding wasteful competition between major powers, each of which has often bid for prestige by supporting projects of doubtful long-range utility to the recipients. As a consequence of the rivalry implicit in bilateral aid programs, rulers of underdeveloped societies have been able to play developed countries against each other (threatening to support one superpower if the other did not provide funds as requested). Multilateral programs would reduce this element of rivalry for short-range objectives—or rather, would transform it into a less dangerous kind of international bargaining.

It is sometimes argued that multilateral approaches are particularly advantageous because they also strengthen the basis for world government, but this result need not follow.[9]

[9] See especially James Patrick Sewell: *Functionalism and World Politics* (Princeton Univ. Press; 1966). Sewell's analysis is an exhaustive treatment of this problem based on a careful study of recent experiences in multilateral financing for economic development.

Assistance through the UN (especially the Special Fund) is only possible when major powers are fundamentally agreed on objectives (or are tacitly willing to accept programs they oppose). Although the United States has chosen not to withdraw from UN developmental activities merely because the Special Fund has granted assistance to Castro's Cuba, one can imagine circumstances in which this tolerance would end.

The primary justification of multilateral assistance lies in the ability to reduce direct American commitments to specific regimes, and hence to remove the element of ideology and responsibility in the relationship between backward and developed societies. From this perspective, American toleration of UN assistance to Cuba may be more than compensated for by Soviet toleration of UN assistance to Yugoslavia; by reducing the bipolar political conditions attached to aid, multilateral assistance may permit the use of political pressure to maintain local stability without creating risks of direct confrontation between major powers.

The case for multilateral aid is therefore a complex one: whatever the long-range hopes that it would encourage the development of a stronger UN, such policies must be defensible from the perspective of the interests of the states involved. Hence multilateral assistance cannot be considered as a total substitute for bilateral aid (especially because there may be situations where the United States, as a major power, is compelled to make binding commitments to a specific underdeveloped regime, partly to balance similar commitments of other major powers). Even within the area in which multinational agreements are sought as a mechanism for distributing assistance, the play of rivalry between the major powers will determine the extent and character of our contributions.

It was suggested in Chapter iv that the goal of transforming the UN into a world government is neither likely to be achieved nor necessarily desirable; the alternative conception of a suzerain power, not unlike that of a medieval monarch capable of residual peace-keeping functions, was proposed as a more realistic long-range objective. It is therefore necessary to specify the characteristics of such a development of the UN and the means by which the United States could contribute to it.

The American attitude toward the UN has always been strangely ambivalent: on the one hand, we have sought the development of an international organization that could prevent war and end the morally suspect need for power politics; on the other, we have been all too willing to use the UN wherever it furthered our own policies and national interests. The clearest case of our support for the UN as an instrument of American policy was the Korean War, in which American troops fought under the international organization's flag; during the Hungarian revolution we used the UN as a forum for denouncing Soviet policies. On other occasions, such as the Suez crisis or the Congo, the UN has been used to avoid great-power confrontations and minimize the risk of major war, not merely as a device for building world order but more fundamentally because such solutions were in our interest.[1]

Three tendencies have characterized the development of the UN over the last two decades: first, the emergence of a large number of newly independent nations, each having a vote equal to that of the great powers in the General Assembly; second, the frequent paralysis of the Security Council and demands that the Assembly, rather than the Security Council, take the initiative in proposing solutions to pressing world problems; and third, the increasing importance of the role of the Secretary General.[2] It is, however, also necessary

---

[1] "During the past twenty years, both superpowers have tried to use the UN as a vehicle for the advancement of their individual, and often antithetical, foreign-policy interests. In this quest, the Organization has been a more important vehicle for the U.S. than for the Soviet Union. The UN has often been persuaded to do collectively what the U.S. might have had to do individually." John G. Stoessinger, with Robert G. McKelvey: *The United Nations and the Superpowers* (New York: Random House; 1965), pp. viii-ix.

[2] See ibid. and John G. Stoessinger: *The Might of Nations,* rev. edn. (New York: Random House; 1965), pp. 255-69.

to take into account the insistence of some of the permanent members of the Security Council, notably the USSR and France, that the last two trends be checked lest they undermine the interests of major powers and destroy the UN.

According to the UN Charter, all members are bound to observe certain basic rules of international behavior; these lofty principles forbid aggression and interference in the domestic affairs of other states, and if realized would produce a more peaceful world.[3] But the UN Charter can bind member states only if it can be enforced. Although the Charter makes provision for the establishment of peace-keeping forces that could be used against any aggressor,[4] failure to implement fully these provisions is hardly surprising because they would imply the subordination of major powers to something approaching a world government. In order to assess the future of international organization, therefore, one must first consider the institutions of the UN and how they were originally intended to operate.

The General Assembly, in which each member state was to have an equal voice, received essentially advisory powers; according to Chapter IV of the Charter, the Assembly may "discuss," "make recommendations," "call the attention of the Security Council," or "initiate studies," but not take definitive action (except with reference to the Trusteeship system and the UN budget). Final, potentially binding decisions were to be made by the Security Council, in which the five permanent members—the USSR, Great Britain, France, China, and the United States—were to have a veto.[5] Although the institution

[3] See Chapter I of the UN Charter, reprinted as an appendix in Stoessinger: *The Might of Nations*, pp. 413-44.

[4] See especially the UN Charter, Article 42 (". . . the Security Council . . . may take such action by air, sea, or land forces as may be necessary to maintain or restore international peace and security") and Article 43, paragraph 1 ("All Members of the United Nations, in order to contribute to the maintenance of international peace and security, undertake to make available to the Security Council, on its call and in accordance with a special agreement or agreements, armed forces, assistance, and facilities, including rights of passage, necessary for the purpose of maintaining international peace and security").

[5] The subordination of the General Assembly to the Security Council

of the veto has been frequently attacked because the Soviet Union used it liberally to prevent the West from using the UN as an agent in the cold war, the United States has often exercised a "hidden veto" in the Security Council by the simple device of marshaling the support of its allies (who formed a majority of the Council); moreover, such criticisms assume that binding international decisions will necessarily be in America's interest, thus misunderstanding the role of the UN.

The United States was originally one of the strongest proponents of the veto in the Security Council, precisely because it was felt that the international organization should not be used to force any major power to follow the desires of a coalition of minor states; it was taken for granted that the United States Senate would never approve the UN Charter if the consequence would be an abandonment of American sovereignty. This principle was shared by other major powers, for it was assumed that the organization could not impose its will on a state unless there was a consensus of the most important nations. In this sense the UN was often perceived as a continuation of the wartime alliance against the Axis (an alliance that had significantly been called the "United Nations" on occasion).

Only when the Soviet Union blocked American or Western proposals in the early years of the cold war did this original conception seem faulty, for during World War II it was hoped that major confrontations between the allies could be avoided; when the Soviet Union walked out of the Security

---

is made clear in Article 12, Paragraph 1 of the Charter: "While the Security Council is exercising in respect of any dispute or situation the functions assigned to it in the present Charter, the General Assembly shall not make any recommendations with regard to that dispute or situation unless the Security Council so requests." The veto provision occurs in Article 27, Paragraph 3: "Decisions of the Security Council on all other matters [except procedure] shall be made by an affirmative vote of seven members [of the original 11 members] including the concurring votes of the permanent members." According to Article 24, Paragraph 1, the Security Council has "primary responsibility for the maintenance of international peace and security"; according to Article 25, "The Members of the United Nations agree to accept and carry out the decisions of the Security Council in accordance with the present charter."

Council in 1950, the United States took advantage of her inability to veto proposals and attempted to shift the center of power of the organization to the General Assembly (where the communist bloc could be easily outvoted). The result was the "Uniting for Peace" resolution of 1950, permitting the United States to use the UN as a cover for our commitment in Korea.

The subsequent enlargement of UN membership has produced demands on the part of smaller powers that this new importance of the General Assembly be maintained. But the increased number of African and Asian states, along with the possibility of a General Assembly majority based on an anticolonialist stance supported by the USSR, has created fears that the United States would be outvoted. Not surprisingly, Washington has come in recent years to emphasize again the desirability of acting in the Security Council, where we have a veto. Nonetheless, the implications of this shift have often not been fully recognized, especially during the periodic crises that have threatened to paralyze the UN completely.

Two such crises are instructive: first, the Russian proposal to replace the Secretary General's office with a "troika" of three executives (representing the West, the communist bloc, and the uncommitted states); second, the refusal of the Soviets and French to contribute to UN financing in support of peace-keeping missions that they have not approved. In each case, a major power was insisting that its veto in the Security Council is absolutely essential to the effectiveness of the UN, on the completely defensible ground that no major power will sustain a defeat merely because it has been outvoted by a coalition of weaker states. American ambivalence on this issue has been possible because we have not yet been massively defeated in the UN, but this immunity cannot be expected to last indefinitely. For example, if the American bombing of North Vietnam were subjected to a vote in the General Assembly, we might be condemned by a majority of the UN membership.

It is therefore of the utmost importance that the United States return to the view that the international organization can implement settlements or mediate disputes only when all the major parties are willing for it to do so. This means primarily that we cannot hope to avoid responsibility for defending our national interests by shifting the burden to the UN, nor can we insist that peace-keeping functions must be financed by unwilling members.

Once it is made clear that the UN is not an agency for compelling major powers to be peaceful, our attitude to international organization can be more consistent and less hypocritical. In particular, we should be perfectly willing to use the veto in the Security Council as a means of defending our own interests, because we—and other major powers—have no conceivable reason for seeking to involve the UN in conflicts that cannot be resolved by an accommodation between sovereign states. On this basis, admission of Peking to a permanent seat on the Security Council becomes more reasonable and less dangerous, for it is no longer assumed that mere membership in the UN implies the complete commitment to the ideals of the Charter—ideals that would mean the end of international politics and a surrender of sovereignty that the United States itself is unwilling to make.

One of the crucial dangers that will have to be avoided if the UN is to function effectively lies in the office of the Secretary General. The ill-fated Soviet proposal to institute a troika established, as a minimal condition for the persistence of the UN, that the occupant of the Secretary Generalship be acceptable to all permanent members of the Security Council. Moscow's toleration of U Thant was predicated on his discretion and caution in exposing himself as a "tool" of any bloc of powers—and, indeed, on Thant's image as an Asian from a noncommitted nation. It seems relatively unlikely that the Soviet Union (or for that matter China) would accept a Secretary General from a European state, even from a neutral nation; Trygve Lie and Dag Hammarskjöld may well be the only European secretaries in the UN's history. The resulting requirements of the office of the Secretary General need to be emphasized, for they modify somewhat the image of the UN as a medieval suzerain. It would be more accurate to view the powers of the international organization as analogous to the council of chiefs among the Iroquois; although one individual might have temporary authority over the Iroquois as a whole (for example, during a battle), basic decisions such as war and peace were determined by a council in which all chiefs had a veto. While the relationship between this council and the individual tribes of the Iroquois nation was somewhat similar to the role of the monarch in medieval Europe, the suzerain was a collective body, not an individual.

In this sense, the Security Council appears as the most likely holder of the UN's suzerain powers, for without at least the tacit support of the major powers it is hard to see how the Secretary General or the General Assembly could intervene effectively in international disputes. Once the UN's purpose is viewed as being limited to moderating conflicts between minor powers, on the assumption that the mechanisms for restraining violence between major powers will rest decisively on their own ability to balance each other, the principle of great-power veto and collective decision-making becomes less objectionable because it is less important.

This approach implies a rejection of the so-called functionalist argument, according to which the UN would develop into something approximating a world government by first establishing international cooperation in noncontroversial matters and subsequently expanding supranational decision-making to more fundamental political issues. Despite scholarly defenses of the idea that habits of collaboration and international responsibility would "spill over" from marginal issues to decisive ones, neither the experience of the Common Market nor of the UN itself indicates that this process is an automatic means of transcending national sovereignty; on the contrary, a multilateral institution can expand its competence and power only when it is supported by the most important member states or powerful private interests of a transnational extent. In other words, great powers will continue to hold an effective veto over the operations of the UN, especially as they touch on basic political issues, and any hopes for world peace must accept this fact as unavoidable.[6]

The UN as a whole could approximate the role of a medieval suzerain only by emphasizing the Security Council as the organ which, through the provisions of the Charter, can act directly or tacitly delegate authority wherever great powers tolerate international decision or intervention. Because situations must be created in which rivals compromise out of their own self-interested desire to avoid all-out war, considerations of power will have an increased importance whenever the UN is used to moderate conflict. It also means that attempts to keep any state outside of the UN will be self-defeating because they mask the primary fact that the international organization is neither an alliance of like-minded states nor a world government.

Emphasis on the Security Council as the organ that should respond to threats to the peace is not the only consequence of viewing the UN as a residual but effective means of increasing international stability, on the analogy of a plural suzerain. Equally if not more important is the role of the UN in multilateral economic assistance and international economic policy. According to the UN Charter, "international economic and social cooperation" is "vested in the General Assembly and, under the authority of the General Assembly, in the Economic and Social Council."[7]

Unlike the Security Council, the Economic and Social Coun-

[6] See Sewell: *Functionalism and World Order,* esp. Chs. vi and vii. On the extent to which the International Bank for Reconstruction and Development has achieved a measure of autonomy by relying primarily on Western nations and private international bankers, see pp. 270 ff. Sewell concludes: "What emerges . . . are not so much organs in a nascent world community as new instrumentalities born of the play of international politics" (p. 291).

[7] UN Charter, Chapter IX, Article 60 (in Stoessinger: *The Might of Nations,* p. 430).

cil (ECOSOC), composed of eighteen members elected by the General Assembly, has not received much attention; again unlike the Security Council, no specific states are guaranteed membership by the Charter, nor do the major powers have a veto.[8] Although the permanent members of the Security Council (except China) have tended to be elected to ECOSOC by the General Assembly, it is entirely possible for the major powers to be outvoted. As the problems of economic development tend to divide the developed and underdeveloped states more sharply, these provisions give rise to the possibility that poor nations, dominating the General Assembly by their numbers, will easily outvote the wealthy countries that are the only source of economic assistance.

If the UN is to be used as the channel for effective policies that might moderate the problems of economic development, it will be necessary to secure the support of the highly industrialized states of the West. To date, this has effectively occurred within such agencies as the International Bank for Reconstruction and Development (which depends on Western financial sources for its capital). Unfortunately, there are a number of issues like commodity price stabilization that sharply divide the developed and underdeveloped nations; as such questions come to the fore, it is possible that the underdeveloped states will attempt to wrest greater concessions from the developed ones.

At present, many multilateral agencies are either effectively autonomous or subject to token supervision by the Economic and Social Council. This has been both possible and advisable since it was feared that debates over specific decisions in ECOSOC would give rise to self-defeating ideological debates; hence, for example, the list of aid programs financed by the UN Special Fund has habitually been approved as a whole. Since more contentious matters will probably arise as the underdeveloped nations seek concessions from all industrial-

---

[8] Ibid., Chapter X, Articles 61 and 67 (pp. 430, 432). Hence, according to Article 67, Section 2, "decisions of the Economic and Social Council shall be made by a majority of the members present and voting."

ized states, this device of delegating decisions to technical administrators may become unwise or impossible.

The UN Conference on Trade and Development, which gave birth to a permanent Trade and Development Board, is perhaps a forerunner of such problems. This type of multi-lateral negotiation, conducted under the authorization of the UN but not within it, has the advantage of permitting non-members of the UN (e.g., West Germany) to participate on a voting basis. But it should not be assumed that a procedural device can in itself resolve political issues; the alignment of interests that was revealed at the UNCTAD meetings of 1964 is thus a good indication of conflicts that are likely to be repeated in the future.

On many issues, a group of seventy-seven delegations from the underdeveloped (or, as they called themselves, "developing") nations acted as a bloc; their prime purpose was to secure concessions from the more developed states in order to improve the terms of international trade. On a number of votes, industrialized Western nations were opposed by a coalition of the developing nations and the communist bloc; on some, the United States alone objected. But in a few very revealing cases, the Soviet Union and it allies joined with the developed nations of the West in refusing to support the demands of the developing states.[9]

The danger to American interests arises from the ability of the underdeveloped states, voting as a unit and often gaining communist support, to form a massive majority in any UN agency that grants an equal vote to all participating states. It follows that, for certain purposes, we could insist that the provisions of the Charter emphasizing the decision-making role of the Economic and Social Council be reinforced and

[9] *UNCTAD Final Act*, Annex A, pp. 25, 88, 95, 97, 108. It should be added that the tacit alignment of Communist and Western nations manifested itself in votes on which the USSR and its allies abstained (whereas the United States and some of its allies voted no). This difference indicates the persistence of ideological conflict (and the Russian attempts to pose as the champions of the underdeveloped nations) even on issues that divide all developed states, regardless of ideology, from the poorer countries.

altered; more specifically, we could combine an offer to increase considerably our contributions to economic aid administered through the UN with a demand that the ECOSOC come to approximate the Security Council in membership and voting rules.[1]

Such a change in the Charter would have been extremely dangerous at a time of bipolar confrontation between East and West; as power is diffused throughout the world, however, it becomes essential as a means of insuring UN decisions that can be effectively implemented. Since developed states, regardless of ideology, feel threatened by the voting majority of underdeveloped countries, both superpowers (as well as the Western European nations) have a common interest in insisting that binding decisions be taken or at least approved by a body in which they have a weighted vote (if not a veto).

This device would doubtless greatly reduce the range of economic programs that could be enacted by formal UN decision. By that very token, however, proposals that could gain the support of the permanent members of the Security Council would be far easier to implement; in contrast, many of the resolutions adopted at the UNCTAD meetings represent the pious hopes of the underdeveloped nations, and could not possibly be carried out since they were opposed by the United States and other developed countries (whose participation is indispensable).

If the assent of a reformed ECOSOC, modeled on the Security Council, were required, debates on the economic relationship between developed and underdeveloped countries would therefore become more acrimonious. In part, this would be healthy, because it would indicate that the negotiations were truly meaningful attempts to settle disputes. More important, the common interests of developed nations regard-

---

[1] It would probably be impossible to enact a Charter revision that gave permanent members of the Security Council a veto in ECOSOC, since the underdeveloped nations would doubtless object strenuously. Nor would this be advisable if Peking were to gain the Chinese seat in the Security Council, for the Chinese communists could thereby paralyze UN development efforts that were acceptable to both Washington and Moscow. Some scheme for weighted voting would therefore seem preferable.

less of ideology would necessarily become more apparent; indeed, such a device would be an exceedingly useful way of demonstrating conflicts within the communist bloc.[2]

Since weak powers will predictably resist such initiatives as means of undermining their power (especially insofar as this device would further limit the importance of the General Assembly), concessions could be made in two forms. First, the Assembly's power of "recommendation" could be utilized to permit the smaller powers to place on record their demands concerning decisions delegated to the Economic and Social Council; for example, before formally endorsing an agreement on international monetary reform, ECOSOC could receive a resolution from the General Assembly that might indicate the interests of the smaller states.

A second means of creating an interest among the smaller powers for increasing the authority of the major powers in ECOSOC lies in the expansion of mutilateral aid. While it would be folly to expect major powers to abandon bilateral economic or military assistance, especially since in some cases aid promotes political leverage, the giver of aid may often want to cut down his responsibility to the recipient. Use of the UN as a channel for multilateral assistance and commodity price stabilization would therefore help to relax ideological tension between major powers and backward countries and force the latter to agree on means of allocating assistance among themselves.

To be effective, such a development of the UN requires that most if not all major powers contribute to multilateral aid funds which are then dispensed according to some formula of "log rolling" in international agencies. The prerequisite for using the UN as an instrument of limited cooperation between major powers is their willingness to forego the advantages as well as responsibilities of conducting bilateral

[2] For example, the communist bloc was split on a number of votes at the UNCTAD meetings of 1964. On four occasions, Yugoslavia supported a resolution on which the USSR abstained (*UNCTAD Final Act,* Annex A, pp. 25, 88, 95, 97). More important, Tito's representative was joined by Rumania on three of these votes (pp. 25, 88, 95), by Cuba on two (pp. 25, 88), and by Albania on one (p. 25).

aid programs. But this requirement can be fulfilled only if a mutually acceptable balance of power exists between the great powers, so that the risks of direct confrontation would outweigh the possible gains of a more traditional diplomacy.

It follows—though this may seem unconventional—that the most important means of increasing the influence of the UN is to achieve an effective political balance between the major powers. Whereas in its original conception, the UN was to end the era of power politics, it may well be that only through power politics will international organization come into its own. Even in the past, "part of the UN's growth in strength has actually taken place *because* of superpower conflicts."[3] If the result is less than hoped for by optimists, it may still be a far greater contribution to international stability than pessimists expect.

It is instructive to consider the extent to which the UN has already developed along the lines suggested here. Where the balance between great powers has been roughly acceptable, the UN has on occasion been able to intervene to prevent direct confrontations; where such a balance has not existed (as in Vietnam), the organization has been helpless. Peace-keeping activities, such as the United Nations Emergency Force (UNEF) created during the Suez crisis and the United Nations Operation in the Congo (UNOC) have, moreover, followed a pattern typical of a political system whose central authorities have suzerainty but not sovereign authority. As among the Iroquois or in a medieval monarchy, conflict between small groups was progressively enlarged as each side sought powerful allies; the role of the suzerain was to discourage major political forces from committing themselves in such a way as to create uncontrolled violence.[4] The UN

---

[3] Stoessinger: *The UN and the Superpowers*, p. 172.

[4] "One striking similarity between UNEF and UNOC was the environment in which each crisis developed. In each case a local dispute escalated into a conflict between nationalism and colonialism that, in turn, led to a major confrontation between the superpowers. . . . But at the outset of both crises, the United States and the USSR both saw their interests better served through UN action than through direct conflict" (ibid).

has therefore been a means of preventing a direct Russo-American intervention in localized rivalries wherever the two superpowers have deterred each other sufficiently to make a UN presence tolerable as an alternative to war.

The financing of such peace-keeping efforts has been a grave issue, however, and one that threatened to destroy the UN. Both France and the Soviet Union have rejected the principle of a "collective responsibility" to pay for UN peace-keeping forces, especially insofar as these activities have been conducted under resolutions of the General Assembly or on the initiative of the Secretary General. The United States faces a dilemma in this regard, since we favor the principle of collective responsibility and realize that a UN "presence" may be in the American interest, but we must now be aware that a majority of the General Assembly could take actions over our strongest objections. Any solution to the problem of financing the UN must take these dual concerns into account.

There is much to be said for developments that would assure the international organization of a modicum of income not dependent on the pleasure of the major powers (and especially the United States). UN peace-keeping forces will often be simultaneously in the interest of the major states and minor powers, and yet one or the other of the superpowers may find it impossible to vote for a peace-keeping mission in the Security Council. This need not prevent UN action, since a great power may abstain in the Security Council or the Secretary General may decide to act on the basis of a General Assembly resolution; recent precedent indicates that as long as the major powers limit their opposition and at least passively tolerate UN action, international intervention is possible.

But whereas the UN can send a peace-keeping mission as long as the permanent members of the Security Council refrain from certain kinds of active opposition, the UN's ability to pay for such forces depends in large measure on the willingness of wealthier and more powerful states. International sources of financing UN operations, no longer dependent on the immediate approval of the major powers, are therefore very much in the interest of the weaker states, for the UN might then be more readily used to limit great-power intervention in local rivalries. Sources of money might come from the natural resources in areas that are technically subject to international rather than national law; should these be considered as belonging to the UN, they could be exploited only if royalty and license payments were made to the international organization. Hence undersea oil deposits outside the territorial waters of states, raw materials that might be found in Antarctica or on the moon, and the like might become sources of independent revenue for the UN.

This idea may seem futuristic, but it is precisely the limited exploitation of such resources to date that makes the idea even remotely feasible; once nation-states begin to utilize them, the international status of these sources of wealth might be permanently eroded. The disadvantage of other possibilities, such as a surtax on international mails, is that they impinge on established economic procedures and hence encounter the hostility of governments and important private interests. Even the use of outer space as a source of international revenue, on the ground that it belongs to mankind as a whole and not to any one nation, has already been somewhat undermined by the use of communications satellites (which could in this view be taxed by the UN).

The development of novel sources of UN revenue should be viewed as part of the organization's evolution and not as an end in itself. Such means of financing are most evidently in the interest of the weaker powers, for these new sources of capital could be used not only for UN peace-keeping missions but also for economic development. The major powers, however, cannot be expected to acquiesce in independent financing should it create the risk that the UN would intervene militarily against their vital interests; to be effective, the exploitation of new sources of UN revenue must therefore be combined with the assurance that such funds will not be used in ways that are intolerable to the great powers. It follows that the United States (and other permanent members of the Security Council) might accept innovations in financing on condition that the UN return to those provisions of its Charter that give the Security Council final authority in threats to the peace and that the Economic and Social Council be reformed along the lines suggested above.

Such a combination would be perhaps the best way to satisfy the contradictory interests of the major and minor powers, and would make it more likely that the UN could survive without either continued economic dependence on the United States or temptations to intervene in direct clashes between great powers. In particular, an increased emphasis on the UN as an institution providing economic aid endowed by independent revenue (as well as by the assessments levied on members) would be particularly healthy as a means of reducing the ideological tension in world politics.

To appreciate the feasibility of these developments and the changes in American attitudes to the UN required for their realization, let us consider the UN's Special Fund as a model. In the past, it has become customary for political considerations to be excluded in determining the countries which will receive assistance from the Special Fund; the only relevant criteria have been technical, and the list of proposed projects has been voted on as a whole. The process therefore includes something analogous to the "log-rolling" that occurs when the American Congress passes a Rivers-and-Harbors appropriations bill that the President must sign or veto as a unit.

Special Fund projects in communist nations have therefore been approved by Western votes, just as projects in pro-Western states have been voted by the communists. In 1962, however, the United States objected strenuously to a small project of agricultural assistance to Castro's Cuba. Although our effort to block this project failed because other UN members refused to depart from the principle of voting on all projects as a single package, from time to time bitter attacks are made on the Special Fund for its support of enemy regimes.[5] Because it is both possible and desirable to channel economic assistance to underdeveloped societies through the UN, such criticisms are regrettable and ignore our long-range interest in reducing ideological rivalries when they threaten to

[5] On this issue, see Stoessinger: *The UN and the Superpowers*, Ch. ix.

cause great-power conflicts in situations beyond our control.

An increased role of the UN as a channel for economic assistance is especially desirable because of the likely use of nuclear technology in underdeveloped areas. If the principle of multilateral assistance through the UN is adopted, with particular reference to nuclear reactors it will become easier to demand controls on the use of nuclear materials without which proliferation to all nations can hardly be prevented. Hence local rivals, like Israel and Egypt, will be less tempted to engage in a nuclear arms race and major powers will not have to contribute assistance that threatens to trigger explosive rivalries.

It is not appropriate here to go into detail concerning further desirable modifications of the UN, although some form of weighted voting may one day be workable in the Security Council. For example, a voting arrangement in which the United States and Russia each had five votes, the other permanent members had two votes, and nonpermanent members had one vote each might be a means of insuring that votes in the Council reflect political power; should a West European confederation be formed and desire to be represented by a single delegation, it too could be allotted five votes. Over the long run such a scheme might even permit a qualification of the veto principle, at least on some matters.

While flexibility on these questions is desirable, we should be fully aware of the risk that alterations of the UN's institutions may not turn out as expected. The UN has managed to play an effective if marginal role in world politics, in good part due to the initiative of those participating in it, but its role has presupposed a reasonable balance between the major powers and their toleration of its initiatives. We should not deceive ourselves that tinkering with the formal institutions and rules of the UN will end the era of power politics; on the contrary, only by maintaining our own strength and encouraging international stability can we see to it that international organization has a role to play in keeping the peace and encouraging economic development.

PART III

THE PAST
IN THE LIGHT
OF THE FUTURE

———

*Un peuple ne devient célèbre que quand sa
législation commence à décliner.*

Jean-Jacques Rousseau, *Du contrat social*

CHAPTER NINE

American Traditions

and World Politics

IN THE LIGHT of trends in international politics, American policy has been criticized in the foregoing chapters. But my specific policy proposals, even if adopted, would not secure perpetual peace by the end of the century. On the contrary, conflict, war, and revolutionary social change seem inherent in world politics, especially as Western technology is spread to previously unindustrialized or backward societies. Since the crises of the future will be increasingly difficult for the great powers to control, the primary consideration for American policy is that our national interests be disengaged from ideological commitments and directed more openly to the maintenance of a pluralist balance of power.

This theme, which has run throughout my analysis, involves a sharp divergence from most American attitudes about foreign policy. The view that the United States should establish as its goal a stable balance of power will strike many as an abandonment of our ideals, since it implies that we no longer consider the fostering of democracy, peace, or international cooperation as our prime goal; instead, it will be said, I propose a Machiavellian manipulation of power that is inimical to our traditions.

To fulfill my intention of exploring the constraints within which American foreign-policy makers will operate in future years, therefore, it is important to examine the traditional opposition to power politics. Before so doing, I should emphasize that the proposed frame of reference is not taken as an end in itself. Those who treat foreign affairs solely in terms of power sometimes fail to consider the relative importance of domestic and international affairs; moral ideals may be insufficient as a guide to foreign policies, but they have a greater role in internal politics and can only be realized domestically if our country is secure against external threats. In the broadest sense, American foreign policy is a means of preserving our democratic institutions, and this end must of necessity distinguish between our own citizenry and the rest of humanity.

In other words, the pursuit of an international balance of power, without primary regard to the ideology or domestic institutions of other nations, is both tolerable and morally defensible because it serves to strengthen American democracy. Insofar as we are convinced that our political order is worthy of imitation, our foreign policies can and should frankly emphasize our national interests in a world that is neither a global state nor a single human community. This approach to international relations assumes that morality can be politically implemented only within a community that shares not only historical traditions and a common sense of justice, but also legitimate governmental institutions.

The assertion that the highest human ideals can be realized through political action only in domestic affairs will seem curiously anachronistic to many Americans. Since the presidential campaign of 1940, Americans have been accustomed to consider the United States as part of "one world" (to use Wendell Willkie's famous phrase); we have become aware that the fate of our own political institutions depends on what happens beyond our shores. This broadening of our perspective has often had a strongly humanitarian tone, doubtless derived in part from our Declaration of Independence: "We hold these truths to be self-evident, that all men are created equal, that they are endowed by their Creator with certain unalienable Rights, that among these are Life, Liberty and the pursuit of Happiness." If all men are essentially equal, the fundamental concern for human rights cannot end at our borders; for some, the logical conclusion is that the United States should orient its foreign policy to the establishment of a better life for all.

The nobility of such an objective is undeniable, but its attractiveness should not blind us to the fact that the political differences between nations have not usually been treated as artificial impediments to the unity of mankind. Throughout history, societies have considered themselves distinct entities whose way of life sets them off from their neighbors; to view the human race as a single community, therefore, one must assume that each country's traditions are merely human inventions or accidents, subject to manipulation, change, and removal. Even more important, it follows that political life can only be understood in terms of the fundamental identity of all human beings, so that a world government could conceivably replace separate and warring states.

In the history of Western civilization, several strands of thought have reinforced this image of the equality of all men (and hence the residual or artificial character of the political differences between one nation and another). In ancient Greece and Rome, Stoic philosophers spoke of the sense in which mankind forms a single "commonwealth"; Christianity radically emphasizes the equality of men in the sight of God. During the Middle Ages, the concept of a "Christian Republic" embracing the entire human race and securing peace on earth was a forceful ideal.

The rise of the modern state, especially in the sixteenth and seventeenth centuries, was in part a reaction against the notions of a universal political community (whose fate had become entwined with the question of the temporal power of the popes); the Protestant Reformation created such deeply divergent interpretations of Christianity that attempts to unify Catholics, Lutherans, and Calvinists led to brutal warfare. As a consequence, it became both tolerable and necessary to admit the autonomy of each state and diversity between states. Since what was legitimate for the French could not be accepted by the English, the rights of Englishmen—not the rights of man—predominated in the evolution of English constitutional government during the seventeenth century.

Emphasis on the uniqueness of each political society is indeed far more deeply rooted in our traditions than many realize today. To appreciate this fully, it is enough to read the Old Testament, for the Hebrew Bible represents not only the root of the Judeo-Christian heritage but also a pervasive strand in Protestant thought. The very term "Old Testament" refers to the covenants Abraham and Moses made with God—covenants that set the Hebrew people apart. Hence the assumption that the natural equality of men is somehow less important than the specific character and principles of each society has had continuing importance in Western thought, especially since the Reformation.

Nowhere was the feeling of political uniqueness more striking than in Puritan New England, for the Plymouth Plantation and later settlements were originally viewed by their members as superior communities based on the true understanding of the divine word. These colonists were so far from believing in the political equality of all human beings that to vote in Massachusetts it was long necessary to be a member of the Congregational Church; as in Calvinist Geneva, the community was bound together by its understanding of Christianity. Since the proper worship of God was considered man's highest duty, religious differences were far more important than the physical or natural similarity between one individual and another.

These historical comments reveal two distinct sources of

American thought about man and the status of his political duties. Although the underlying Christian orientation of the West, as well as specifically American traditions, include a belief in the equality of all men in the sight of God, the Protestant and English origins of our colonization emphasize the uniqueness of one's own political community. These two strands of thought persist to the present, as can be seen in the image of an Atlantic community based on shared democratic traditions but separated from communist states by an insuperable gulf. This may explain why many Americans who are suspicious of agreements with the communists have also found it hard to tolerate de Gaulle's demands for autonomy within NATO; since the French seem to share our notion of human equality while the Russians have adopted strange and antithetical political principles, national differences should be of minor significance within the West and of overriding importance between any Western society and the communist world.

The division of the international arena into "good" and "bad" states is a frequently noted aspect of American political opinions. Again and again congressmen denounce our nominal allies for their failure to support us in Vietnam or their willingness to trade with China or Cuba. According to such "conservative" or "nationalist" attitudes, neutrality in the cold war is a sign of unreliability or treachery; formal allies should demonstrate their sincerity by continued support for specific American commitments throughout the world. In contrast, there is also a more "liberal" outlook in the United States, willing to tolerate divergences with our allies in the name of international cooperation. This more universalistic approach, connected in recent years with the attempt to achieve agreements with the Soviet Union, has been the source of American support for the UN and the ideal of collective security, not to mention economic assistance to the backward nations.

Because these two opinions stem from Western political traditions (and each shares a measure of truth), it should not be surprising that both are commonly held in various combinations by the same individuals. Hence those who condemn our intervention in Asia reflect our nineteenth-century reluctance to be entangled in world politics together with a criticism of the immorality of our use of force; those who insist that we must check "communist aggression" in Vietnam combine an acceptance of America's role as a global power with an emphasis on the fundamental difference between Western democracy and Marxist principles. To clarify this merger of opposed attitudes, one could say that the "doves" combine the "conservative" assumption that the United States should not intervene in foreign wars with the "liberal" assumption that both the Vietcong and our allies in Saigon have an equal right to hold their political views. In turn, the "hawks" combine the "internationalist" assumption that events elsewhere in the world are a legitimate American concern with the "nationalist" assumption that the distinction between our allies and our enemies is a matter of highest principle that cannot be compromised.

It would appear that the distinction between "left" and "right" is misleading, for there are liberal and conservative assumptions on both sides of most foreign-policy issues. This may explain why America's role in world politics can create bitter domestic conflict, dividing both parties internally. Although the tradition of a "bipartisan foreign policy" is one way of preventing this danger, mere consensus need not be an adequate guide to effective decisions, especially if the United States is faced with problems that require generally unpopular and unaccustomed calculations of power; a democracy cannot permanently and thoughtlessly delegate questions of the highest importance to a select few whose decisions are passively ratified by the populace.

Since a degree of controversy is healthy, it is most important to reconsider those attitudes shared by all parties (rather than the specific arguments between hawks and doves). If most

Americans simultaneously hold both "liberal" and "conservative" assumptions (albeit combined in different ways), public understanding of foreign policy can best be improved by a deeper awareness of the common basis of American attitudes. More specifically, we must become conscious that some of our most cherished assumptions about world politics are inadequate.

Recently, the dualism of American opinions concerning world politics has produced domestic harmony and agreement in two situations: major wars (where the world-wide challenge to Western traditions also seemed a direct military threat to the United States), and peaceful cooperation with our favored allies (whose goals were consistent with ours, and whose regimes have been tolerably democratic). During World War II and in the initiation of Marshall Plan aid to Europe, therefore, the nationalist and humanitarian assumptions of most Americans have coincided, and a bipartisan foreign policy was easily established. Conversely, whenever the question of peace and war, or the identity of allies and enemies, has been confused, domestic division has necessarily followed.

As has often been noted, Americans are reluctant to go to war, but once committed they fight with a common devotion to the goal of total victory. War and peace seem to be viewed as polar opposites with no intermediary condition; just as nations are either our allies or our enemies, so we are either at war (in which case there is "no substitute for victory," to use General MacArthur's phrase) or at peace. In peacetime, moreover, we tend to assume that our differences with foreign nations can be resolved amicably by the process of "reasonable" negotiations, and that our sincerity will be reciprocated by others. This attitude can, like many others, be traced to our Declaration of Independence from the British: "We must, therefore . . . hold them, as we hold the rest of mankind, Enemies in War, in Peace Friends."

However reasonable a sharp distinction between war and

peace may appear, the post-World War II situation has not conformed to our traditional image; the term "cold war" connotes a situation of formal peace between more or less declared enemies. The most profound foreign-policy debates of the last twenty years—the demands to settle the Korean War after it degenerated into a military stalemate and the furor over our commitment in Vietnam—reflect frustration with our participation in wars that are not total. Because domestic life has continued on a more or less peacetime basis during both the Korean and Vietnamese wars, there were widespread cries that we either defeat the enemy completely or stop fighting.

One aspect of the broadly held view that war and peace are diametrically opposed conditions is American reluctance to accept the notion of a "limited war."[1] With the emergence of a nuclear stalemate, escalation could result in national suicide; military restraint has become absolutely essential. Despite this obvious fact, many Americans remain bewildered by our inability to convert massive firepower and fabulous national wealth into military victory. As a consequence, the public wavers between fears of a third world war and bitter condemnation of those who, by criticizing the administration, "sabotage" the successful prosecution of a limited war. The Johnson administration has demonstrated this ambiguity by insisting on its desire to avoid escalation in Vietnam while proclaiming that we must prove that communist-led wars of national liberation can be defeated.

Behind this ambivalence lies the hope that military defeat of the enemy will restore the peace and teach the aggressors that violence is not a permissible means of achieving political goals. Successful wars—even limited wars—are thus perceived as a means of returning to a peaceful situation in which reasonable negotiations will solve outstanding international problems. This view is shared by those who seek a negotiated settlement and those who demand miltiary victory, with the difference that the former consider reasonable negotiation possible and necessary before the enemy has been defeated.

[1] See esp. Robert Osgood: *Limited War* (Univ. of Chicago Press; 1957).

Hence both hawks and doves share the assumption that a peaceful world is intrinsically different from a condition of war; the fundamental debate revolves merely over the possibility of military victory and the desirability of assuming that our enemies will accept an honorable settlement.

It is at this level that American attitudes concerning foreign affairs are open to the strongest objection. As long as the sovereignty of a world government is not universally accepted, international relations will be an ambiguous and tense condition of neither perpetual war nor assured peace. Our allies will insist on defending their national interests, often using arguments which (like those of General de Gaulle) seem "unreasonable" to most Americans; our enemies will resort to diplomatic and political as well as military maneuvers that show warlike hostility even in periods of nominal peace. Negotiated settlements will be reached only to be violated by our rivals—and, in our own self-interest, we will be forced to violate such agreements ourselves.

For example, the Korean truce was generally perceived as an end to a war that had become unpopular within the United States. Communist violations of the specific terms of that agreement have been denounced from time to time by Americans, but it is not usually admitted that we ourselves have provided our troops in Korea with new weapons (in violation of the Panmunjom agreements). The Vietcong are bitterly attacked for not obeying the spirit as well as the letter of the Geneva Agreements of 1954, but critics of our commitment to Saigon point to similar violations on our part (notably our advice to Diem that he not permit general elections in 1956).

Americans usually have a bad conscience about our failures to observe international treaties, justifying this behavior on the ground that the enemy was the first to break the agreement. There is nothing novel about such rationalizations; both Sparta and Athens said much the same thing in breaking their truce at the outset of the Peloponnesian War.[2] What is dan-

---

[2] Here again, Thucydides' *History of the Peloponnesian War* provides invaluable insight into the nature of international politics and the role of morality and power in the relations between states. With reference to the

gerous, however, is the self-righteous assertion that only the enemy is at fault and that only we uphold standards of morality by conforming to our international commitments. Any sovereign state will feel compelled by necessity to defend itself against potential enemies in time of peace, and fundamental conflicts of interest may prevent the most enlightened statesmen from resolving their differences by sincere negotiation.

Since true peace is a characteristic of the political life within an organized society, the relations between states are never totally devoid of the basic hostility that finds its purest expression in war. A peace treaty does not convert former enemies into friends—unless, as with Western Germany after World War II, there are compelling reasons of national interest which make alliance mutually desirable. War is not a fundamental distortion of the natural relationship between independent societies, for no government can ignore the potential threat to its interests from states that have different ideologies or goals. As long as no world government exists so that treaties could be enforced like domestic laws and contracts, international politics will remain a condition of potential war and insecure peace.

The cold war therefore reflects the essential character of international politics rather than an unusual situation. Because public opinion could conceivably tolerate the realities of power, it is necessary to explain American frustration with our inability to secure total military victory or with the apparently unreasonable refusal of other nations to abide by their agreements. Why do our political traditions lead us to expect that all mankind will be "enemies in war, in peace friends"? Why is it that Americans persistently hope that victory in war can make the world "safe for democracy," ushering in periods of peace during which international disputes can be resolved on the basis of mutual respect, sincerity, and understanding?

---

violation of the Thirty Year Truce and the origins of the war, see Book I (Modern Library edn.), esp. pp. 65-83.

Scholars generally agree that the philosopher whose understanding of politics most influenced our Founding Fathers and has remained most characteristic of our political opinions was John Locke. Because the American colonies were absolved, by historical accident, from the need to overthrow a previously established feudal order, Locke's notions of private property and limited government have been uniquely effective in the United States; Marxism has never been more than a minor sect among us, whereas it has been and remains a widespread popular movement in most of continental Europe.[3] To gain perspective on our own attitudes, therefore, let us consider briefly Locke's political ideas and the reasons for their persisting vitality in our society.

Without attempting an exhaustive analysis of Locke, several aspects of his thought are relevant.[4] First, Locke argued that all men are by nature equal and free; from this natural freedom and equality flowed the natural right of every man to preserve himself as he sees fit. For Locke, this meant that all men have a natural right not only to "life" and "liberty," but also to property; without the right to property in money and material objects, civilized man's right to life and liberty is essentially meaningless (since he would then depend on the good will of others for his survival).

Locke set forth principles for the kind of society that would most completely protect man's natural rights and secure his property. He did this by emphasizing the importance of the consent of the governed in any decent civil society; if a government can tax or confiscate private property without the consent of a popularly elected legislature, the citizen can be

---

[3] See esp. Louis Hartz: *The Liberal Tradition in America* (New York: Harcourt, Brace; 1955). For example, Hartz summarizes the striking impotence of socialist movements in the United States as follows: "A society which begins with Locke, and thus transforms him, stays with Locke, by virtue of an absolute and irrational attachment it develops for him, and becomes as indifferent to the challenge of socialism in the later era as it was unfamiliar with the heritage of feudalism in the earlier one" (p. 6).

[4] The following pages will focus on Locke's *Second Treatise of Civil Government,* his best-known political work. Appropriately enough, many editions are currently available.

at the mercy of his rulers. But since all men have a natural right to be free and to acquire property, a government that violates the rights of its citizens need no longer be obeyed. In the words of the Declaration of Independence, "to secure these rights, Governments are instituted among Men, deriving their just powers from the consent of the governed. That whenever any Form of Government becomes destructive of these ends, it is the Right of the People to alter or abolish it, and to institute new Government. . . ."

It is not hard to see why the principles of Locke were particularly appealing to the colonists in 1776. "No taxation without representation" follows directly from Locke's theory; since the colonists had been taxed without representation in one way or another, they appealed increasingly to their rights as men—not their rights as Englishmen. But we should never forget that most of those who signed the Declaration of Independence were born English subjects; Locke, the English theorist who defended the Glorious Revolution of 1688, was a fitting source for the principles of the American Revolution because he was an Englishman whose writings justified a break with England.

One aspect of John Locke's political thought is of particular importance in explaining American attitudes toward domestic and foreign politics. Locke's notion of man's natural rights is based on the situation that exists wherever there is no established government; he calls this condition the "state of nature," adding:

> But though this be a state of liberty, yet it is not a state of licence . . . The state of nature has a law of nature to govern it which obliges every one; and reason, which is that law, teaches all mankind who will but consult it that, being all equal and independent, no one ought to harm another in his life, health, liberty, or possessions.[5]

The claim to man's natural rights must therefore be consistent with the law of nature—or, as Locke describes it elsewhere,

[5] Locke, *Second Treatise*, Ch. ii, §6.

the law of reason; as long as men are reasonable, therefore, the state of nature, in which men live without a common government, can be peaceful.

This conception is especially important because Locke explicitly describes international politics as a state of nature. Since the government of each society is sovereign and does not recognize a higher authority or world ruler, the relationship between states can be peaceful, just as the state of nature among individuals can be peaceful, as long as all participants are reasonable in claiming their natural rights. But since there is no common government in the state of nature, each individual or government judges for itself whether its claims are in fact just; as a result, the state of nature can easily become a state of war whenever the laws of nature (or reason) do not produce mutual agreement.

Locke therefore distinguishes between war and peace in much the way that has been described in contemporary American opinions: even without a government that would impartially enforce the laws, peace is possible (though not assured) as long as men are reasonable. War and peace are fundamentally different precisely because in warfare there is an attempt to secure one's rights by force and violence, whereas peace is a condition of natural harmony between those who recognize the same principles of justice.[6] Although the peaceful state of nature can easily become a state of war as long as there is no common government, this "inconvenience" does not contradict the underlying difference between the two situations.

Not only do American attitudes about foreign policy echo Locke's notion of international peace as a relationship be-

[6] "And here we have the plain difference between the state of nature and the state of war which, however some men have confounded, are as far distant as a state of peace, good-will, mutual assistance, and preservation, and a state of enmity, malice, violence, and mutual destruction are one from another. Men living together according to reason, without a common superior on earth with authority to judge between them, is properly the state of nature. But force, or a declared design of force, upon the person of another, where there is no common superior on earth to appeal to for relief, is the state of war" (Ibid., Ch. iii, §19).

tween reasonable governments, to be contrasted with war; we also share Locke's conception of the only way to avoid the danger that a peaceful state of nature would degenerate into a state of war. On the level of individuals, Locke argues that men avoid the "inconvenience" of the state of nature by forming a social contract and establishing a government. In this way, man's freedom and his natural right to property are protected by political institutions that can punish domestic violence and enforce contracts between individuals. If applied to the relations between states, this theory implies that peace and security are only possible if international organizations like the UN are empowered to enforce treaties and resolve conflicts.

Ever since becoming a world power, the United States has placed more faith in international organizations than have other nations; from Woodrow Wilson's eloquent pleas in favor of the League of Nations to the establishment of the UN, this theme has been of increasing prominence in American foreign policy. Why then did we fail to join the League? Simply because it was felt that the United States could be secure in isolation—that is, that we did not have to play a central role in the international arena. Just as Locke argued that the state of nature could be peaceful as long as there were but few men who had little contact with each other, those who rejected American membership in the League of Nations believed that our security was assured by the Atlantic and Pacific Oceans.

Before World War II, isolationism seemed not merely feasible but reasonable; after World War II, an international organization that would secure the peace through collective security seemed equally necessary and desirable. We have therefore oscillated between the extremes of assuming that we could simply ignore conflicts between other nations and of thinking that only through an impartial UN could we prevent a global holocaust—extremes that represent a transference of Locke's principles concerning domestic politics into the area of international politics.

But although Locke describes the relationship between sovereign states as a state of nature, he does not consider international politics and the state of nature between individuals identical in all respects. Although the individual can escape the "inconveniences" of the state of nature by forming civil societies, Locke does not propose world government as a similar solution in international politics. Each "whole community is one body in the state of nature in respect of all other states or persons out of its community"; as a consequence, the international state of nature constantly threatens to become a state of war.[7] Since the relations between states are not naturally pacific, like the original state of nature among individuals, Locke's philosophy is completely consistent with a balance-of-power approach to world politics.

It is for this reason that Locke excludes foreign affairs from his general principle that actions of the executive should be subordinate to laws reflecting the consent of the governed; in contrast to domestic affairs, where the populace can judge adequately and must be represented through the legislature, Locke treats foreign policy as the "Federative Power," normally exercised by the executive without subordination to previously enacted law.[8]

American political traditions have therefore diverged from Lockean principles in assuming that foreign policies, like domestic ones, should reflect a popular consensus. Locke asserts that "it is almost impracticable . . . that the executive and federative power should be placed in persons that might

[7] Ibid., Ch. xii, §145. Some commentators have argued that, for Locke, the international state of nature is essentially a perpetual state of war (like the war of all against all which Hobbes described as the natural condition of man). See Richard Cox: *Locke on War and Peace* (Oxford: Clarendon Press; 1960).

[8] ". . . the power of war and peace, leagues and alliances, and all the transactions with all persons and communities without the commonwealth . . . may be called 'federative' . . . And though this federative power in the well management of it be of great moment to the commonwealth, yet it is much less capable to be directed by antecedent, standing, positive laws than the executive, and so must necessarily be left to the prudence and wisdom of those whose hands it is in to be managed for the public good." Locke: *Second Treatise,* Ch. xii, §146-7

act separately, whereby the force of the public would be under different commands, which would be apt some time or other to cause disorder and ruin"; the American doctrine of separation of powers partly contradicts this advice, requiring the "advice and consent" of the Senate on matters that Locke viewed as best managed according to the prudence of the executive.[9]

This divergence from Lockean principles may help explain why Americans have tended to apply his teaching concerning the state of nature between individuals to the international sphere. Since our legislature must give final approval to fundamental orientations in foreign policy, domestic and international affairs are subject to the same institutional division of powers in the American constitutional system; because the relevant institutions are similar, the problems must somehow be similar. As a result, our traditions have viewed world politics as an essentially peaceful state of nature; where Locke could accept considerations of the balance of power as necessary to any prudent foreign policy (because the state of nature between foreign states is implicitly also a state of war), Americans have rejected the notion of a balance of power because they view war as an abnormal disturbance in the naturally peaceful relations among states.

If, as has been argued, this distinction between war and peace is unrealistic, our reliance on international organization is as misleading as our prior faith in security through isolation. Why, then, have Locke's principles—and particularly his principles concerning the origin of a civil society among individuals—had such a persistent hold on American minds as a guide to foreign policy? Of the many answers that might be given, one stands out: as if by fate, America's national ex-

[9] Ibid., §148. On the powers of the American president in foreign affairs, and the extent to which his authority is less than that of the English king in the seventeenth and eighteenth centuries (obviously Locke's model), see *The Federalist Papers,* No. 69.

perience has closely paralleled Locke's doctrines of the state of nature and the state of war.

The relationship between the original colonists and the American Indians could easily be conceived of in later years in terms of Locke's principles. Whenever the Indians were "reasonable"—and especially if they signed and abided by treaties with the colonists—the virgin continent appeared to be a factual example of Locke's peaceful state of nature. When the Indians were hostile, this state of nature had the "inconvenience" of degenerating into a temporary state of war. As in Locke's principles, no government existed to arbitrate the differences between the Indians and the colonists; as a consequence, the original settlers could only have recourse to arms.

By the time of the Constitutional Convention of 1787, therefore, it was no accident that Americans used Locke's doctrine of the state of nature to describe the relations between sovereign states. For evidence that this was the case, one need only consult Madison's notes of the debates at the Constitutional Convention; as Luther Martin put it, explicitly citing Locke (and other political thinkers), "the States like individuals were in a State of nature equally sovereign and free."[1]

The use of violence to deprive the American Indians of lands became increasingly necessary as the United States expanded inland. While it could be justified in terms of the cultural and religious superiority of our growing country, the expropriation of Indian lands fits perfectly into Locke's doctrine that property is only truly acquired by labor within a civil society governed by law. The belief in man's natural

[1] Madison's notes are available in *The Federal Convention and the Formation of the Union of the American States*, ed. Winton U. Solberg (New York: Liberal Arts Press; 1958), p. 180. Others referring to the concept of the state of nature included James Wilson (p. 118) and Alexander Hamilton (p. 158). Indeed, at the Convention the issue was not whether the state of nature was an adequate concept for describing international relations; rather, debate concerned the sovereignty of the thirteen states of the Confederacy, and whether or not they had been placed in a state of nature *with each other* by the Declaration of Independence.

right to gain possession of land that is still unclaimed in the state of nature thus gave free play to the self-reliant and pragmatic spirit of the settlers as they moved westward.

This principle clarifies the connection between the underlying beliefs of Americans and their practical ability to solve problems. The national spirit of our people is not, as is sometimes asserted, based solely on a moralistic attitude toward internal or external political issues. On the contrary, within the framework of an unquestioned belief in the natural virtue of individualism, hard work, and the sanctity of private property, Americans customarily approach specific obstacles without many of the preconceptions that long characterized continental Europe. In a sense, the rise of the United States to its present power is a revealing consequence of the hardy pragmatism of our people; although the Industrial Revolution originated in Great Britain, it has reached its flowering on our shores in no small part owing to that famed "American ingenuity."

In foreign policy, the counterpart of our pragmatic approach in domestic affairs has been a tough use of power based on the immediate needs of each situation. Eschewing theories of the balance of power, we have shied away from long-range planning and approached problems one by one; in crises, American power has been committed with a practicality and vigor that permitted us to win every war in which we were involved (at least up to 1950).

The dispossession of the American Indians, who were ultimately "contained" on limited reservations, is a model we have followed in subsequent external policies. When treaties could be made, we were willing to purchase lands and allow them to move farther west in peace; thus far the state of nature remained peaceful and reasonable. When the Indians refused and fought, we sent cavalry and infantry to defeat them and insure the security of our settlements. But in most cases our actions were a direct response to specific crises or threats rather than a settled long-range policy implemented by a central bureaucracy.

Our national experience in the nineteenth century merely repeated and confirmed this combination of short-range pragmatism and the view of international affairs as a Lockean state of nature. Westward expansion was the result of a series of distinct actions, some by those who sought to increase our national power, others in order to extend the territories open to slaves, others as a means of weakening the domestic control exercised by the Eastern seaboard. Whatever the reasons, when opportunities for acquiring new territories appeared, they were eagerly seized. Hence Jefferson consummated the Louisiana Purchase (though in so doing he strengthened the national orientation of American society, in contradiction to principles of states' rights that many of his supporters had championed). We purchased Alaska in 1867, despite vigorous debate (which must now seem almost incomprehensible considering how Russian possession of that territory would have affected world politics in the twentieth century).

The pragmatic aspects of our movement across the North American continent did not exclude a sense of mission; even at the Constitutional Convention of 1787, some delegates spoke of the inevitability and desirability of expansion over the "new extensive Country" in which Americans found themselves. As Jefferson put it in 1801, "it is impossible not to look forward to distant times, when our rapid multiplication will . . . cover the whole northern, if not the southern continent."[2]

But in pursuing such long-range plans—which, characteristically enough, were not universally shared—American statesmen and politicians have from the beginning based specific policies on a straightforward calculation of the play of selfish interests and the art of the possible. We have sought to achieve our immediate objectives by persuasion where possible and force where necessary, being careful to use the threat of our power to reinforce the persuasion. As Gouverneur Morris said

[2] See Solberg: *The Federal Convention*, esp. p. 169 (speech of Mr. Pinckney), p. 205 (speech of Governeur Morris, who "looked forward also to that range of New States which would soon be formed in the West"), and pp. 293-6. Jefferson is quoted in William Miller: *A History of the United States* (New York: Dell; 1958), p. 161.

at the Constitutional Convention: "This Country must be united. If persuasion does not unite it, the sword will."[3]

Such pragmatic threats, backed up by military action where persuasion and money failed, were of course the basis on which we combined commercial development and territorial expansion throughout the nineteenth century. For example, when Spain seemed reluctant to cede Florida, Jefferson confidently stated: "If we push them strongly with one hand, holding out a price in the other, we shall certainly obtain the Floridas, and all in good time."[4] Much the same methods were evident in the annexation of Texas in 1845, leading as it did to the Mexican War of 1846-8.

These events are in many ways characteristic of American experiences in foreign affairs. Annexation of Texas and war with Mexico were most strongly favored by slave-holding Southerners and opposed by Northerners who feared any further extension of slavery; attitudes to our use of force were largely determined by the varying practical interests within the country rather than by concerns for the global balance of power or long-range planning. Once determined upon, our policy was frankly backed up by military intervention, though with a willingness to settle outstanding issues amicably; having demonstrated that we could force Mexico to cede the territories of New Mexico and California in 1848, we rounded out our borders by negotiating the Gadsden Purchase of 1853.[5]

Hotly debated, these actions had implications that were not always clearly perceived at the time. The same could be said of the Spanish-American War of 1898, which led to our almost unexpected acquisition of the Philippines and Hawaii (thereby making the United States a power in the Pacific). Our reaction to the supposed brutality of Spanish

---

[3] Solberg: *The Federal Convention*, p. 203.

[4] Quoted in Miller: *A History of the United States*, p. 162.

[5] It should be added that where persuasion, money, and American force were insufficient, the desires to acquire new territory (notably Cuba and Central America) failed. Such disappointments were not serious, however, because ample space was available for asserting the growing power of the country.

repression in Cuba, transformed into a nationalist outrage with the sinking of the battleship *Maine,* was based on the same spirit as our attitude toward the American Indians and the Mexican government. In each case, the peaceful state of nature, in which acquisitive Americans had a natural right to increase their possessions and power, was disturbed by an opponent who did not behave "reasonably"; each time, we felt culturally superior to the enemy and responded to his opposition by a frank resort to force.

The impulse to "send the marines" was thus hardly an invention of Theodore Roosevelt; the combination of Locke's political principles and our national experience has conspired to produce a strong confidence in the successful use of our power in foreign affairs. Where possible, peace is preferable because American initiative grants us sufficient control over our neighbors through commercial superiority; when the interests of American business are checked in such a way as to create an apparent threat, military force can be used (as it was against the Barbary pirates at the beginning of the nineteenth century and against Spain at the end of it).

It must be added, however, that the success of this national experience depended upon a global balance of power of which most Americans were simply unconscious. Prior to World War I, the Atlantic and Pacific tended to guarantee American security (though only after we had successfully defended the principle of the freedom of the seas in the War of 1812 and declared our intention to exclude European powers from the Western Hemisphere under the Monroe Doctrine). Isolationism—which is to say, the assumption that the United States could ignore considerations of European power politics while pursuing its national objectives—in fact presupposed a specific balance of power, based in part on Britain's maritime superiority; unaware of this, we were led by tradition and experience to interpret international affairs in terms of Locke's notion of the relations between free individuals in an essentially peaceful state of nature.

Our involvement in World War I was therefore quite consistent with the frame of mind underlying an isolationist policy. We could believe that our intervention was necessary to preserve the freedom of the high seas—a principle which Americans view as a reasonable international law (if not a reasonable law of nature); we did not have to think of ourselves as attempting to restore a global balance of power. This attitude explains the easy return to isolationism in the 1920's, for having exorcised the threat of German violations of our neutrality, we could assume that a peaceful world order would once again be restored without our active concern from day to day.

The United States has therefore become fully conscious of its status as a world power only since World War II. Even during this war, many felt that the defeat of the Axis would permit a new return to "normalcy"; only the exhaustion of Great Britain and the rest of Europe, combined with the threat of communism based in the USSR, made it evident that our presence in Europe was necessary to preserve the peace. Those who realized, before the end of the war, that we would play a continued role in world politics tried to minimize this necessity through the creation of the UN; later, when Soviet hostility indicated that the international organization would be paralyzed by great-power disputes, we hastened to establish NATO as an institution that would defend the West against attack and insure us of peaceful dealings with our European allies.

Our willingness to act as a great power has thus coincided with a determination to base our involvement on formal institutions that regularize the relations between states. In the 1950's, we entered into a series of so-called "collective security" treaties—after NATO came the ANZUS and SEATO pacts as well as a host of bilateral treaties. What has derisively been called the "pactomania" of John Foster Dulles is, however, merely an extension of the Lockean principles widely accepted by Americans; when one's security is threatened by the degeneration of peaceful relations into a state of war, the natural solution is to establish formal institutions. In more recent years, the same reflex has been apparent in proposals to settle differences of interest within NATO by the establishment of a multilateral force or a consultative committee on nuclear strategy, on the assumption that reasonable allies need only establish common institutions within which they can settle their mutual differences.

Our attitude toward the UN as a global organization is thus similar to our view of regional institutions joining allies against a common enemy (like NATO, SEATO, or the OAS). Americans have described both as institutions protecting the "collective security" of member states; in the American mind, support for the UN and for NATO is completely consistent. Hence we have fled from the brutal realities of power politics even in playing the role of a world power: whether in the era of isolation or in the present day, our tendency is to avoid any conception of foreign affairs based primarily and decisively on the need to manipulate a balance of power between rival states. Transposing Locke's conception of domestic politics onto international relations, we instinctively responded to the continuous threat of war by establishing international organizations, hoping that they would resolve conflicts peacefully (on the model of our own federal government).

It may be thought that the connection between our commitment to international collective security and our attitude toward domestic political institutions, framed as it is in Lockean terms, has been exaggerated. Yet in an important diplomatic exchange with the President of France, Lyndon Johnson wrote:

> Let me begin with the American conception of the purpose of the North Atlantic Treaty and the alliance it creates. Under our Constitution the treaty is the law of the land. Like our Constitution, it is more than a legal document. It is the outward and visible form of a living institution— not an alliance to make war but an alliance to keep the peace.[6]

Here one sees clearly the American image of an international alliance that is tolerable because it mirrors our view of

[6] *The New York Times,* March 25, 1966, p. 7.

domestic society; treaties that are oriented to making war are presumably evil, for they reflect the transient needs of power diplomacy rather than a community having "a political integrity and an identity of interests," based on "bonds of culture, of political institutions, traditions and values."[7]

The insufficiency of this attitude can be quickly perceived if one compares the North Atlantic Alliance and the United States Constitution. Under NATO, each member state has the legal right, on or after April 4, 1969, to denounce the basic treaty and leave the alliance; it is hard to imagine the remaining members attacking a state that utilizes this privilege in order to force it to return to the Atlantic community. This was of course exactly what Lincoln did when the South seceded from the Union in 1860, for the United States is a single nation, not an alliance of sovereign states. That our federal system is also composed of units called "states" should not blind us to the fundamental difference between Virginia and France; international politics is an arena of independent societies whose governments have a legal right to make or break alliances whenever they find it in their self-interest to do so.

It may now be somewhat easier to show why Americans are peculiarly accustomed to speak in moralistic terms when discussing foreign policy. As has been remarked, our actions are ultimately pragmatic, being based on what appears to be the most effective response to the problem at hand (be it the incursions of Indian tribes, the desire of slave-owners for new territories to the west, or the Kaiser's unreasonable sinking of American ships on the high seas). This approach to external affairs has been eminently successful, but only because it has

[7] See President Johnson's address to the Foreign Service Institute, quoted in *The New York Times*, March 24, 1966, p. 18. This address repeats the comparison between NATO and the U.S. Constitution used in the letter to President de Gaulle and explicitly refers to "the design of collective security protecting the entire Atlantic community." Popular opposition to admitting Peking to the UN rests on the similar assumption that UN membership, like participation in NATO, represents a wholehearted acceptance of commonly shared political principles; for most Americans, the UN Charter is a social contract in the Lockean sense.

seemed to us legitimate and right; the Lockean principles so widely accepted on our shores have been used to justify whatever action our leaders chose in order to solve immediate problems to our best advantage.

Locke's principles of the natural equality and freedom of all men not only encouraged the self-reliant attempts to solve problems on the part of individuals; they also counseled governments to abstain from undue interference in private affairs, thereby permitting the acquisitive passions of man to contribute to the strength and power of the community. In the American context, therefore, Lockean traditions and pragmatism went hand in hand, allowing us to combine forceful political rhetoric (which in Europe was usually the sign of ideological rigidity and impracticality) with inventiveness and a spirit of political compromise. This may explain the apparent contradiction between the fundamentalist or Puritan tone of American Protestantism and the self-seeking if not corrupt activities of American businessmen; similarly, it suggests why the passion of political oratory throughout the nineteenth century (which often surprised European observers) did not produce a social revolution like those on the continent.

The compatability of moral fervor and practical effectiveness, here attributed to the underlying political principles our founders derived from Locke, was of course equally evident in foreign affairs. In isolation from global power politics, the use of force to remove obstacles to our expansion could give rise to bitter debate (as did the Mexican War), but these controversies were not lasting because the object in view was short-range advantage; in general, everyone has profited from our expanding power, including those who opposed the specific steps that made it possible.

American pragmatism was of course not primarily oriented toward international affairs. On the contrary, our traditional distrust of balance-of-power politics rested on a profoundly inward-looking orientation. Charles Pinckney echoed the thoughts of many Americans (then as now) when he told the Constitutional Convention:

Our true situation appears to me to be this:—a new extensive Country containing within itself the materials for forming a Government capable of extending to its citizens all the blessings of civil and religious liberty—capable of making them happy at home. This is the great end of Republican Establishments. We mistake the object of our Government, if we hope or wish that it is to make us respectable abroad. Conquest or superiority among other powers is not or ought not ever to be the object of republican systems. If they are sufficiently active and energetic to rescue us from contempt and preserve our domestic happiness and security, it is all we can exect from them,—it is more than almost any other Government ensures to its citizens.[8]

Yet in a setting that led men to equate international affairs with a normally peaceful state of nature, this pursuit of "domestic happiness" led to an industrial progress so astonishing that we have now attained "superiority among other powers" without having established it as our "object."

Our straightforward use of persuasion and power has been rewarded by history in no small part because it has rested on confidence and self-reliance, which in turn depended on an unquestioning acceptance of our popular beliefs about human nature and politics; as Tocqueville noted, nineteenth-century Americans did not seem given to philosophic reflection. America's rise to the status of a world power thus rested, perhaps necessarily, on a failure to understand the peculiar conditions that made our approach to political life so successful. Because the United States refused to enter into "entangling alliances" on the European continent, we were free to expand—using force where necessary; as in Locke's state of nature, we acquired property and power by means of our labor and initiative.

Since the vital interests of other major powers were not challenged by the foreign wars in which the United States engaged during the nineteenth century, the costs of erroneous policies were minimal. Now, however, that we have been

[8] Solberg: *The Federal Convention*, p. 169.

forced to play the role of a world power, Americans are confronted by a tension between their traditional pragmatism—entailing as it does the uninhibited use of force to remove external obstacles—and the hazards of nuclear war. For this reason, it is of particular relevance to consider the major example of a short-range foreign-policy decision that had catastrophic consequences for the United States. In so doing, we may discover why both the traditional distrust of power politics and the moralistic rhetoric that often accompanied it are today extremely dangerous.

The Civil War represents the only occasion on which American institutions proved incapable of resolving domestic conflicts; the debate concerning the injustice of slavery could not be settled by compromise and delay because it became clear that either the North or the South would come to dominate the Union as a whole. Each section sought to impose its interests and conception of justice on the other, and neither was willing to tolerate defeat. As some have argued, civil war was inevitable once Lincoln posed this problem boldly in 1858 by declaring that "this government cannot endure permanently half slave and half free."[9]

It was not, however, totally inevitable that the American Union collapse on the issue of slavery; many of the Founding Fathers had expected this "peculiar institution," so contradictory to the principles of human equality established in the Declaration of Independence, to wither away. Both at the Constitutional Convention and in the Missouri Compromise of 1820, our pragmatic ability to resolve immediate problems seemed adequate to settle the conflict of interest, at least temporarily. Why then did civil war result in 1860?

A strong case could be made for the proposition that the annexation of Texas in 1845 and the Mexican War of 1846-8 were the decisive links in the historical chain of events leading

[9] See esp. Harry V. Jaffa: *Crisis of the House Divided,* (Garden City, N. Y.: Doubleday; 1959).

to the secession of the South. Once before in our history the acquisition of new lands had produced the threat of secession; when the Louisiana Purchase threatened to alter the sectional balance of power between North and South, New England Federalists talked of leaving the Union. Because the new states carved out of the Louisiana Purchase were not intrinsically bound to any one section or interest of the original states, compromise was possible; in contrast, the acquisition of Texas and the territories of New Mexico and California seemed to be solely in the interest of the slave-holding South.

It is understandable that Southern politicians sought to increase their power by extending the portion of the United States in which slavery seemed economically feasible; their ability to gain broad support for this policy is equally comprehensible, for the desire for territorial expansion, by violence if need be, was widely shared and confirmed by past American experience. But the ad hoc decision to annex Texas and the Southwest had long-range effects on the balance of power within the American political system; once it was recognized that the addition of many new slave states along our southern border would lead to the introduction of slavery in the territories of the Great Plains, then approaching statehood, the North saw that it was in danger of becoming a permanent minority.

The Mexican War indicates how the typically American view of foreign affairs, in which the use of force is a reflexive response to obstacles in the state of nature, can have disastrous consequences. Short-range decisions, like the annexation of Texas, led almost imperceptibly to commitments that altered the configuration of power on which the United States rested. As a result of these changes, it became impossible to compromise on the issue of slavery without effectively defeating, on a permanent basis, one or the other of the major sectional interests in American politics.

In the nineteenth century, therefore, the Achilles' heel of the American political system was the source of our power— namely, a self-confident pragmatism, resting on Lockean principles, that encouraged the use of persuasion, money, and force to secure maximum immediate advantage without reference to long-range strategies. Even the Civil War was not as disastrous as similar crises in Europe, because the resulting dominance of the North opened the way to rapid industrialization during the late nineteenth century. The unself-conscious quest for power and wealth redounded to the economic benefit of all, including the waves of immigrants after the 1870's; whereas the French Revolution left social cleavages that were to be ignited once again by the revolutions of 1830, 1848, and 1870 (not to mention the further constitutional changes represented by the Vichy regime and the Fourth and Fifth republics), our institutions survived intact.

One condition for the longevity of the American Constitution and its ability to survive the storm of the Civil War has unquestionably been the limited impact of world politics. The subsidiary importance of foreign affairs can no longer be taken for granted, however, because the very purpose of American commitment in world affairs has radically changed since 1950. No longer are we primarily concerned with "domestic happiness and security"; rather, as President Johnson phrased it, we have come to believe that the cause of freedom is "indivisible" throughout the world.

This shift has been an unforeseen result of foreign commitments that, following American experience, were practical responses to immediate crises. But now that the United States has embarked on a new role as a world power, the responsibilities involved can be expected to create vigorous domestic controversy. Moreover, the resulting debates probably will become increasingly bitter, for each side defends an aspect of our national traditions.

Those who insist that the threat of world communism be met with force where persuasion fails are in effect responding to America's status as a global power in the same way that our leaders acted in the nineteenth century; just as President Polk dispatched troops to occupy parts of Texas contested by the Mexicans and President McKinley ordered the fleet into

Manila Bay, so President Johnson did not hesitate to send American troops to the Dominican Republic and South Vietnam.

In contrast, those who feel that they have yet to reap "all the blessings of civil and religious liberty" at home argue that the domestic objectives set forth by Pinckney in 1787 should be fully achieved before we spend billions in defense of the South Vietnamese. For the American Negro and the most vocal supporters of the civil rights movement, the social consequences of the Civil War should be remedied before we attempt to win the cold war by exporting the "Great Society" to foreign lands.

It is to be feared, therefore, that the unplanned role of world power will place extraordinary strains on American political life. However one judges the particular issues as they arise, the central problem lies in the persistence of the traditional approach to foreign affairs. As long as we treat international affairs as we have in the past, there is great danger in the contradiction between current conditions and the Lockean notion of a peaceful state of nature (which occasionally requires the use of force against the unreasonable and less civilized enemy).

For example, we have long refused to recognize Peking as the government of China, despite the evident facts, because it has acted as an international "outlaw"; like the American Indians or the Mexicans, the Chinese seem to reject rules of international behavior that we find reasonable and just. As a consequence, persuasion and if need be force should be used to induce the Chinese to adopt a more peaceful, friendly attitude. In recent debates on our China policy, the persistence of habitual attitudes is remarkable; indeed, the major difference seems to be that the doves insist that the Chinese will be reasonable if only we try peaceful persuasion, whereas the hawks intimate that only force will teach them the error of their ways.

Unfortunately, an all-out attack on China is no longer comparable to our uninhibited wars against the American

Indians or the Mexicans, and the possibilities of persuading the Chinese to alter their policies, even under the stimulus of financial advantage, are reduced by the impact of Marxist ideology. As this example shows, moralistic rhetoric, whether of the right or the left, has become increasingly dangerous. When viewed in the light of the future, the American past is no longer an adequate guide to the foreign policy of a nuclear superpower.

Conclusion

BECAUSE our traditional beliefs about international politics
need to be reconsidered, I have proposed the advisability of
viewing foreign affairs in terms of a balance of power. More
to the point, especially since the tough-minded use of force
is an American tradition, our attitudes must be directed toward the necessity for long-range policies; as a nuclear superpower, the United States can no longer afford the luxury of
ad hoc decisions that meet crises as they arise.

American commitments, originally made on a pragmatic
and short-range basis, can lead to alterations in the global
balance of power with unforeseen and dangerous consequences.
Just as the Mexican War seems to have unintentionally
brought about a shift in the domestic equilibrium of North
and South (thereby setting the stage for the Civil War), so
the Spanish-American War established the United States as
a power in the Pacific Ocean (thereby making us vulnerable
to the Japanese attack on Pearl Harbor and forcing us to fight
World War II in Europe and Asia simultaneously).

The parallels with more recent events are not difficult to
find. It is generally conceded that President Kennedy's decision
to send more military "advisers" to South Vietnam was not

intended to be the forerunner of a major commitment; Kennedy hoped to show Khrushchev that we were willing to oppose wars of national liberation while avoiding direct American involvement. In less than five years, however, over 300,000 American troops were directly engaged in a guerrilla war that was not the result of long-range planning. Like the Athenian expedition to Sicily, the Vietnamese war seems destined to alter the global balance of power regardless of the outcome.

Mere repetition of the traditional American resort to persuasion, money, and force will not, even if successful in the short run, lead to a satisfactory outcome now that the United States is a superpower. Whereas many have argued that an American withdrawal from Southeast Asia would have catastrophic results (because the Chinese would expand and threaten to dominate Asia as a whole), few have wondered what would happen if our efforts to contain Peking proved to be as successful as our containment of the American Indians. Despite the contrary argument in Chapter vii, it is within the realm of possibility that the United States gain a total victory in Vietnam (just as the Anglo-French, almost to their own surprise, were victorious in the Crimean War).

Should we inflict military defeat on the Vietcong and their communist allies, our success would obviously be due to the combination of our superior firepower (reflecting American wealth and industrial strength) and our traditional self-reliance in times of crisis; as in the protracted campaigns against the Indians, our willingness to use force where persuasion fails would then pay off. Here the similarity with the past would end, however, for the consequences would be incalculably different from our victories in the nineteenth century.

Total victory in South Vietnam would mean that the Vietcong had ceased to be in any way a threat to the government of Saigon. This would mean that the communists were incapable not only of large-scale military operations but also of the kind of widespread and persistent terrorism that drove the French out of Algeria. Given the number of North Vietnamese troops now in the South, therefore, total victory implies that both the Vietcong and Hanoi would have been forced to surrender.

Assuming that our military strategists could devise practical means of achieving this end, our success would be a massive defeat for both the Soviet Union and China. Indeed, the loss of prestige to Peking would be so severe that the Chinese might well intervene with large ground forces in order to avert such a reverse, just as they intervened in Korea when our generals, following tradition, equated the practicability of total victory with its desirability.

Since we are here imagining the complete success of our traditional reliance on force based on short-range pragmatism, let us envision an all-out American response to Chinese intervention. It is not impossible that the United States would resort to a nuclear attack on China, which might seem preferable to a protracted land war against superior numbers in unfavorable geographic conditions. It is also possible that the Soviet Union, faced with the threat of nuclear destruction, would not retaliate in any way after we had devastated China. Should this happen, it would become clear to all that our power could rarely if ever be challenged; our pragmatic efforts to resolve immediate crises might then have effectively established an American empire—or at least world hegemony.

Despite the fears of the left, we may be able to defeat any conceivable enemies without sustaining direct attack on ourselves. If a nuclear war on China were successful, we would demonstrate to the world that the Soviet Union was impotent to defend other communist states; by the same token, it might appear that even the industrial powers of Western Europe could not openly oppose us without risk. Aided by the indirect influence of our economic power, we could then hope to restrain any remaining threats to world peace. Washington might even try to export the Great Society by massive economic assistance, perpetually to the advantage of the American businesses that would furnish the materials and financing needed by the developing societies.

Such world dominance, if it came about, would be the unintended product of a perfectly traditional American policy of using persuasion, force, and money to insure the defeat of unreasonable enemies that block our naturally expanding power; to our victories over the American Indians, the Mexicans, the Spaniards, the Germans, and the Japanese would be added our defeat of China. Yet this success of past methods of foreign policy would surely alter the basic character of our political system because American hegemony would not be a return to the peaceful state of nature.

Omnipotent rulers are rarely popular; we would be plagued by minor wars and revolutions throughout the world. To maintain our position of dominance, increased governmental control over the private lives of American citizens would necessarily be called for. The spirit of individualism and free enterprise would continuously be contradicted by demands for centralized governmental planning, and the combination of national pride and enormous wealth could as easily corrupt our populace as it did the Athenians and Romans after they rose to empire. Political freedom as we know it might cease to exist, again as occurred in both Athens and Rome.

Hence even the most unexpected success of our nineteenth-century outlook on foreign affairs would decisively contradict and undermine our political traditions. On the other hand, if (as seems more likely) we fail to achieve unchallenged world hegemony, we must also abandon our belief that long-range calculation of the balance of power is unnecessary. While traditional American methods of persuasion and force will remain valid means of acting toward other states—a necessity recognized by sober thinkers since the time of the Greek city-state—we will be forced to admit that international politics is not essentially a peaceful state of nature that is only disturbed by unreasonable or savage men.

Re-examination of the adequacy of our political traditions as they apply to international politics is therefore today indispensable. It was argued in the last chapter that the principles of John Locke, which explain our insistence on each American citizen's natural right to "life, liberty, and the pursuit of happiness," have also colored our perception of foreign affairs; our national experience has led us to consider world politics as if they were domestic affairs. Just as every reasonable man should be aware that private property is a natural right that cannot be replaced by socialism, so reasonable statesmen should abide by certain international laws. If they do so, the peaceful accommodation of political differences among states, like the peaceful state of nature among reasonable individuals, need not degenerate into a state of war.

This approach to world politics assumes, as Locke does, that it is possible to understand political rivalries in terms of the rational calculations all men are likely to make. But this notion of human reasonableness is open to an important objection. Locke treats the "law of nature" as a set of rules that will be agreed upon by equitable men who think alike; his principles seem universally applicable. Yet in fact his political doctrines have been of great impact only in the Anglo-Saxon world; the conception of man's natural rights took a very different form in the French Revolution of 1789, and private property has never been as sacrosanct on the continent as in England and the United States. In part, this is due to historical accident; the connection between democracy and local self-government, so strong in our own traditions, has been largely absent in European societies, where democratic governments could only be established by the revolutionary overthrow of a highly centralized monarchy.

Constitutional democracy in Western Europe has therefore developed along lines that frequently diverge from our own experience. Not only have central governments been more powerful on the continent, but the principle of the separation of powers has been less well established; in contrast to the two-party systems of England and the United States, European democracies have most often had a large number of parties, not to mention a conception of the parliament as the sole representative of the people. The Bonn regime in West Germany since 1949 is perhaps the most striking exception to—and confirmation of—this generalization, for the new German constitution was largely a conscious imitation of the Anglo-Saxon model, adopted during our military occupation.

It is therefore dangerous for Americans to assume that our political principles are totally shared by other democratic nations. Even apart from communist states, most other countries do not share our conception of what is reasonable or unreasonable. Leaving aside the English (and some former British colonies like Canada and Australia), our attitude toward war and peace is relatively unique; most statesmen do not expect that international conflicts can be resolved if rivals negotiate in good faith, for they are aware—if only from their own domestic experiences—that agreements will often be violated whenever individuals or groups have the power and self-interest to do so.

Our moralistic denunciations of communist aggression, for example, must strike statesmen like General de Gaulle as rationalizations that justify our pursuit of America's national interests. The more we refuse to see the depth of this divergence of assumptions, the more others feel that we seek to establish our hegemony over them; since we consider reasonableness as agreement with our notion of reason, governments that view the world from very different perspectives cannot help but distrust or misunderstand us. Lacking our belief in the principles of John Locke, they naturally doubt the sincerity of our actions based on these principles.

This fundamental gulf between the moral and political principles of nations cannot be ignored, nor can it be attributed to the stubbornness of our allies and the hostility of the communists. On the contrary, men are social animals who naturally live in groups; it is natural to distinguish between those who are part of one's own society and those who are aliens. Moreover, it is characteristic of virtually every human society that it inhabits a territory which it will, under threatening circumstances, defend against outside attack.[1] The philo-

---

[1] For a popular statement of the anthropological evidence concerning human nature, see Robert Ardrey: *African Genesis* (New York: Atheneum; 1961), and *The Territorial Imperative* (New York: Atheneum; 1966).

sophical principles of John Locke are not confirmed by modern science, for the rise of society cannot be attributed to a social contract concluded between previously isolated men. Hence it becomes vital to reinvestigate our own traditions with a full awareness that many of our assumptions about foreign affairs are neither shared by others nor necessarily valid.

It is by no means easy to alter commonly held opinions which have been the basis of generations of political experience. Indeed, it may be simply impossible for Americans, having acted upon views that reflect Lockean principles, to subject these principles and opinions to searching criticism. This is particularly so because Locke's political teaching has a peculiarity which it shares (surprisingly enough) with Marxism.

Marx's political ideas have one characteristic that contributes to the tremendous effectiveness of communist ideology: he claimed to have discovered a scientific theory of human history that was at the same time a guide to political practice. We fail completely to understand communism if we do not see this unity of theory and practice, for Marx provided both an explanation of the human condition and a recipe for improving it.

The development of a scientific theory of politics that is simultaneously a practical political program should not be dismissed lightly as a minor aspect of Marxism. On the contrary, it explains the paradoxical success of Marxist principles despite the failure of Marx's own predictions. He expected that the working class in the industrialized Western democracies, spurred on by inevitable class conflicts that would produce economic disaster, would revolt against the capitalist order and abolish private property; instead, continued economic progress has led to the emergence of a welfare state combining private capital with public assistance to the less fortunate.

While Marx's scientific predictions have thus not been fulfilled, his doctrines have successfully inspired those who initiated revolutions in Russia, China, and other economically underdeveloped countries. A teaching that was developed within the West has become the dominant ideology in the East. Our curious reason for this success of Marxist ideology is that it is a Western theory that can be used to criticize the West (just as Locke's was an English doctrine used by the colonists to justify our independence from England). As such, Marxism is admirably suited to the needs of rulers who seek industrial development, in imitation of the West but in opposition to Western domination.

Marxism would not, however, be such an effective ideology if it was merely a convenient vehicle for the mixture of admiration and hostility toward the West that marks the underdeveloped world. Other Western thinkers criticized their own societies but have not had the same impact as Marx. The decisive aspect of Marxism is its claim to provide the scientific truth concerning man in a form that simultaneously indicates the proper and desirable course of political action. Since underdeveloped nations seek to imitate Western science, here is a scientific doctrine, developed in the West yet critical of capitalist institutions, which supposedly outlines the route to political success. Especially as reformulated by Lenin and Mao, this fusion of theory and practice attracted many who are frustrated by the seeming inability of backward societies to catch up to the industrialized democracies of the West.

The Lockean principles so long accepted in the United States are, on the surface, totally antithetical to Marxism. For Locke, men have a natural right to private property, and only on this basis can the just society be established; for Marx, it is through the abolition of private property that man will end the tyranny of one class over another, ushering in true human decency and justice. Despite these fundamentally divergent assumptions, Locke shares Marx's belief that the theory which fully explains political life is a tenable guide to political practice. Not only did Locke argue that his principles explained fully the political settlement of 1688, upon which English constitutional democracy was and still is based; he also attempted to realize these principles in practice by writing the constitution of the colony of South Carolina.

Locke's theory is intended to be fully consistent with the realities of life (as is Marx's); beginning from the desire of every man to preserve himself, Locke tries to show how the natural laws of human behavior can be channeled into prosperous and stable societies. His emphasis on limited government according to the law is intended to realize, in practice, the truths of philosophy that he attempted to establish for all time. There is a sense, however, in which Locke's principles presuppose that men will be aware of their natural rights; if they continue to believe that kings rule by divine right, Locke indicates that the proper limits on civil society will be difficult if not impossible to establish. As we have seen, Locke must ultimately assume that all men—or at least all members of a just society—share the same view of reason and understand the same laws of nature.

History shows that Locke's principles are not held by all men. They have, instead, become the ideology of the Anglo-Saxon, or at most the Western, democracies. Rather than establish a theory that applies without question in all times and all places, Locke developed a set of ideas that characterize certain societies as distinct from others—and, most particularly, as distinct from communist states. This occurred because Locke sought to have a direct effect on contemporary politics; unlike Plato, whose description of the best political order in the *Republic* is presented as virtually impossible to achieve (and hence as a proposal that will be laughed at), Locke seriously tried to set forth principles that could justify and govern day-to-day political practice.[2] On this score, if no other, Locke and Marx seem to share a common view that a scientific theory of human nature can lead to a feasible program of action.

[2] Compare the Preface to Locke's *Two Treatises of Government* with Plato's *Republic*, 473CD, 502C, 592AB (and Plato's *Laws*, 736B, 778B, 858AC). Aristotle stated clearly the view of the classical Greeks: "It is evident that philosophic wisdom and the art of politics cannot be the same" (*Nicomachean Ethics*, 1141A).

The persistence of international rivalry that we habitually describe as the cold war gives rise to doubts about the sufficiency of both the Marxian and the Lockean attempts to develop a philosophy that is simultaneously a practical guide to statesmen. It seems that such an attempt produces instead an ideology which is inevitably opposed by other ideologies. On the deepest level, it is the necessary incompleteness of any set of popular political beliefs, including those most Americans accept unquestioningly, which compels the observer to insist that an effective foreign policy must be oriented to a balance of power.

Our political traditions and national experiences seem to have prepared the United States poorly for its new role as a major world power. Nor can one minimize the difficulty of adjusting deeply rooted opinions to a changing international situation. It can hardly be expected that the publication of a book would persuade American politicians and citizens to change their attitude toward power politics. Even if that book were demonstrably true in every respect, it would not be easy to convince many of the inadequacy of present beliefs and past habits.

Serious errors in our foreign policies remain a persisting threat to American democracy as we have known it. Perhaps the mood with which I end this book is best captured by the words of Max Weber. Reinhard Bendix (in *Max Weber, an Intellectual Portrait*, p. 30) quotes the conclusion of a speech he delivered in 1893 as follows:

I am at the end of my remarks. Perhaps you will have been impressed by a certain resignation in what I have said . . . I do not know whether all my contemporaries have this same intense experience as I do at this moment: the nation is burdened with the heavy curse on those who come afterwards. The generation before us was inspired by an activism and a naïve enthusiasm, which we cannot rekindle, because we confront tasks of a different kind from those which our fathers faced.

Index

Abraham, 282

Aden, 132

Adenauer, Konrad, 135

Africa: relations with other countries, 5, 130, 163, 255; primitivism, 20, 24; development, 24, 26, 31, 82; as power, 41, 110; tribalism, 94–5; United States policy toward, 249; South, 40, 60, 250

Alaska, 297

Albania, 112, 249, 271 n.

Algeria, 7, 210–11, 312

Alliance for Progress, 101

American Motors Corporation, 53

American Revolution, 290

Antarctica, 274

anti-Americanism: in Asia, 36, 188, 243, 244; in South America, 251

anticolonialism, 34, 253, 264

anticommunism: in United States, 11–12, 13, 38, 106, 108, 126, 193; in Western Europe, 88

Anzus Treaty, 300

Arab League, 253–4

Arab states, 31, 36, 250, 253

Ardrey, Robert, 79 n., 215 n., 315 n.

Argentina, 32, 87

Aristotle, 7, 121, 318 n.

Asia: relations with other countries, 5, 102, 229; communists in, 8, 204–5, primitivism, 20, 24; development, 26; United States policy toward, 102, 221, 225–7, 233, 235-45, 248, 284; as power, 163, 224, 245; historical background, 207–9; confederation, 244–5; see also Southeast Asia and names of specific countries

Asian and Pacific Council (ASPAC), 244-5

ASPAC: see Asian and Pacific Council

Assyrians, 23, 30

Athens, 35, 45, 115-18, 287, 313

Atlantic alliance: see NATO

Atlantic community, 98–9, 101, 140, 161–2, 163, 283, 302 and n.; see also NATO

Atlantic Nuclear Force, 133, 147, 153, 161

atomic bomb, 6, 48

Australia, 40, 315

Austria, 11, 75

Axis powers, 12, 263, 300

Ayub Khan, 240

balance of power: nuclear, 6; global, 13, 36, 38–43, 44–5, 76, 99, 102–3, 105, 108, 114, 119, 183, 189, 190, 204, 279–80, 310; European, 27, 194–5, 198, 207–8; great power, 79, 98, 272; Asian, 209, 224, 238, 245; regional, 254

Balkan conflicts, 207, 208

Baruch Plan, 81

Bay of Pigs, Cuba, 252

Beaufre, General André, 55 n., 157–9, 210 n.

Belgium, 29, 131, 138, 155

Benda, Harry J., 203 n.

Bendix, Reinhard, 319

Berlin, 64, 65; see also West Germany

Berlin Wall, 136, 194; see also Germany

Bernstein, Eduard, 170

bipolarity: present status, 32, 43, 160; in 18th–19th centuries, 44–5; and nuclear power, 47–8; risks in, 75; weakening of, 167, 183, 192, 200

Bolsheviks, 168

Bonn: see West Germany

Bonner, James, 23 n.

Borah, William, 106

Brazil, 32

Britain: see Great Britain

British Atlantic Nuclear Force, 126

Brown, Harrison, 23 n.

Buddhists, 212

Burma, 47, 89, 218, 229

Burns, Arthur Lee, 159 and n., 238 n.

California, 298, 306

Caligula, 91

Calvin, John, 174–5

Calvinists, 282

Cambodia, 89, 219, 229, 235

Canada, 29, 40, 193, 315

capitalism, 91, 103, 169, 171, 172 and n., 201

Caribbean area, 252

cartels, 75

Castro, Fidel, 34, 86, 191, 250; see also Cuba

Catholic Church, 174–5

Catholicism, 12, 212, 282

Central America, 298 n.

Central Intelligence Agency; see CIA

China, 21

China (Red): United States policy toward, 11, 77, 87–90, 102–5, 108–9, 187–91, 204–17, 220–7, 229–30, 231–4, 240, 265, 283, 308–9, 312; as power, 32, 38, 42, 44, 45–6, 57, 78, 80, 103–5, 109–12, 178–9, 185, 189, 208, 213, 219, 221–2, 231, 232–4, 242, 302 n., 312–13; policies, 43, 100–1, 103 n., 119, 172, 187–90, 207, 208 and n., 214–15, 225, 227, 230, 231, 236, 239, 249, 265, 270; as threat, 89–90, 103, 187, 189, 237 n., 240, 243–5, 311; development, 103–4, 179, 231–2; European policy toward, 113, 144; and South Asia, 213, 238–9, 240, 242–3, 312; see also communists, Chinese; Sino-Soviet split

Christianity, 13, 175, 281–3

Chrysler Motors Corporation, 52, 53–4, 55
Church, Frank, 192 n.
Churchill, Winston S., 12
CIA, 241
city-states, 30, 44–5, 116, 313
Civil War (U.S.), 305, 307, 308, 310
cold war: cooling of, 4; early stages, 10, 84, 167, 263, 286; future status, 22, 177; strategy, 38, 190 n., 191, 193, 288
colonialism, 20, 21, 187, 272 n.
Comecon, 28
Common Market: function, 28, 127, 138–9, 156, 244, 266; African or Latin American (proposed), 31; United States role in, 130; dissent involving, 131 and n., 133, 143, 145, 147; future role, 196
communism: threat of, 5, 14, 64, 135, 175, 186–7, 191, 193, 199, 236, 300, 307; in Soviet Union, 12, 85, 231; as ideology, 35, 43, 91, 168–80, 182–3, 185, 186, 188, 190–1, 230–1, 245, 317; containment, 84–90, 112, 117, 123, 172–3, 183, 185, 189, 235, 243, 250, 252; expansion, 85, 86, 99, 101, 102, 103, 179, 233, 252; in West, 141, 168–71, 184; revisionism, 170–3, 178; Soviet control, 178, 203, 312; in Asia, 233, 237, 241–2; see also Leninism; Marxism
communist bloc: Marxism in, 31, 172, 177–9, 185; power of, 63; and NATO, 70; Russian strength in, 81, 85, 100, 163, 182, 186–7; split in, 86, 101; United States policy toward, 193, 201; and polycentrism, 195, 202, 233; in United Nations, 264, 269, 271 and n.
communists: in Vietnam, 5–6, 8, 87, 99, 185, 209–17, 218–20, 287, 311–12; Russian, 6, 10, 21, 188; Chinese, 6, 8, 9, 11, 17, 34, 88–90, 183–5, 218, 227; Cuban, 10, 87; and nuclear power, 89; European, 170–1, 176, 193–4, 196; American, 175; Asian, 191, 215–17, 241–2
Concert of Europe, 75
"Concorde" jet transport, 131–2
Confederacy, 295 n.
Conference of the New Emerging Forces, 225
Congo, 37, 95, 97, 250, 261
Congregational Church, 282
Congress (U.S.), 129, 193, 275
Conservative Party (British), 132 n.
Constitution (U.S.), 301–2, 302 n., 307
Constitutional Convention of 1787, 295 and n., 297–8, 303, 305
continent-states, 79, 96
Counter-Reformation, 175
Crimean War, 207–9, 311
Cuba, 10, 34, 107, 112, 193, 199, 213, 250, 259, 271 n., 283, 298 n., 299; see also Castro, Fidel
Cuban crisis, 4, 9, 37, 49, 100, 111, 143, 181, 95, 215

Cyprus, 34, 95, 97
Czarist regime, 10, 21
Czechoslovakia, 40, 171

de Gaulle, General Charles: government, 7, 10, 15, 65, 129, 133; policies, 77, 88, 127 n., 131 and n., 137, 139, 144–7, 149, 161, 164, 211, 287, 315; and NATO, 126–8, 131 and n., 137, 139–47, 163, 283, 302 n.; see also France
Declaration of Independence, 281, 285, 290, 295 n., 305
Delian League, 116 n.
democracy: United States as, 3, 59, 177, 247, 280; Western, 4, 13, 43, 134, 174, 175, 176, 178, 284, 314, 318; in underdeveloped countries, 26
Dien Bien Phu, Vietnam, 241, 287
disarmament, 79–82
Discourses on Titus Livy (Machiavelli), 206
Dominican Republic crisis, 76, 86–7, 99, 101, 111, 161, 213, 250, 252, 308
Dulles, John Foster, 136, 300

ECOSOC: see United Nations Economic and Social Council
East Germany: nuclear power, 40; government, 89; and reunification, 134–5, 199–200; and Russia, 173; future of, 197
EDC: see European Defense Community
EEC: see European Economic

Community
EFTA: see European Free Trading Area
Egypt: ancient, 23, 30; as power, 36; and Israel, 37, 78, 253–4, 276; and Russia, 38; as future nuclear power, 41, 53, 72–3, 113
England: see Great Britain
Europe: historical background, 11, 56; Eastern, 28, 85, 111, 152, 156, 192–3, 196–8, 233; United States relation to, 123–7, 128, 136, 138–9, 193–200; United States business investments in, 139, 193–4, 233; proposed division, 195–8; see also Western Europe
European Coal and Steel Community, 28
European Defense Community (EDC), 129, 136
European Economic Community (EEC), 130, 131, 139
European Free Trading Area (EFTA), 131
extremism, 7

Fascism, 176
Federalists, 306
Fellner, William, 51 n.
Fifth Republic (French), 307
Florida, 298
Ford Motor Company, 52, 53–4
foreign aid: to industrialize underdeveloped countries, 25, 248; to Egypt, 38; to Europe, 233; to India, 238; as moral commitment, 246–8; to Middle East, 254; agencies, 256–60,

268–71, 283; *see also* underdeveloped countries, United
States aid to
Formosa: *see* Taiwan
Fouchet plan, 154
Fourth Republic (French), 126,
143, 307
France: historical background, 11,
13, 45, 312; in Vietnam, 18,
58, 241; industrialization, 19;
policies, 38, 39–40, 43, 76–7,
78, 95, 99, 100, 125–8, 138–55,
273, 283; as power, 59, 74, 89;
United States policy toward,
129, 138–57, 161–3; *see also*
de Gaulle, Charles
French Revolution, 168, 307, 314

Gadsden Purchase, 298
Galbraith, John Kenneth, 52 *n.*
Gallois, General, 157
General Motors Corporation, 52,
53–5, 58
General Principle Seven (UNC-
TAD), 257
Geneva: agreements, 287; conferences, 144, 209
German Democratic Republic,
136
Germany: United States policy
toward, 4, 133–7; Nazi, 12,
176, 206, 234; as power, 27,
70, 125, 152, 208, 300; division,
89, 193–4, 226; reunification,
125, 129, 133–8, 151–2, 153,
156–7, 193–4, 197; policies of,
153; current status, 193–5; *see
also* East Germany; West Germany

Ghana, 9
Gomulka, Wladyslaw, 184
Gorden, Morton, 140 and *n.*
Great Britain: policies, 11, 38,
39–40, 76, 78, 108, 128, 132–3,
207, 315; industrialization, 19–
20; colonialism, 21; as power,
47, 72, 74, 75, 89, 155, 299, 300;
Commonwealth, 99, 130, 318;
Anglo-American relations, 129–
33, 157; relations with Europe,
132–3, 154–5
Greece, 34, 76, 87, 165, 213, 281,
318
Gross National Product, 29, 47
Guatemala, 34, 87, 252
guerrilla warfare: in Vietnam, 6,
18, 87–8, 215, 218, 245, 311;
as strategy, 33, 67, 73, 210 and
n., 219, 220; defense against,
71, 79, 114, 230
Guinea, 191

Hallstein, Walter, 139
Hamilton, Alexander, 295 *n.*
Hammarskjöld, Dag, 266
Hanoi: *see* communists, in Viet-
nam
Hanoi harbor, 216
Hawaii, 298
Hazard, Leland, 237
Hebrew Bible, 282
Henry IV (king of France), 90
Himalayan frontier, 239
*History of the Peloponnesian
War* (Thucydides), 80 *n.*, 116 *n.*,
117, 287–8 *n.*
Hitler, Adolf: racism, 5; policies,
12, 56, 60, 91, 205, 215; rise to

Hitler, Adolf (*Continued*)
power, 176; expansionism, 206–7
Ho Chi Minh, 150, 216
Holland, 129, 131, 138–9, 155
Honolulu conference on Vietnamese situation, 211
Hot Line Treaty, 10, 75, 85, 167, 192
Hungarian revolution, 33, 76, 172 *n.*, 195, 261

imperialism (U.S.), 243
India: industrialization, 21; as power, 32, 40, 41, 44, 47, 60, 73, 74, 78, 110, 112, 225, 236, 238; policies, 36; and Asia, 229; and Pakistan, 235–42; United States policy toward, 236–8, 240; *see also* Indo-Pakistani war
Indians (American), 227, 295–6, 298, 308–9, 311, 313
Indochina, 207, 241; *see also* Vietnam, French in
Indonesia: policies, 37, 235; as nuclear power, 40; and Red China, 62, 191, 228, 232, 243; communists in, 241–2, 249
Indo-Pakistani war: effects, 36, 240; strategy, 38; Russian mediation during, 76, 97, 181; United Nations policy toward, 114; and SEATO, 235–6
Industrial Revolution, 20, 24, 168, 196
industrialization: dynamics of, 18–20, 22–32, 200–1, 247; early growth, 20–2; in Western

countries, 42, 171; in United States, 54–5; in Russia, 168–9; in China, 231; in underdeveloped countries, 234, 248
International Bank for Reconstruction and Development, 256, 259, 267 *n.*, 268
International Monetary Fund, 256, 259
Iron Age, 15
iron curtain, 64, 167, 183, 187, 192, 193–5, 199
Iroquois, 266, 272
isolationism: United States policy of, 105–7, 163, 292, 294–301, 303; Red Chinese, 232
Israel: and Egypt, 37–8, 72–3, 113, 276; as nuclear power, 40; United States policy toward, 77–8; and Arab states, 250, 253–4
Italy, 40, 45, 59, 89, 131, 155, 176

Jakarta: *see* Indonesia
Japan: United States policy toward, 4; and World War II, 10; industrialization, 20, 25, 27, 45–6; as nuclear power, 40 and *n.*, 41; as power, 60; present status, 243–5
Java, 242
Jefferson, Thomas, 297, 298
Johnson, Lyndon B.: on world affairs, 102, 307; on NATO, 141, 301, 302 *n.*; on Vietnam, 142, 211, 215, 217, 286; policies, 145, 308

Kant, Immanuel, 90
Karachi: *see* Pakistan
Kashmir: *see* Indo-Pakistani war
Kennan, George, 84–6, 84 *n.*,
 85 *n.*, 88, 173–4, 175 *n.*, 195
Kennedy, John F.: assassination,
 10; European policies, 98, 127;
 on peace, 100; policy toward
 Russia, 167, 177, 192, 195;
 policy in Vietnam, 215, 310–11
Khrushchev, Nikita S.: policies
 of, 81, 85, 100, 173, 179; and
 Kennedy, 167, 192, 311; and
 Sino-Soviet split, 185; and
 Tito, 202
Kissinger, Henry A., 118 *n.*,
 124 *n.*; *Nuclear Weapons and
 Foreign Policy*, 213
Korea, 226, 312
Korean War, 5–6, 9, 118, 143, 228,
 250, 261, 264, 286, 287
Kosygin, Aleksei, 180–2, 255
Kremlin: *see* Soviet Union
Kuomintang: *see* communists,
 Chinese
Ky, Nguyen, 211

Labor Party (British), 132
Laos, 34, 89, 220
Lassalle, Ferdinand, 170
Latin America: Common Market,
 31; nuclear power in, 41, 82;
 United States policy in, 101,
 106, 163; communists in, 102,
 250; and OAS, 251, 252–3;
 nuclear deterrence, 255
Le Monde, 146, 147 *n.*
League of Nations, 61, 292
Lebensraum, 207

Leites, Nathan, 143
Lenin, Nikolai, 5, 168, 171, 176,
 317
Leninism: as ideology, 43, 91,
 203; disciple of Marx, 168, 171;
 dogma, 174; modern applica-
 tion, 179–81, 184–6
Lerner, David, 140 and *n.*
Lexington and Concord battles,
 34, 210
Lichtheim, George, 27 *n.*, 132 *n.*,
 171 *n.*
Lie, Trygve, 266
Lincoln, Abraham, 117, 302, 305
Liska, George, 59 *n.*, 76 *n.*, 77 *n.*,
 113 *n.*
Locke, John: philosophy, 93 *n.*;
 303–4; influence on United
 States politics, 289–92, 294–5,
 299, 300–1, 306–7; modern ap-
 plication of philosophy, 293,
 302 *n.*
Louis XIV (king of France), 12,
 56
Louisiana Purchase, 297 *n.*, 307
Luther, Martin, 174–5
Lutherans, 282
Luxembourg, 131, 155

MacArthur, General Douglas, 5
 and *n.*, 285
Macedonia, 45
Machiavelli, Niccolò: *Discourses
 on Titus Livy*, 206 and *n.*; 280
Madison, James, 295 and *n.*
Maginot Line, 5
Maine (battleship), 299
Malaya, 34, 89, 112, 210 *n.*, 211,
 235; *see also* Malaysia

Malaysia, 37, 130, 132, 233, 235, 241

Malaysian Federation, 241; *see also* Malaysia

Manchuria, 21, 224; *see also* China (Red)

Mao Tse-tung: policies, 5, 187–8, 189–91, 190 *n.*, 226, 230; government, 11, 34, 86, 224, 231; communism of, 91, 168, 184–5, 317

Manila Bay, United States fleet ordered to, 308

Marshall Plan, 233, 285

Martin, Luther, 295

Marx, Karl, 12, 87, 168–72, 172 *n.*, 186, 188, 316–18

Marxism: modern application, 5, 31, 43, 173–5; as ideology, 91, 172 *n.*, 177–80, 199, 201–3, 284, 309; early history, 168–72; in Red China, 231; in United States, 289; and Locke's principles, 316–19

Massachusetts, 282

Max Weber, An Intellectual Portrait (Bendix), 319

McKinley, William, 307–8

McNamara, Robert S., 65, 130, 145, 165

Mensheviks, 171

Mexican War, 303, 305–7, 309, 310, 313

Mexico, 298–9

Middle Ages, 92–3, 96–7, 281

Middle East, 37, 78, 110, 163, 253–5

missiles: Egyptian, 37–8, 41; production of, 39; nuclear, 46, 72, 128, 130–1; in war, 48, 49, 82, 179, 189; Soviet, 63; Red Chinese, 221 and *n.*, 228, 229

Missouri Compromise, 305

MLF (multilateral force), 148, 152 *n.*

Mohammedans, 13

Monnet, Jean, 149

Monroe Doctrine, 299

Morris, Gouverneur, 297–8, 297 *n.*

Moscow: *see* Soviet Union

Moses, 282

Munich, 5, 166, 205

Mussolini, Benito, 176

Napoleon (Bonaparte), 56, 109, 206

Nassau agreement, 131

Nasser, Gamal Abdel, 38

nation-states, 27–8, 30–1, 44, 61, 96, 110

nationalism: as political force, 28; in underdeveloped countries, 31, 44, 272 *n.*; de Gaulle's, 128, 146; German, 151; European, 155; in satellite countries, 183, 185; Vietnamese, 219

NATO: *see* North Atlantic Treaty Organization

Nazi-Soviet Pact, 232

Nazism, 5, 7, 12, 176–7

Near East, 130

Nero, 91

Netherlands: *see* Holland

New Delhi: *see* India

New Mexico, 298, 306

New York Times, The, 180, 181 *n.*, 192 *n.*, 248 *n.*, 301 *n.*, 302 *n.*

Norris, George, 106

North Atlantic Alliance, 302

North Atlantic Treaty Organization (NATO): membership, 8, 89; function, 63, 64, 66–71, 98, 123, 129 n., 155, 164, 194, 196, 197, 198, 199, 200–2, 302 n.; United States position in, 90, 123–9, 140–1, 144–5, 146–7, 152–3, 162–5, 193; policies of, 99, 163, 245, 255; Western Europe's position in, 124–7, 130–1, 133, 134–8, 141–5, 147–51; Council of Ministers, 150; future of, 156–7, 163–6, 224

North Korea, 219, 228, 233

North Vietnam: see Vietnam

Nth Country Problem: see nuclear power

nuclear power: weapons, 3, 4, 5, 33–4, 46–7, 48–9, 63, 65, 68–9, 77, 79–80, 88, 195, 216–17, 228–9; Russian, 6, 49, 62–71, 100, 105, 110, 124, 158–9; Chinese, 6, 8, 10, 31, 40, 41, 62, 63, 66–7, 71, 73–5, 79, 100, 104, 159–60, 221–2, 227–30; diffusion, 6, 39–42, 45–83, 113, 152–4; American, 9, 49–50, 62–71, 105, 110, 115, 125, 152–3, 158–9, 216, 311; war, 15, 17–18, 22, 23 and n., 48, 50, 54, 57, 58, 64–74, 82, 105–6, 113–14, 179, 194, 213, 222–4, 229, 234, 312; in underdeveloped countries, 39–43, 237, 238, 241, 255; nuclear club, 40, 60–3, 66–7, 69, 70, 73, 78–9, 229; control measures, 41–2, 49–50, 53, 59–63, 75, 113–14, 124–6, 144, 148, 154, 157–61, 165, 230, 255; Nth Country Problem, 48, 50, 157, 238 n.; treaties, 60 and n., 61–3, 82, 100, 255; British, 62, 68, 80, 116, 131, 132–3, 154, 159; French, 62, 66–7, 68, 116, 142, 145, 157–9; conferences, 69

Nuclear Weapons and Foreign Policy (Kissinger), 213

OAS: see Organization of American States

Oder-Neisse line, 134

Old Testament, 282

Operation in the Congo (UN), 272 and n.

Organization of African Unity, 253

Organization of American States (OAS), 94, 101, 250–3, 301

Ottoman Empire, 207–8

Pakistan: and India, 36, 38, 235–42; nuclear power, 40; as power, 47, 78, 219; policies, 229; United States policy toward, 238–40; see also Indo-Pakistani war

Panama, 191–2

Pankow, 197

Panmunjom agreements, 287

Paris, 33, 64; see also France

Peace Corps, 256 n.

Pearl Harbor, 10, 176, 215, 310; see also World War II

Peking: see China (Red)

Peloponnesian War, 35, 45, 117, 287 and n.

People's Republic of China: *see* China (Red)
Pericles, 117
Persia, 115
Philippines, 102, 235, 299
Pinckney, Charles, 303-4, 308
Plato: *The Republic,* 318 and *n.*
Plymouth Plantation, 282
Poland, 184, 195, 233
Polk, James, 117, 307
polycentrism, 183, 185, 187, 195, 200, 202
Prince, The (Machiavelli), 206
Protestantism, 175, 282–3, 303
Prussia, 11, 75
Puritans, 282, 303

Rapacki, 195
Rapallo, 134 and *n.*, 153
Red Sea, 254
Reformation, 174–5, 282
Renaissance, 30
Republic, The (Plato), 318 and *n.*
Reston, James, 180–1
Rhodesia, 132, 250
Rockefeller Committee report, 8
Roman Catholic Church: *see* Catholic Church
Roman Empire, 91, 118
Rome (ancient), 45, 115, 206, 281, 313
Roosevelt, Franklin D., 176
Roosevelt, Theodore, 299
Rousseau, Jean-Jacques, 90, 93 *n.*, 119
Rumania, 40, 59, 151, 208, 271 *n.*
Rural Development Associates, 256 *n.*
Rusk, Dean, 144, 209

Russett, Bruce M., 35 *n.*, 42 *n.*
Russia, 75, 207, 208 and *n.; see also* Soviet Union

SAC: *see* Strategic Air Command
Saint-Pierre, Abbé, 90
Sarajevo, 166
SEATO: *see* Southeast Asia Treaty Organization
Senate (U.S.), 263, 294; *see also* Congress (U.S.)
17th parallel, 211, 216
Sino-Soviet split: effect on West, 100–1, 223; and balance of power, 103 and *n.*, 238; as nuclear deterrent, 159–60, 230; ideological basis, 172 and *n.*, 177–8, 183–5, 231–2; restraint on Russian aggression, 203; effect on bipolarity, 205, 214
Social Contract (Rousseau), 119
Social Democrats, 168, 171, 187
socialism, 31, 188
Socialists, 169, 172 *n.*
South Africa, 40, 60, 250
South America, 24, 26, 99, 102, 110, 111, 191
South Carolina, 318
South Vietnam: *see* Vietnam
Southeast Asia: wars in, 71, 235, 237, 310; communism in, 89, 90, 111, 160, 204–5, 206–8, 219, 220, 229, 236; anticommunism in, 106; negotiations in, 142, 215, 220, 236–7; United States policy toward, 227, 241–3; *see also* underdeveloped countries, Vietnam, *and names of specific countries*

Southeast Asia Treaty Organization (SEATO), 107, 236, 245, 300, 301

Southern Rhodesia: see Rhodesia

Soviet Russia: see Soviet Union

Soviet Union: opposition to United States policies, 5 n., 37, 181, 214–15; policies in Europe, 10, 109, 134–5, 137, 145–7, 148, 151, 156–7, 160–3, 193–200; diplomatic relations with United States, 11–13, 100–1, 167–8, 173–86, 190–3, 199–203, 221, 283, 311; as military power, 17, 46, 49, 63, 74, 80–1, 115–16, 158, 213, 217, 311; industrialization, 19, 21, 27; as nation-state, 30; and underdeveloped countries, 32, 39; as superpower, 32, 42–3, 97, 102, 109, 110, 183, 234; policies in Asia, 38, 235–8, 238 n.; intervention in other countries, 73, 76–7, 254; policies in Africa, 78; and communist bloc, 85; and Red China, 86, 90, 103–4, 159–60, 183–5, 187–9, 221, 223–4, 230–3; role in United Nations, 95, 255, 262–4, 269 and n., 273; satellite countries, 111, 125, 249; internal politics, 119; communism in, 168, 171–2, 177–86

Spain, 45, 76, 299

Spanish-American War, 298, 310, 313

Sparta, 35, 45, 115, 116 n., 117, 287

Stalin, Joseph: as leader, 85, 172 n., 174, 183–4, 231–2; policies, 168, 185, 188, 233

State Department (U.S.), 143, 145

Stone Age, 15

Strasbourg, 139

Strategic Air Command (SAC), 222, 223

Straus, Franz Josef, 144

Suez Canal, 254

Suez crisis, 9, 37, 38, 73, 78, 100, 130, 181, 261, 272

Sukarno, Achmed, 37, 62, 233, 241–2

Sweden, 12, 40, 159

Syria, 78, 253

Taiwan (Formosa), 226 and n., 229

Tashkent, 76, 77, 236–7

technology: industrial, 15–30, 39, 45, 54, 108, 174, 276, 279; military, 33, 36, 41, 42, 48, 81, 105, 106, 179

Test Ban Treaty, 10, 75, 85, 167, 192

Texas, 298, 305, 306, 307

Thailand, 102, 229, 235

38th parallel, 228

Thucydides, 80 n., 116 n., 117, 287–8 n.

Tilman, Robert O., 210 n., 235

Tito, Marshal (Josip Broz), 85, 184, 202, 219, 271 n.

Tocqueville, Alexis de, 304

Tokyo: see Japan

totalitarianism, 12, 13, 173, 174, 176–7, 202

Trade and Development Board, 269

Treaty of Rome, 131

Trotsky, Leon, 188

Truman, Harry S., 5
Turkey, 12, 165, 207–8

U Thant, 265
Ulbricht, Walter, 136
UN: *see* United Nations
underdeveloped countries: communism in, 4, 26, 87–8, 98–9, 177, 186–7, 191, 251, 317; and bipolarity, 15–16, 23, 53–5; economy of, 18–19, 21, 45–7, 234, 256–9, 257 *n.;* problems in, 24–8, 33–4, 248–56, 270; nationalism, 31–2, 44; great power intervention in, 36–8, 76–9; in United Nations, 38; and nuclear proliferation, 39–43, 47–50, 59–62, 71–3; United States aid to, 247–9, 256; *see also* foreign aid *and names of specific countries*
United Arab Republic, 40
United Nations (UN): function, 8, 36, 53, 55, 61, 250, 254, 255, 256, 264–76, 292, 300; United States policy in, 38, 81, 90, 261–5, 261 *n.,* 269–70, 273, 275–6, 283, 301; General Assembly, 38, 97, 226, 261–4, 266, 267–8, 271, 273; future of, 90–7, 270–6; Security Council, 90, 97, 114, 225, 261–5, 267–8, 270 and *n.,* 273, 274–5, 276; Red China's admission to, 224–6, 243, 302 *n.;* Charter, 225, 238, 262 and *n.,* 263 and *n.,* 265, 267, 269–70, 270 *n.,* 274–5, 302 *n.;* Special Fund, 256, 259, 260, 268, 275; Conference on Trade and Development (UNCTAD), 257–8, 257 *n.,* 269 and *n.,* 270, 271 *n.;* development, 261–4; Secretary General, 261, 264, 265–6, 273; Economic and Social Council (ECOSOC), 267–71, 270 *n.,* 275; Emergency Fund, 272 and *n.;* Operation in the Congo, 272 and *n.*
United States of Europe (proposed), 126–7, 138, 155, 165
USSR: *see* Soviet Union

Vichy regime, 307
Vietnam: North, 6, 17, 88, 159, 214–17, 219, 229, 233; South, 8, 18, 58, 205, 206, 209–14, 219, 235; division of, 89; American commitments in, 99, 104, 144, 145, 151, 166, 204–5, 207, 209–13, 210 *n.,* 217, 220, 264, 283–4, 286; French in, 211, 241; future of, 212–13, 217–20, 235; *see also* Vietnam war
Vietnam war: ideology, 3, 9, 193, 207; military strategy in, 6, 109, 118, 142, 210–13, 241; anti-Americanism, 36; European attitude toward, 7, 76, 132–3, 143, 200; Russian attitude toward, 86, 167, 185; communists in, 114; possible settlement, 122, 208–9, 217–21, 310–12; policies, 161, 205 and *n.,* 308; escalation, 209, 213–17; Honolulu conference on, 211
Vietcong: *see* communists, in Vietnam; Vietnam war
Virginia, 302

Waltz, Kenneth, 32 *n.*

War of 1812, 299

Warsaw Pact, 151, 197, 198

Weber, Max, 319

Weir, John, 23 *n.*

West Berlin, 74, 158, 194, 198

West Germany: development, 40, 41; as power, 62, 99, 125, 144–5, 148–9, 314–15; defense of, 64, 137, 150–1; United States policy toward, 124, 134–8, 165; policies of, 193–4; relations with Europe, 156–7, 193–4, 199, 236, 244, 288; United States armed forces in, 158, 196, 197, 223; *see also* Germany

Western Europe: development, 20, 27–8, 30, 32, 45; as power, 30–1, 41, 42, 44, 57, 75, 98, 99, 101, 102, 105, 110, 312; defense of, 64–8, 66, 80, 84, 88, 223; relations with other countries, 111, 137, 140, 201–2, 270; relations with United States, 116, 123–6, 126 *n.*, 128, 129, 147–52, 162, 199, 200; political confederation, 196–8, 276

Western European Union, 244

Wilhelm, Kaiser, 170, 303

Willkie, Wendell, 280

Wilson, Prime Minister Harold, 131, 132–3

Wilson, James, 295 *n.*

Wilson, Woodrow, 292

World War I, 5, 10, 12, 118, 170–1, 208, 222, 299–300

World War II, 3, 4, 5, 10, 11, 12, 27, 34, 45, 75, 89, 115, 118, 133, 135, 164, 177, 193, 234, 244, 263, 285, 288, 292, 300, 310, 313

Yale University, 134 *n.*, 235 *n.*

Yalu River, 5, 6

Yemen, 34

Yugoslavia, 40, 85, 233, 249, 260, 271 *n.*

A Note About the Author

ROGER D. MASTERS was born in in Boston in 1933 and received his A.B. from Harvard in 1955 and his M.A. (1958) and Ph.D. (1961) from the University of Chicago. He served in the U. S. Army from 1955 to 1957 and was a Fulbright fellow in France in 1958-9. Since 1961 he has taught political science at Yale, where he is now an assistant professor. In 1964-5 he was awarded a joint Yale Junior Faculty grant and Social Science Research Council grant for study in France. He was editor and co-translator (with his wife, Judith R. Masters) of Rousseau's *First and Second Discourses;* his book *The Political Philosophy of Rousseau* will be published later this year. Mr. Masters's articles have appeared in the *New Republic, Yale Review, Reporter, New Leader, Commonweal,* and scholarly journals both here and abroad.

A Note on the Type

THIS BOOK was set on the Linotype in a type face called "Baskerville." The punches for this face were cut under the supervision of George W. Jones, the eminent English printer and the designer of Granjon and Estienne. Linotype Baskerville is a facsimile cutting from type cast from the original matrices of a face designed by John Baskerville, a writing-master of Birmingham, for his own private press. The original face was the forerunner of the "modern" group of type faces, known today as Scotch, Bodoni, etc. After his death in 1775, Baskerville's punches and matrices were sold in France and were used to produce the sumptuous Kehl edition of Voltaire's works.

The book was composed by Electra Composition Corporation, New York City. Printed and bound by The Haddon Craftsmen, Inc., Scranton, Pa., designed by Victoria Dudley.